The Barn Owl

Guardian of the Countryside

The Barn Owl
Guardian of the Countryside

Jeff R. Martin

Whittet Books

Whittet Books Ltd
1 St John's Lane
Stansted
Essex CM24 8JU

First published 2017

Text © Jeff R. Martin 2017
See page 239 for picture copyright details.

This publication is in copyright. Subject to statutory exception and to the provisions of relevant collective licensing agreements, no part of this publication may be reproduced, transmitted or stored in a retrieval system, in any form or by any means, without permission in writing from Whittet Books Ltd.

Whittet Books Ltd has no responsibility for the persistence or accuracy of URLs for external or third party internet websites referred to in this publication and does not guarantee that any content on such websites is, or will remain, accurate or appropriate.

A catalogue record for this book is available from the British Library.

ISBN 978 1 873580 89 9

Designed by Lodge Graphics

Cover and frontispiece paintings: Terance James Bond

Contents

Foreword by Heimo Mikkola   1
Acknowledgements   3
Introduction   7

Part 1
The world of the barn owl   **9**
  1: An early history of the barn owls   11
  2: The barn owl described   41

Part 2
At home with the barn owl   **61**
  3: The farmland owl   63
  4: Prey and habitat diversity   81
  5: Aspects of behaviour   105
  6: Roosting and nesting habitats   123
  7: Nesting   143
  8: The Owlets   151
  9: Dispersal and migration   163

Part 3
Quis custodiet ipsos custodes?   **171**
  10: A fragile relationship   173
  11: Weather and climate   193
  12: Perspectives, thoughts and conclusions   209

Appendix: The problems of sex identification   231
Scientific names   235
Useful addresses   237
Credits   239
References and bibliography   241
Index   245

Foreword
by Heimo Mikkola

My interest in owls started when I was a boy growing up in my homeland of Finland. Not only did I enjoy watching these attractive birds, but I went on to study and write about them. Since that time I have been fortunate in being able to visit many countries over the years to see, and hear, many of the world's owls. Jeff Martin and I first became acquainted through correspondence while I was working in Africa some years ago. It was to be 22 years before we met in person, when I returned to live permanently in Europe. It soon became evident that he shared my passion for studying owls, and I am honoured and delighted to be able to introduce Jeff's book on that most popular of owls – the barn owl.

As a family, the barn owls are fascinating creatures. Until recently it was thought there were only eight species distributed throughout the world, but now, through phylogenetic analysis (DNA) and vocal analysis, we know that there at least 24, and that number looks set to rise in the future.

Yet all around the world barn owls are under threat from man's activities. Vital nesting places are lost as large trees are destroyed through logging, which is a particular concern in the tropics. In the northern hemisphere we can, to some degree, counter that loss by putting up nest boxes, though they do not fulfil the role of trees in helping to battle climate change. The loss of habitat for small mammals is another threat, as is the poisoning of rats and mice. Barn owls are at the top of the food chain, and any poisoned rodents that are eaten by them may have fatal consequences.

There is also the problem of road traffic, which kills many barn owls each year not only in Britain but elsewhere, but road deaths are only part of the problem. In this book, Jeff draws attention to the problem of road traffic noise and the likely affect that it may be having on hunting efficiency. Barn owls rely heavily on their hearing to catch their prey so any such noise can be a hazard.

While acknowledging these problems, this latest contribution to barn owl conservation is a positive one. It lays out a vision for Britain in which this popular owl can firmly establish itself in well-managed areas, as safe as they possibly can be, away from the damaging effects of man's activities. Slowly, but surely, the mysteries that surrounded our owls when I was a young man are being unravelled, and the importance of the owl as an indicator of the planet's health is being revealed. Perhaps no other owl is as important as the barn owl in performing that role.

Each published study heightens our interest in this splendid bird, and this book will ensure that, as a species of conservation concern, the barn owl will remain in the public's eye for many years to come. This book deserves to be read in its entirety and not just dipped into from time to time, as we so often do with the other books on owls. I warmly recommend Jeff Martin's book to both the layman and to the professional ornithologist.

Heimo Mikkola
Danube Delta, Romania

Acknowledgements

Throughout its preparation, I have been constantly supported and helped with this book by a great many people. I have been fortunate in being able to draw upon the works of a number of photographers, artists and fellow authors, and I cannot adequately express my sincere thanks to them all.

I am most grateful to Peter Hewitt who has very kindly allowed me to use some of his excellent photographs. They highlight the photogenic qualities that ensure barn owls are one of the most sought after species to photograph. I am also grateful to him for his cordial and enthusiastic correspondence.

I am indebted to David Hosking for allowing me to use some of his photographs as well as those of his late father. I have included some of Eric Hosking's magnificent historical portraits as they not only tell an informative story of the barn owl's lifestyle, they also provide the evidence that barn owls look good in black and white, as well as in colour.

I am most grateful to Michael Daniels for providing not only interesting conversation but also the photograph of barn owl bones.

Thomas Harris came in at the last moment and provided me with some of his fine photographs and I very much appreciate his help and cooperation.

Alan Sieradski has kindly provided me with encouragement and assistance with various matters. As work is progressively thrown onto this interesting group of birds, his work with the Global Owl project (Glow) and the World Owl Bibliography (WOB) is becoming increasingly valuable.

This book has its origins in Suffolk when in 1983 I first set out to study this interesting bird, though my interests now go beyond that county's borders. I am, therefore, delighted to be able to include a splendid picture by Suffolk photographer Jonathan Wright, and I thank him very much for allowing me to use it.

Some years back Essex farmer Mark Hollingsworth introduced me to Oxford naturalist Ian Richardson who has not only provided me with some interesting correspondence with regard to the Wychwood Project in Oxfordshire, but also readily made available to me his useful collection of photographs. I am greatly indebted to him.

While in Essex, I should like to thank Nigel Clarke for drawing my attention to the barn owls using the buildings at his work place, and which are probably breeding there. The records that exist in Essex of barn owls using buildings for nesting over the years are very few, so this record is particularly noteworthy.

It was always my intention to highlight the plight of our small mammals in the countryside for without them there are no owls for us to enjoy. Pat Morris has supplied me with pictures of a number of these delightful, interesting and important creatures. My thanks also go to John Dobson for allowing me to use some of his photographs. John has not only provided me with some excellent images, he continues to provide useful, interesting and friendly exchanges.

Sir David Attenborough needs no introduction and he has been kind in allowing me to quote from his interesting and useful volume *The Life of Mammals*. Apart from their obvious relationship with small mammals, barn owls can sometimes provide an interesting comparison with other mammal species, and this is something I touch on here and there.

Derek Bunn read an early draft of the manuscript and, as always, has provided valuable comment. As a friend and correspondent for more than 30 years, he continues to provide interesting and sometimes alternative views on barn owls and their conservation. Where we disagree, it is always in the most amicable manner. I also thank Peter Rose in Northumberland for some interesting and informative correspondence.

The South West Lancashire Ringing Group is perhaps the longest running barn owl conservation group in Britain. I am, therefore, most grateful to Tony Duckels for providing me with a potted history of the group and its successes, and details of their study.

In Portugal Artur Vaz Oliveira has been most helpful in providing a number of attractive and useful photographs, and I thank him for his kind and helpful correspondence. He is associated with ALDEIA, a non-profit, non-governmental organisation, providing guidance on nature conservation within sustainable development and helping to preserve the traditions and cultures that survive in rural areas. It is currently responsible for the management of two wildlife rehabilitation centres (CERVAS and RIAS). STRI (Nocturnal Raptors of Portugal) is a project of ALDEIA that aims to gather information about the existing nocturnal birds of prey in Portugal.

Germany is one of the countries which are foremost in the study of owls. I thank Dr Michael Exo, at the Institute for Avian Research at Wilhelmshaven, northern Germany, for his views on owl conservation and for allowing me to quote from his foreword to *The Little Owl*. Dr Thomas Bachman at the Institute for Fluid Mechanics and Aerodynamics, Darmstadt, has also been very helpful in providing me with an insight into his fascinating work on the flight of barn owls and how that might be applied in today's world. I thank Jarosław Wiącek of the Maria Curie-Skłodowska University, Lublin, Poland, for useful comment and kind assistance.

Archaeological digs are not only great fun, they are also very interesting, and they can provide important information on many aspects of history. I am most

It is in the light of these factors that this book has been written and, although it has been enjoyable to write, the story it conveys is not a joyful one. It is a message that illustrates quite clearly that, if matters continue in the countryside as they are at present, eventually many barn owls will struggle to survive.

The message also conveys thoughts as to how we view the countryside and gives recommendations for matters that need to be addressed if we want barn owls to return to parts of the countryside from where they have been absent for many years.

In early 2015, it was reported that in 2014 barn owls had their best breeding season ever recorded, though this was in the wake of 2013, which was the worst recorded. It is too early to say whether a corner has been turned. We shall not know that for a numbers of years yet, but pressure continues to grow on our barn owls all of the time, irrespective of how much enthusiasm and effort we put into their conservation.

It is because of this that proposals are presented here for their long-term future. Not everyone will agree with these views, but one thing is sure: barn owls will continue to interest and surprise us from whatever direction you approach them, and, while it might not be thought so, there is still so much to be learnt about these fascinating creatures in the UK, and indeed worldwide.

This book is about barn owls, and, although they hold centre stage throughout, as the reader progresses they will find other animal and plant species entering the story, for barn owls cannot exist in isolation. The RSPB and BTO have publicly broadened their horizons and deepened their interests beyond birds, and surely that must be welcomed. But at the end of the day barn owls have to exist, as they always have done, alongside man in the countryside, and so this book also touches on aspects of their conservation that were initially raised by Iain Taylor in his important study. The influence of farmers and the employment of young people in the countryside is something to be encouraged, while there is much to be discovered by ornithologists with a serious interest in owls, but with an all-embracing approach.

In the light of this, if there is a theme running through this review it is to encourage the further study of Britain's barn owls, and for this we must look to the young and aspirant ornithologists of the future – those who will, one hopes, arrive in the arena of barn owl conservation armed with the tools and background knowledge that their predecessors will have left them but intent on making their own discoveries with an enquiring outlook. It is likely, therefore, that parts of this book will be looked upon as somewhat trivial by the more experienced birdwatcher, but I make no apologies for that; it is my hope that those young naturalists of the future will fill the gaps in our knowledge that previous and present naturalists will have left them, for there is still much to learn. But where does one start? Well, perhaps the best way is to go back a long way in history...

Introduction

In the animal world the human eye is a critical entity in what it regards as a thing of beauty, as a consequence of which many species of owl are looked upon as physically attractive. That may be so, but all is not equal within the owl world, for undoubtedly the barn owls reign supreme. With their striking looks they have, over the years, captivated many people from all sorts of backgrounds. For the naturalist, though, they present an alternative form of attraction, for biologically they form a most interesting group of birds.

Of course, it is not only the naturalists who find barn owls attractive. Authors love to write about them, photographers spend hours photographing them, while artists and sculptors lovingly portray their images. These are just a few of the many people, from all walks of life, who are captivated by their charm. Indeed, it is this following that puts them into a class of their own, and there can be little doubt that if they were pop stars they would probably rival Elvis Presley or the Beatles in popularity. However, while pop stars come and go, the barn owls rock on and will appear as stars on the stage of wildlife for many years to come.

For students of barn owls, though, this fascination goes much deeper than just belonging to a fan club, for it has long been considered that the barn owls' presence in the countryside is an indicator that the environment is healthy and is being managed with wildlife in mind. As a consequence of this, it is through our actions to conserve them that they have, quite unwittingly, become what some might call guardians of the countryside; driving us on to ensure that we maintain their numbers in the belief that by doing so our actions are benefitting wildlife in general. However, at a time when Britain is repeatedly failing to meet its biodiversity targets, are barn owls really proving to be effective guardians of the countryside?

In the UK we know a great deal about barn owls in the north-west of England and the south-west of Scotland, two areas that are relatively close both in geographical proximity and in habitat terms. This knowledge has been acquired through two long-term studies that were carried out there over a period of years stretching from the 1960s through to the early 1990s.

Contrary to this the barn owls of the south and east have received little attention even though it is this part of Britain that has largely borne the brunt of the post-war farming revolution and that is now coming under further pressure from an increasingly demanding human population.

comments on an earlier draft and who continues to provide useful and thought-provoking discussion and encouragement on all aspects of owls. There is, perhaps, no one more fitted to write a foreword to my book than he, and I am most grateful to him for that.

It was Shirley Greenall, my publisher at Whittet Books, who suggested that I might wish to consider writing a new book on barn owls, my first being *Barn Owls in Britain*, also published by Whittet Books when Annabel Whittet was alive. Throughout the preparation of this new book, Shirley has provided me with great support, helpful encouragement and pertinent suggestions for improving the manuscript. I am grateful to her, Faith Anstey, and Frank Lee of Lodge Graphics for turning my manuscript into the published book you are now reading.

At the end of the day, though, the 'buck stops here', so any omissions or errors in the content are entirely down to me.

grateful to Hazel Williams, Janet Sharpe and especially Tom Walker, of the South Oxfordshire Archaeological Group, for providing me with useful correspondence and information regarding the interesting find of small mammal bones at the Roman villa at Gatehampton.

Barn owls cannot be treated in isolation from the wider world, and the effects of climate and weather have in the past, and will in the future, influence their fortunes. I am appreciative of Dr John Kington, formerly of the University of East Anglia, for not only granting me permission to quote from his interesting and absorbing volume *Climate and Weather*, but also for kindly reading and improving some sections of the text to provide the authorative view to my efforts.

The analysis of owl pellets is an important factor in barn owl conservation and so I thank Alasdair Love for allowing me to reproduce some of the information he collected during the course of his lengthy period as the coordinator of the Mammal Society's Owl Pellet Survey. I also thank Richard Austen of the Society for his assistance with this.

I am most grateful to Stanley Dumican for not only allowing me to use some of his photographs but for his kindness and friendship over the years. I thank Dag Peterson, in Sweden, for allowing me to reproduce the Falkland Islands stamp he designed, while Keith Alexander and his fellow authors have given me permission to quote from their writings on hedgerows. Helen J. Read, at the City of London Corporation, has answered my questions and queries with regards to pollard trees in Europe as well as helping with photographs.

The internet is now a part of our daily lives, and, for owl enthusiasts, *The Owl Pages* is a most useful and interesting website. I am most grateful to Deane Lewis, in Australia, for allowing me to use the skeleton and eye illustrations from that site. Apart from the internet, technology of various sorts continues to grow as an important way of monitoring our wildlife, and barn owls are no exception. John Worland has been helpful in providing me with some technological advice with regards to the monitoring of owl boxes. Ralph Hancock has provided interesting and useful correspondence as well as a picture of tawny owls in Kensington Gardens, London.

In my introduction I point out that artists love to paint barn owls, but I have to say that, while many artists make great attempts at capturing the essence of this attractive creature, few excel at it. I am, therefore, most grateful to Terance Bond who has kindly allowed me to use his fine paintings for the cover and frontispiece.

I am grateful to my wife Kate, aka Tina, for her patience and understanding with regards to my incessant ramblings and thoughts on owls. As always she has patiently read (several times) the draft of this book and has provided many useful suggestions and corrections.

I am sincerely grateful to Professor Heimo Mikkola who made important

Part 1
The world of the barn owl

1: An early history of the barn owls
Out of the dinosaurs • Day and night – are you the one? • The emergence of the modern-day barn owls • To the four corners of the Earth – the spread of the barn owls • The worldwide distribution of the barn owls • The barn owl *Tyto alba* • The dark-breasted barn owl • The arrival of barn owls in Britain • Distribution within Britain • Naming the barn owl

2: The barn owl described
General description • Silent flight • Effortless flight • Voice and calls • Sight • Hearing

1: An early history of the barn owls

The barn owls living in Britain today belong to a species that, together with a number of other species, form the worldwide family of owls known scientifically as the Tytonidae, the family of barn owls. It has an ancient history, and to gain some understanding of that we have to go back a long way in time.

Out of the dinosaurs

Since the year 1861, the study of the origins of the Birds has centred upon the extinct species *Archaeopteryx lithographica*, which evolved from the dinosaurs and whose remains were discovered in a quarry in Bavaria, in southern Germany. This first example of a fossilised feathered, bi-pedal therapod dinosaur dates back to about 150 million years ago ('mya') and now resides in the British Museum, London, but several other examples of this species exist, all of which were found in the same area.

The history of *Archaeopteryx*, and how it has come to dominate avian palaeontology, has been described by Birkhead *et al.* (2014) who detailed the scientific controversy that continues to surround this creature. Foremost among those who believe that the Birds evolved as aerial dinosaurs in the trees, and not as terrestrial dinosaurs on the ground as in the case of *Archaeopteryx*, has been the American palaeontologist Professor Alan Feduccia (1996) whose research has received some support but also strong opposition.

Recent discoveries, though, have now shifted the focus of attention to China and elsewhere, so the date and location of the first bird on earth remains questionable. For the present, however, *Archaeopteryx* retains its title.

As far as the family of owls is concerned, the oldest known species is the extinct *Ogygoptynx wetmorei*, whose remains were discovered in North America and are believed to have originated in the mid-Palaeocene, a period which dates back to around 60 mya. However, it is not until about 42–33 mya that we see the first appearance of the real owls, in the form of the extinct *Intutula brevis,* which was also found in North America.

This tended to coincide with the discovery in France of another extinct owl species (Mlíkovský 2002), while further south there have been other finds which date back to the Miocene, the first geological period of the Neogene epoch, which ranged from 23.03 to 2.58 mya.

It was during the Early Miocene, some 23–16 mya, that the Tytonidae first appeared in the form of the Phodilinae, the bay owls, which are still with us but do not feature here. The Tytoninae, the barn owls, came later and emerged during the period of the Lower and Middle Miocene, 20–15 mya.

During the Middle Miocene a series of extinctions occurred, and Mátics (2003) was of the view that the family of barn owls also nearly went that way. He considered their near extinction came towards the end of the Early Miocene as the 'true' owls, the Strigidae (see below), began to overtake the barn owls in evolutionary terms. He believed that it was the diversification of the small mammals, which occurred around 23–15 mya, that prompted this development. It seems, therefore, that barn owls may have been going through some form of transitional period in their evolution.

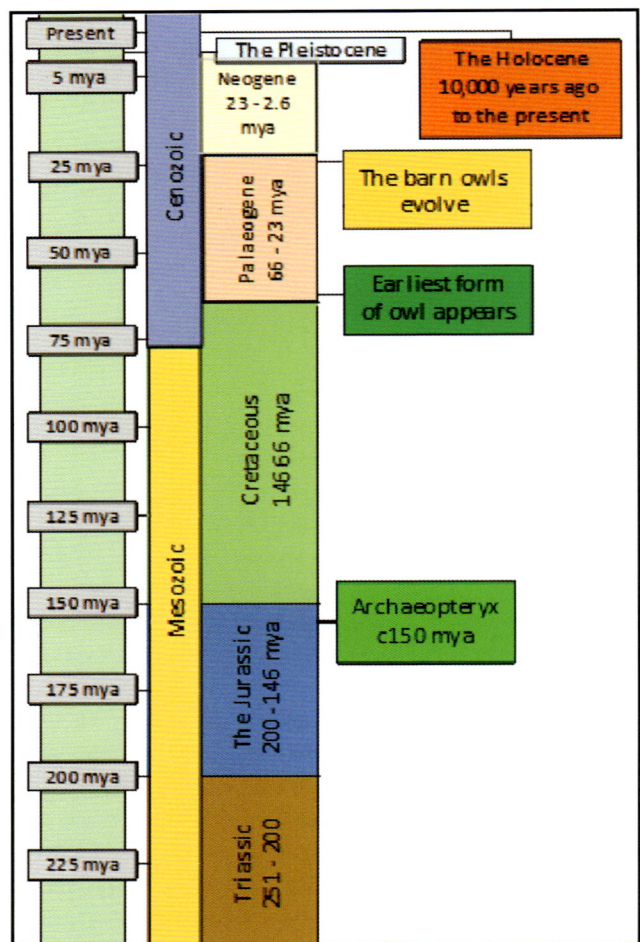

A guide to the evolutionary time period of the owls.
Source of geological time periods: Friend, P., Scotland (Collins, 2012)

Then, around 15 mya, the modern genus of *Tyto* appeared, from which the present-day *Tyto alba* evolved around 1.6 mya. It was to be some considerable time, however, before these classifications were established, and that is an ongoing process even now.

Day and night – are you the one?

While the origin of the Birds is hotly disputed there are controversies within the realms of the day-flying birds of prey – raptors – and owls which continue to rumble on as to whether these two groups are directly related.

Owls do share similar features to the raptors, such as hooked beaks and sharp talons, and it is because of these similarities that it was originally thought the two groups were directly related. But in 1827 the German zoologist Christian Nitzsch found there were differences between the two groups, and this led to the owls being placed into a scientific order of their own – the Strigiformes.

Nearly 200 years later, modern-day research through molecular phylogenetics, or DNA, suggests that the owls are related to the day-flying raptors, as well as to the osprey, the new world vultures, rollers and woodpeckers, but not to the falcons. This, though, is not the end of the story, for, at the time of writing, further research suggests that eventually all of the diurnal and nocturnal raptors (the owls) may be lumped together.

The discovery by Nitzsch was significant but not final, for this was followed by further discoveries in 1828, when the Swedish naturalist Gustaf Billberg revealed that, within the Strigiformes, some of the owls were different. These then formed the sub-family Tytonidae. This family was subsequently divided into two groups, with the recent suggestion that one, the Tytoninae, should comprise the barn, grass and masked owls, the genus *Tyto*, while the second, which consists of the bay owls, should form the sub-family Phodilinae, the genus *Phodilus*. All of the world's other owls remain within the sub-family Strigidae, the typical owls.

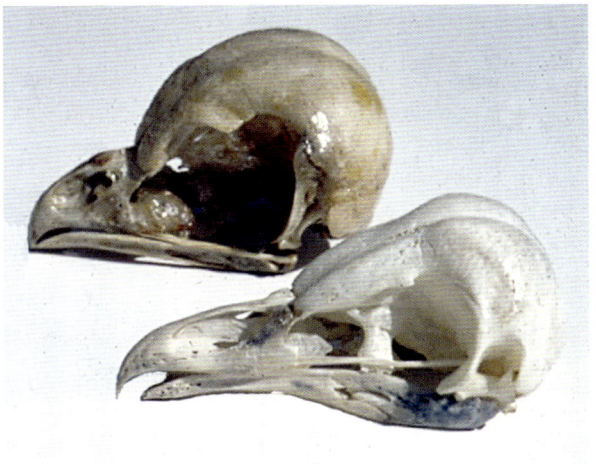

Top: The skull of a typical owl, Strix aluco, the Tawny Owl.
Bottom: The skull of a Barn Owl, Tyto alba.

The division of the owls into two sub-families came through the examination of their skeletons, and through that it was found there were some defining differences. We can see here that the skulls of the two sub-families are very different. Those of the typical owls have a high dome, a short, stubby downward-curved beak, and very large orbits, or eye sockets, when compared to the size of the head. In addition, the inter-orbital septum, which is the interior bone dividing the eye sockets, is narrow. By comparison, the skull of a barn owl is less domed, the beak is longer, and the eye sockets smaller, while the inter-orbital septum is wider. All owl skulls are pneumatic, or hollow, which renders them light in weight.

It is the lower part of the skeleton that perhaps provides a further demonstration of the evolutionary process that barn owls demonstrate in the present day, suggesting that they are at another intermediary stage in the evolution of the owls.

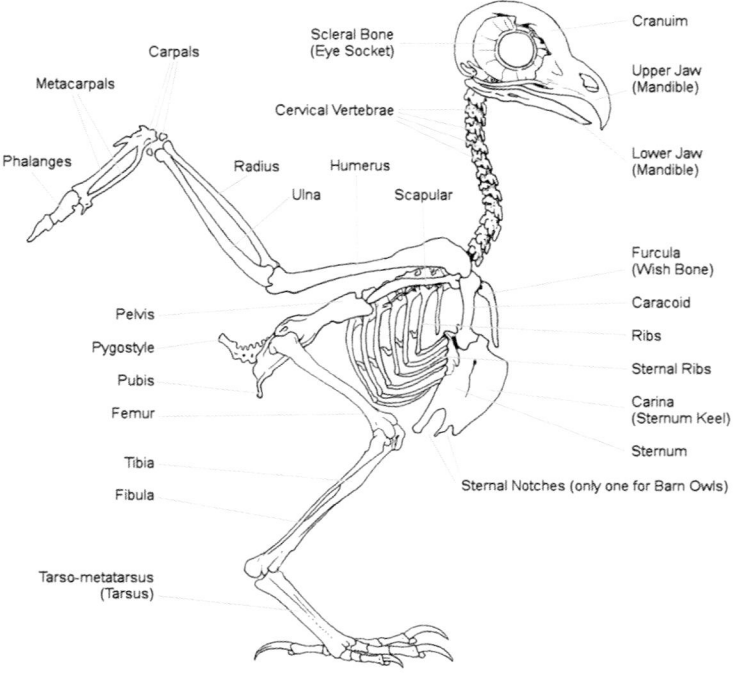

The skeleton of a typical owl.
The long neck contains 12 of the 14 cervical vertebrae. The vertebral artery which carries blood to the head has more free movement in the owls than it does with humans who would be likely to suffer strokes and blood clots if they tried to rotate and move their heads in the manner of owls.

The Carina, or sternum keel, (top left of photograph opposite) has just the one notch unlike the 'true' owls which have two notches (see diagram above). (It is important to note that the sternum in the photograph is incomplete; the bottom left is broken off as a consequence of which the notch cannot be seen clearly.) The long bone (middle) is the fibula and the small bone (bottom left) is the tibula. Little attention has been given to these two bones over the years, probably because, unless the bones are exposed, as here, it is difficult to obtain measurements from feathered examples, either dead or alive.

More attention has been paid to the tarsus (right of photograph). This example is 60 mm which is within the range 54–60 mm (mean 57) for males and the same size range for females (mean 56.8) (Source: BWP). The tarsus of the barn owl is longer than those of other comparative Eurasian owls as the table shows. Only

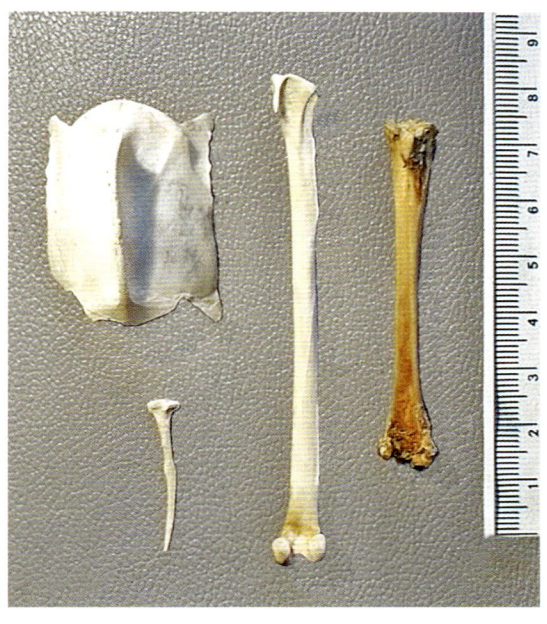

the eagle owl has a longer tarsus (males: 79.3 mm; females: 82.2 mm – source BWP).

The legs are formed of three sections. The upper thigh bone, the femur, comprises one bone. The lower section beneath the knee joint is comprised of two bones, the thickest and most prominent of which is the tibia, while the fibula is the thinner bone. These meet at the ankle joint, below which is the tarsometatarsus.

A distinct characteristic of the barn owls is that the knee joints meet at the knees, giving a distinct 'knock-kneed' impression. Why this should be is not clear, but perhaps this arrangement provides them with a greater spread of the feet when hunting. Short-eared owls also have a slight tendency for their tarsi to come together as well, but it is not so evident as it is with the barn owls.

Average tarsus lengths of five European medium to large owl species (Measurements in millimetres)		♂	♀
Barn owl	*Tyto alba*	57	56.8
Tawny owl	*Strix aluco*	46.5	48.3
Short-eared owl	*Asio flammeus*	44.5	46.2
Long-eared owl	*Asio otis*	38.2	39.9
Great grey owl	*Strix nebulosa*	53.9	55.1
Ural owl	*Strix uralensis*	51.4	53.9
(Source: BWP)			

At the end of the metatarsus are the toes, of which the owls have four. The first of these lies at the rear of the foot and faces backwards, as it does with most bird species. With the typical owls the second toe, which is the inner of the three forward-facing toes, is shorter than the third; but with the barn owls the three forward-facing toes are of the same length while the fourth, or outer, toe is very mobile and reversible.

The toes are variously coloured from dark grey-brown to bright yellow, and the claws are dark brown.

A feature which helps separate the Tytonidae from the typical owls is that on an adult bird the third, or middle forward-facing, talon has a raised flange with a comb-like serrated edge on the inside. On very young birds the flange is not apparent but develops with age. At seven months it is fully developed, and from the depth of the flange a bird may then be sexed. On males it is 1.5 mm and on females 2.0 mm. However, it is not always possible to use this guide on museum study skins because the tarsi and feet can shrink with dehydration.

This brief description provides sufficient evidence to suggest that barn owls are indeed very different from all other known owl species, and, in consequence, it could be argued that the discovery by Gustaf Billberg should stand and that the barn owls should remain a distinct family rather than placed within the general owl assemblage.

The developing pectinate flange of a barn owl.

The emergence of the modern-day barn owls

About 10 million years ago a large inland sea existed to the south of Budapest, Hungary. This was the Pannonian Sea which, over time, progressively dried out and was eventually replaced by a lake known as the Slavonian Lake. Then, about one million years ago, this lake also disappeared as the climate became hotter and drier and the feeds filling the lake dried up.

As the lake contracted, its fringes were covered by forest and grassland, and it was here that the first modern-day examples of the genus *Tyto* – the barn owls and associated species – appeared.

The site of the former Pannonian Sea is now known as the Carpathian Basin.

A Fishing Owl?

During the process of the Carpathian Basin drying out, barn owls may initially have evolved as fish eaters because at that time fish would most likely have been the most available food source in the lake fringes. Then, as the lake continued to dry out, they turned to alternative prey, such as frogs and toads, which they would have found in the lake shallows, and later to other prey in the form of small mammals and birds, which they found in the expanding grass and woodland areas.

The thought of the barn owls evolving as fish-eaters might seem implausible, but, looking at the physiology of the barn owl, we can see that it is perfectly adapted to catching fish. The lower legs are very long and only lightly feathered which has led to this adaptation being described as a necessary feature to assist them when hunting for prey in wet or damp grassland. There are, though, other owl species which also tend to hunt over grassland and which have well-feathered tarsi. The short-eared owl, for example, is one and yet its tarsi are well feathered, while barn owls are by no means restricted to hunting over grass.

Lightly feathered leg.

The lack of feathering, though, would have been beneficial if barn owls evolved primarily as hunters of fish. Catching fish from the surface of a lake or river would leave only small areas of saturated plumage, and it may have been that, in their formative years of evolution, their legs were completely devoid of feathering. The legs of the modern-day fish owls are completely devoid of feathers, but there are other features which tend to support the theory that barn owls emerged as fish eaters.

Beneath the upper surfaces of their toes, barn owls have a series of pads, or 'papillae', which help grip slippery prey items such as frogs, but they would be especially useful in catching fish. The fish owls and the related osprey have similar features, i.e. spiny soles to their feet, to enable the catching of fish and slippery amphibians.

The pectinate (serrated) talons of the barn owl (page 16) are thought to have developed to help them keep their facial discs in fine order so that they can hear their prey. It also seems likely that barn owls developed this flange for the same reason that the distantly related herons and the more closely related ospreys developed similar pectinate flanges – to clean fish slime away from their faces. Interestingly, the more distantly related nightjars also have similar flanges.

So perhaps barn owls initially evolved as fish-hunters rather than hunters of small mammals and other prey, which they only turned to as the Basin dried up. If this were so, it would be a demonstration of their ability to adapt to differing habitats, and alternative prey, which has allowed them to become a successful worldwide group of birds.

They are also superb opportunists when it comes to feeding, as demonstrated by some interesting fish-hunting records. From their exhaustive research, Bunn *et al.* (1982) presented accounts of barn owls catching fish from a variety of sources. One reliable record was of a barn owl taking 'a good-sized Roach from the River Anholme, Lincolnshire'. From trials they conducted, they were able to confirm that captive barn owls will readily eat fish, and they included a description of a tame barn owl that was 'very fond of small trout', which, interestingly, it bolted down tail first (barns owls usually swallow their prey head first). They also mentioned that other fish species, such as perch, brown trout, rudd and small carp, have also been recorded as taken by barn owls. In the USA there is an interesting record in Part Two of A. C. Bent's *Life Histories*

> *of North American Birds of Prey* of a group of 30 barn owls catching grunion fish on a beach in southern California.
>
> The argument that barn owls may have initially evolved as fish eaters might be difficult to believe, but the evidence suggests that the diets of species do evolve when necessary to adapt to local circumstances. For example, there is circumstantial evidence from the period between the Middle Jurassic and the Holocene to illustrate how the behaviour and diets of various bird species have evolved over time (Naish, 2014), and this process is ongoing. A rather startling discovery was made by Čech and Čech (2015) who reported on a common kingfisher which fed on a lizard. The authors considered that the taking of such aquatic prey as beetles, newts and crayfish appeared to be accidental, but this was the first record of an amniotic vertebrae creature being selected as prey by a common kingfisher.

The Carpathian Basin is an outstanding area that holds a wealth of interest for palaeontologists, naturalists and other scientists. During the latter part of the nineteenth century, and more especially in the twentieth century, a great deal of archaeological field work was carried out in this region, and the area still attracts focussed attention (Kessler, 2014).

To the four corners of the Earth – the spread of the barn owls

The eventual drying up of the Slavonian Lake took place during the Pleistocene, which is generally referred to as the 'Great Ice Age', an epoch that started about 2.5 mya and ended about 20,000 bp (before present).

In the Great Ice Age there were intervals of glaciation followed by periods of amelioration, some of which spanned thousands of years, and these intervals of inter-glacial warming were often greater than the period of climate warming that we are experiencing at present.

It was during the periods of glaciation that many species, including the barn owls, were forced down into three main areas of southern Europe, only for them to return north when the climate warmed. This was a process that continued throughout the Pleistocene, and which appears to be continuing.

The bodies of some of those barn owls that did not survive were covered by snow, ice, earth and other debris, waiting for the time when they would be discovered by the palaeo-ornithologists of the future, and it may have been during one of those cold periods that the barn owls nearly died out completely.

The glaciations throughout the Pleistocene were important in helping to form the owl fauna that we have today. At their greatest extent, the ice sheets covered much of the Earth's crust. While it was the northern hemisphere that was mostly affected, the southern hemisphere did not always go entirely untouched, and it is this that might have helped the spread of barn owls around the world.

Barn owls prefer a warmer climate, and the remains of barn owls have been discovered in Mexico, New Zealand (where they were once extinct but have recently been re-introduced), Brazil, southern Europe, the Galápagos Islands and Israel, while other remains have been discovered on the Mediterranean islands of Mallorca and Menorca, as well as in the Caribbean. These also date back to the Pleistocene.

The worldwide distribution of the barn owls

From relative obscurity to the point where taxonomically they have become the most studied group of non-passerine birds, the owls are now the focus of attention by many ornithologists, who are making new discoveries on a regular basis. A little more than twenty years ago there were 130 or so accepted species of owl, but the latest estimate suggests there are now 249, and by the time this book is published it is likely there will be ten more. Although many of these new arrivals are at present yet to be officially recognised, it can only be a matter of time before many, if not all, are.

These changes will feature the barn owls – a cluster of owls that once consisted of just eight species but which now totals many more. The recent advances with the analysis of the owls through DNA have brought many changes and none more so than to the family Tytonidae. In broad terms this dynasty remains at rest with two genera, *Tyto* and *Phodilus*, although the latter now contains only the bay owls, with the grass owls and the Itombwe owl, or African bay owl, *Tyto prigoginei*, having now been moved into the genus *Tyto*. This reclassification is both interesting and remarkable, though these changes are by no means the last word on the subject.

The trait of an owl's vocabulary is that its calls are inherited and not learned (König *et al.*, 2008). In consequence former subspecies of owl are now being assigned full species status of their own through the use of voice sonograms, along with differences in morphology and mannerisms.

Accordingly, the genus *Tyto* now contains 24 or 25 species with a general agreement that there are, at present, 12 known species of barn owl, while the remainder number about 13.

These enjoy a considerable worldwide distribution that ranges from the Americas through to Europe, Africa, Asia and Australasia. Wherever you may be in the world, a member of the barn owl family is not that far away. That is, unless you are in some of the more inhospitable parts of the world, particularly the desert extremes or the desolate polar regions.

Many species of barn owl follow a common trend in that they tend to feed on

The distribution of the world's barn owls.

small mammals, they live in buildings, and they haunt open countryside. Nearly all barn owls rely upon mature large trees for nesting, not only in the northern hemisphere but also in the tropical rain forests, as a consequence of which their survival is threatened by deforestation. In some places forest clearance might actually benefit them as long as they have somewhere to nest, although it might bring other problems in the form of road traffic, disturbance and agricultural poisons.

The remains found in the Caribbean provide us with sufficient information to suggest that barn owls of three different size classes might have once lived at the same time, with the likelihood that one species *Tyto gigantea*, was larger than all three. In addition, it seems that there was another giant barn owl, *Ornimegalonyx*, that existed in the Mediterranean some 10,000 to 30,000 years ago during the Pleistocene.

It is not abundantly clear why those large owls disappeared, though it seems likely that in some instances their prey played a significant role. The remains of a new and closely related species to the barn owls, *Tyto neddi*, were discovered in the 1990s at Barbuda, in the Lesser Antilles. It is believed this owl may well have died out due to the extinction of its main prey, a large and unclassified rodent. Today there are no owls present on Barbuda, thus demonstrating how vulnerable members of the genus *Tyto* can be if they live on a restricted diet.

The barn owl *Tyto alba*

The subject of this book is the barn owl *Tyto alba* whose range, according to present listings, extends around large parts of the world, and comprises some 36 subspecies, with *Tyto alba alba* the nominate race occupying the British Isles, the

How did barn owls colonise far-flung and remote places?

The Ice Age, harsh though it was, may have been of great benefit to barn owls; for as the ice sheets became thicker they locked up vast amounts of sea water, and consequently the level of the sea was lowered. At its greatest extent the ice sheet is considered to have been some 1,500–3,000 metres thick, with a resulting fall in sea level around the world of 130 metres. A considerable amount of submerged land was uncovered as the water level dropped which would then have allowed many isolated areas to connect with others through land bridges. This was likely to have been the way that barn owls colonised many far-flung islands and archipelagos, such as the Galápagos and Australasia.

Of course, barn owls might have colonised islands and other far-off places through flight. A survey of the Falkland Islands in 2003 revealed that there were seven to ten pairs of the barn owl *Tyto alba tuidara*, all of which, along with a singleton on South Georgia, were considered to be arrivals from Argentinian Patagonia (A.Sieradzki *in litt.*).

Whether the forebears of these owls reached the Falkland Isles by flying there is open to discussion, because their flight is not particularly strong, and they are therefore reluctant to cross large expanses of water. The Islands lie about 300 miles to the east of Patagonia on the Patagonian Shelf, so access by a land bridge cannot be ruled out.

It is because of their isolation, after the last period of glaciation, that some subspecies of barn owl, such as the Galápagos barn owl *Tyto alba punctatissima*, will in time be reclassified as species in their own right, for at the time of writing there is a proposal that this barn owl should be reclassified as a stand-alone species and named *Tyto punctatissima*. This 'fluidity' within the barn owl family is why a precise list of species and subspecies cannot be produced here.

Channel Isles, western and southern France, the Iberian Peninsula, Italy, parts of Switzerland, parts of North and southern Africa, as well as the Americas, Middle East and Asia. In Australasia a variety of barn owl related species occupies the continent. The main species is the Australian barn owl *Tyto delicatula*, which is widespread not only across the mainland but also in many of the neighbouring islands.

Some of those subspecies are under scrutiny to establish whether they are

The Australian barn owl. How did barn owls reach Australia? It seems likely that land bridges had a role to play in enabling barn owls to 'cross' the vast Pacific Ocean.

a race of *Tyto alba* or whether they are indeed stand-alone species, and this is especially relevant to those living on islands. For example, Robb *et al.* (2015) have proposed that the subspecies *T. a. glacilirostris*, an inhabitant of the Eastern Canary Islands, Lanzarote and other neighbouring islands, should be named the slender-billed barn owl *Tyto glacilirostris*, while they also suggest that *T. a. schmitzi*, of Madeira, should be reclassified as the Madeira Barn Owl *Tyto schmitzi*.

Subspecies	Date described	Distribution
T. a. alba	Scopoli, 1769	British Isles, western & southern Europe
T. a. guttata	C. L. Brehm, 1831	Central and eastern Europe
T. a. ernesti	Kleinschmidt, 190	Mediterranean region. Merges with *alba* in Spain
T. a. affinis	Blyth, 1862	Africa south of the Sahara
T. a. hypermetra	Grote, 1928	Madagascar and Comoro Islands
T. a. stertens	Hartert, 1929	Pakistan, India, Sri Lanka, east to China, but see *javanica* below
T. a. schmitzi	Hartert, 1900	Madeira
T. a. gracilirostris	Hartert, 1905	Canary Islands
T. a. javanica	Gmelin, 1788	Burma, SW China, Thailand, Cambodia, Laos, Malay Peninsula
T. a. erlangeri	W. L. Sclater, 1921	Middle East, Iraq, Iran, Arabia

On Madagascar *T. a. hypermetra* lives alongside another species of barn owl, *Tyto soumagnei*, the Madagascar Red Owl

Refs: König & Weick, 2008; Mikkola, 2013

Subspecies of Tyto alba

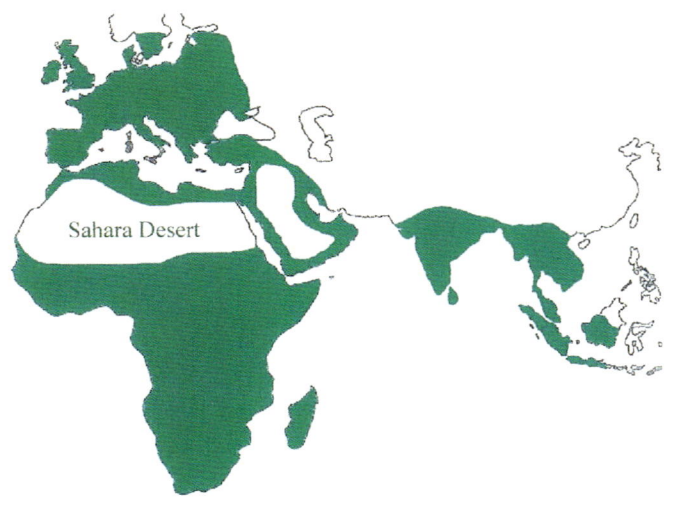

Distribution of the species Tyto alba.

The Barn Owl
1: An early history of the barn owls

Barn owls on the Falkland Islands

The Falkland Islands barn owl Tyto furcata tuidara.

In 1982 the Falkland Islands were at the centre of controversy and warfare.

Since then, the islands have attracted many tourists in search of the wonderful wildlife that can be found there.

Although barn owls are not commonly seen, they are not forgotten, for on 25 October 2004 the Falkland Islands postal authority released a set of stamps depicting the breeding owls that may be found there.

This attractive first day cover depicting the Falkland Islands barn owl is a further demonstration of their worldwide distribution and the enormous appeal that they have.

An African barn owl of the former race T. a. affinis produces a threat display for the photographer.

Robb *et al.* also propose that *T. a. detorta* be assigned full species status and named *Tyto detorta*, the Cape Verde barn owl. This is a very interesting owl in that it has similarities with *Tyto alba guttata*, the dark-breasted barn owl of Eastern Europe. It is a barn owl that is much darker than its nearest neighbour on the African mainland, the African barn owl *Tyto alba affinis*, so it is of great interest and just another example of the complexity of this large family of owls.

The dark-breasted barn owl

In Eastern Europe the subspecies *Tyto alba guttata*, the dark-breasted barn owl, inhabits the Netherlands, Germany, eastern and northern France, Denmark, Poland, western Russia, Austria and Hungary. In nearby Bulgaria both light and dark forms occur, although only dark birds have been found breeding there. The white form is a winter visitor and may be seen during migration periods (Nyaglov and Ignatov, 2003).

Ongoing research may, in time, reveal that *guttata* is not a subspecies at all, but merely a colour morph (variation) of *T. a. alba*. This is demonstrated by the wing and tarsi lengths, along with other biometric measurements, which show there is very little difference between them, while DNA research has established that genetically the two subspecies can hardly be separated (König *et al.*, 2008).

The division of the two colour morphs is an interesting one for which various reasons have been proposed. One theory suggests that the 3 °C January isotherm

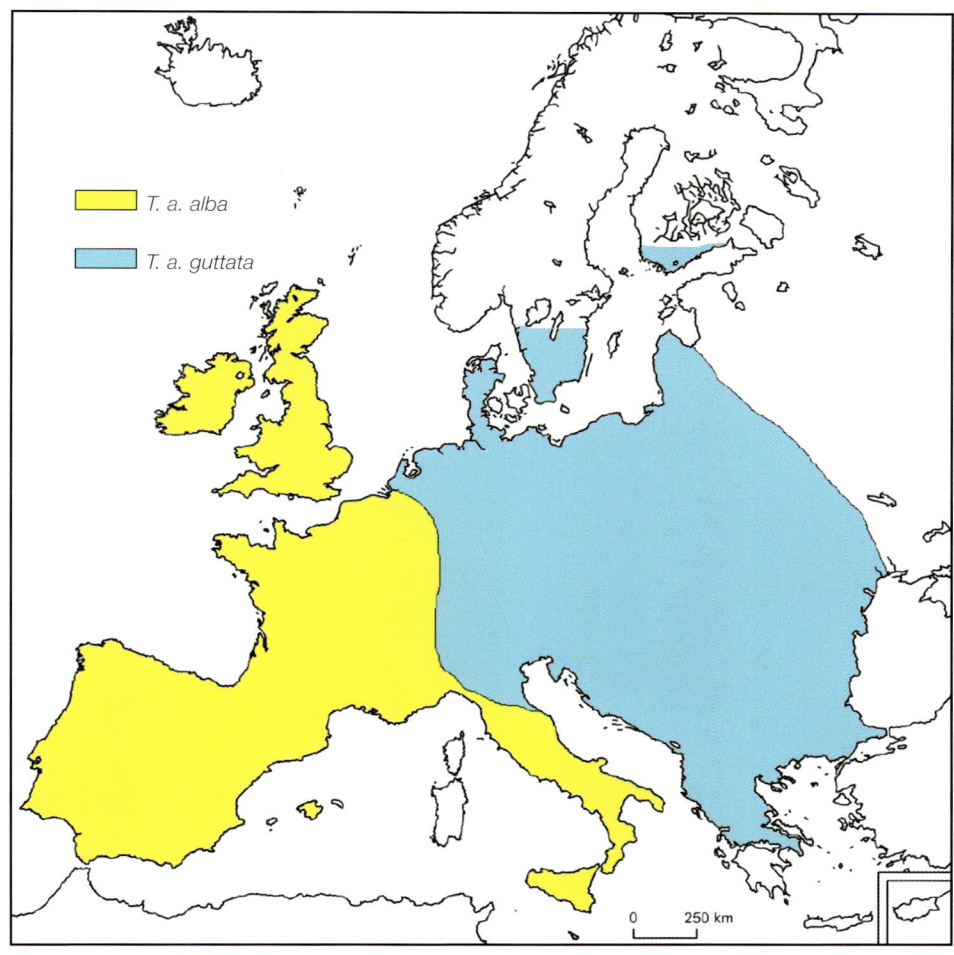

*The European distribution of Tyto alba.
Barn owls have recently moved into southern Finland, and the dark-breasted race guttata
has also been recently recorded in northern Italy.*

is critical in separating the two races (Shawyer, 1998). This runs through the east coast of Britain, the French border with Germany, down through Italy and on into Bulgaria. Thus there is the suggestion that climate is the determining factor.

From Switzerland comes the proposal that these colour variations arose following the Pleistocene and that these have been conserved through their diets: not directly because of what they eat, but through different foraging strategies (Roulin, 2004). This study found that those owls with light breasts feed largely on mice, while those with dark breasts feed mainly on common voles, because historically their colours allowed them to exploit the differing habitats and thus enabled them to hunt more successfully.

Even within the nominate subspecies T. a. alba there can be considerable colour variation. This bird from Portugal has varying amounts of under-wing and body spotting, as well as patches of golden brown on the body and under-wing.

It may be that white-breasted barn owls are so coloured because they hunt by day and it is more difficult for their prey to see them against the sky (Taylor, 1994), which also suggests that foraging strategy is important to them. This does not take into account, though, the white-breasted mice-eating barn owls of southern Europe which usually hunt at night.

As is so often the case with barn owls, there is no straightforward explanation. Across Eurasia, animals in warm and humid areas tend to follow the general rule in being more heavily pigmented than those of cooler and drier areas. Consequently, the owls of south-west and northern Europe, except for the barn owl, tend to be smaller and darker in colouring than those further east, such as in Russia for example, which tend to be much paler. It would seem, therefore, that Europe's barn owls are contrary to the general rule.

The reasons for this have not yet been fully studied, and we still could be some way from establishing the reason for the colour differences between these two barn owl races. To complicate matters further, a study of 318 barn owls found that the females comprised five colour types and that they were predominantly of the race *'guttata'*. Contrary to this, the males tended to be more typical of the race *'alba'*. It was thought this reflected possible immigration from the west. It may be, though, that the explanation is to be found in the Carpathian Basin.

It would appear that during the onset of a period of glaciation, Europe's barn owls moved into southern Spain, Italy and the Balkans. When the climate warmed again, they moved north, with those in the west tracking the nesting opportunities that would have been provided by maturing oaks. Those barn owls that moved north from their Balkan refugia were slower to take advantage of that nesting opportunity due to the drier and cooler climate, which is favourable to spruce but not oak, which prefers a moist temperate climate (Brewer *et al.*, 2002).

This reflects Alexandre Roulin's proposal, in terms of present-day foraging strategies, with barn owls retaining their original dark colouring in the forest environments near to their source of origin, and those that ventured west and south adopting the colour morph that suited the emerging farmland environment, as the wildwood was cleared from western Europe.

In assessing the microevolution of the barn owl in Europe, Mátics (2003) pointed out that there is a narrow transitional area where dark-breasted and white-breasted barn owls meet. Where that occurs 84 per cent of the barn owls to the east of that line were of the dark-breasted *guttata* subspecies.

Contrary to the popular view, it was felt that the colour forms of *Tyto alba* did not evolve separately from the south-east and south-west glacial refugia of the Ice Age but from a central area based around Hungary.

In recent years there have been two instances of female dark-breasted barn owls, *guttata*, nesting with males of the white-breasted race *alba*. One of the females had been ringed in The Netherlands, and the second was not ringed. Both of the males were originally un-ringed. On the assumption that there had been no human involvement in these two cases, this could herald an invasion of *guttata* from the east, so that in time the white race alba may disappear and a new species, or sub-species, will emerge.

The arrival of barn owls in Britain

The most widespread of the barn owls is the species that inhabits the British Isles, the common barn owl *Tyto alba alba*, the white-breasted barn owl. It has a wide distribution throughout much of the Western Palearctic, which ranges from Ireland and Portugal in the west through to a line south from Lithuania to Ukraine in the east of the region. From its tentative hold in southern Fennoscandia, the barn owl can be found throughout Europe all the way down to the northern parts of Morocco and Algeria. There are a number of small populations in the Middle East, including Jordan, Syria, State of Palestine, Israel, the Nile Delta and southwards along the fertile banks of the River Nile to Aswan.

The subject of how barn owls arrived in the British Isles after the last ice age is an important part of our story, for it demonstrates their ability to colonise a land mass very quickly if the conditions are right, as they were as the ice receded before the rising sea finally cut Britain off from Europe.

Before that happened vast sheets of ice periodically covered much of Europe, stopping every now and then as the climate warmed, only to restart the process later as it cooled. It may be that the world is going through such a process at present.

During the last glaciation the ice covered much of Britain, and at its furthest extent it reached as far south as the Gower, in south-west Wales, and across to north Norfolk. It was upon this landscape that small mammals such as lemmings lived, and there they were hunted by short-eared and occasionally snowy owls. It was too cold for barn owls, due to their lack of body fat, and any that were present as the glaciation approached either moved south or died out.

The severity of the weather at that time, even in some southern parts of Europe, is shown by the finding of snowy owl remains on the northern fringe of the Iberian Peninsula, in the Pyrenees, but other remains have been found to the south in Gibraltar, although the tundra did not extend quite that far. It is likely that, at the furthest extent of the Ice Age, those barn owls that had survived the icy conditions were concentrated into southern Spain, North Africa, southern Italy, the Balkans and perhaps elsewhere, such as the Middle East.

Then, about 20,000 bp, the climate warmed and the ice started to melt, although every now and then the freeze restarted and the ice increased, though never to its earlier levels. Gradually the ice sheet receded until it reached its present position in about 11,700 bp. As it moved rapidly northwards, vast amounts of water that had been held in the ice packs were released. As the climate continued to warm, those species which had sought refuge in southern Europe began their journeys northward to colonise or recolonise areas lost during the Ice Age.

Pioneering plants were among the first life forms, and one of the trees to start the journey would have been birch, a species capable of producing lots of seed from an early age. Initially it formed areas of scrubland, as it still does, and these provided food for small mammals, such as wood mice and bank voles. Field voles would also have been present, but their numbers would have been controlled by the amount of available grassland which may not have been great in those early stages. Flowers also began to appear, and their pollen and nectar attracted many insects which in turn enticed insect-eating mammals such as shrews as well as the aforementioned wood mice and bank voles.

Following the small mammals were the creatures that feed on them: stoats, weasels, kestrels and, of course, barn owls. All of these species required not only food to sustain them, they also needed places to live. Initially barn owls nested in caves and rocky crevices, but in time various cavity-producing tree species, such as oak and elm, appeared, while those tree species which prefer an even milder climate, such as beech and hornbeam, followed later.

As the climate warmed, further amounts of melt-water were released which brought about a corresponding rise in sea level, the outcome of which was to progressively flood or erode many coastal areas.

The rise in sea level was so extensive that it brought about the separation of the British Isles from mainland Europe. In some places the parting was quite abrupt, but in others the process was much slower. Land bridges enabled plants and animals to continue colonising the British Isles before it was totally separated by the sea.

Ireland was the first piece of land to separate, but it is unclear whether the separation took place over a short period of time or whether it was a more protracted event which left a short-lived land bridge between Ireland and what is now Britain. The absence of such species as common shrews and voles suggests the separation was abrupt, although the ubiquitous wood mouse made it while the origins of pygmy shrew remain debatable.

Barn owls appear to have made it naturally to Ireland, no doubt due to their adaptability to eat a wide variety of prey, but also to nest in a wide range of habitats. However, the more selective tawny owl did not and although it too eats a wide variety of prey (Southern, 1954) its preponderance for nesting in mature deciduous trees with suitable holes probably meant that Ireland was separated from what is now Britain before mature trees became established (Martin, 2008). It is true that on occasion tawny owls will nest on the ground, but an environment fraught with danger from ground predators would have made that a dangerous habit. To date, no tawny owl fossil remains have been found in Ireland.

Even though the remains of sunken forests indicate that forested land extended well out from the Welsh coast, there appears to be little indication that a land bridge existed between the two land masses as the sea level rose and quickly separated Ireland from Britain.

As the ice continued to melt and the sea level rose, more coastal land became inundated until finally the land bridges that existed between what is now Britain and the rest of Europe were finally severed. It was at that juncture that Britain became an island, and any further colonisations by terrestrial species stopped. Only creatures that were capable of sea crossings were able to reach Britain, although, with man's assistance, others did arrive later. It seems possible that if barn owls had not made it to Britain before the separation their general unwillingness to cross large expanses of water in sufficient numbers, at any one time, might have precluded them from taking up residence here, but we shall never know that for certain.

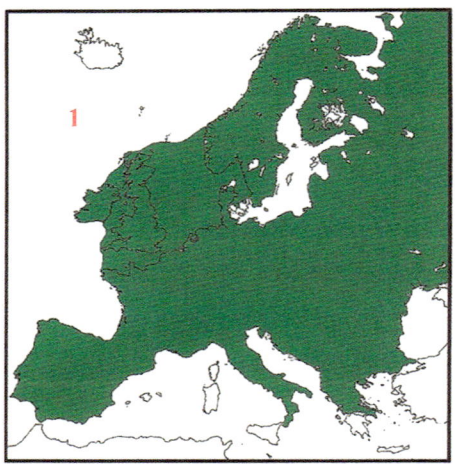 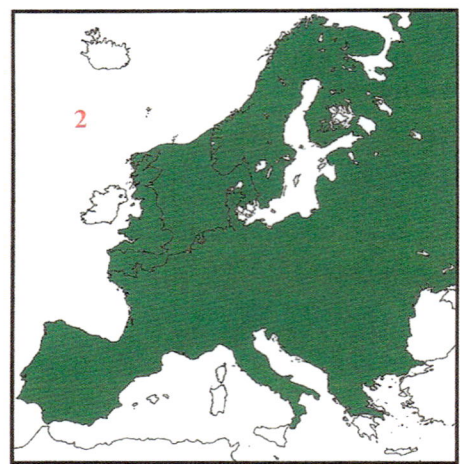

At its furthest extent, the presence of the ice lowered the level of the sea, so that both Ireland and the UK were connected to the mainland of Europe (Map 1). As the ice began to melt, the sea level rose, and Ireland became isolated (Map 2).

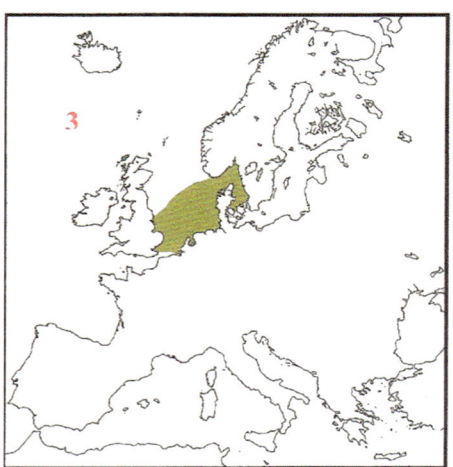 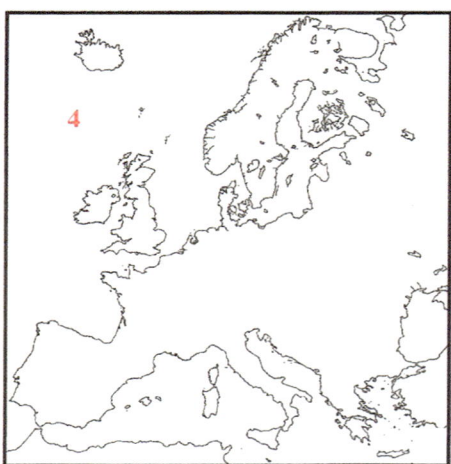

As the ice continued to melt, sea levels continued to rise until the UK was virtually isolated form the European mainland. A bridge, called 'Doggerland', (Map 3) did exist for some while and continued to allow other colonisations. Eventually the sea rose sufficiently high enough for Britain to become isolated also (Map 4), after which it became difficult for barn owls to reach the UK.

The separation of the British Isles from mainland Europe after the Ice Age.

There seems little doubt that other small mammal species would have made it to the British Isles had it not been for the separations, but for thousands of years Irish barn owls had to sustain themselves on a diet largely restricted to wood mice and pygmy shrews, and no doubt birds. Rats and bank voles were introduced much later. On mainland Britain the root vole did make it, only for it to die out some 9,500 years ago, but the widespread common vole, now found at the French coast, did not, although interestingly it is present on the Orkney Islands.

It was while all this was going on that a period of landscape transformation was taking place across Eurasia, as natural growth took place and trees began to cover much of the land. This was the time of the wildwood.

Trees did not cover all of the land, for there were lakes and wetlands along with clearings caused by tree fell which were kept clear by grazing animals. It did mean, though, that the predominant habitat across most of Britain and continental Europe was woodland of some form. Even places that were formerly dry, such as the fen lands of eastern England and the wetlands of Somerset, for examples, were not devoid of trees before the rising sea level flooded the land and made it inhospitable for them.

It was during this Mesolithic period that tawny and probably long-eared owls were more common in Britain than they have ever been since. A recent study, based upon present-day knowledge, has calculated that during that era there were some 160,000 pairs of tawny owls in Britain compared to an estimated 1,040 pairs of barn owls (Yalden and Albarella, 2009). The population of tawny owls at present is now much lower, at round 20,000 pairs, while present estimates suggest a healthy 5–6,000 pairs of barn owls.

It was about five to six thousand years ago, that the wildwood went into decline as the forests and woodlands were cleared to make way for farming. Although much of the clearance was due to human actions, the relatively quick clearance may have been too great for it to have been achieved by people alone. Working with the primitive tools at their disposal, clearing the wildwood would have been an immense task, so it is likely that elm disease also played its part (Coleman, 1998). Whatever the cause, the woodland clearance created an open landscape which suited a creature that would go on to dominate the wildlife scene six thousand years or so later. The day of the barn owl had arrived.

The woodland clearance was not restricted to the British Isles, for throughout Europe many of the forests that once existed were swept away for agriculture and for cities, towns and villages. This type of land management went on elsewhere, such as in large parts of the Middle East and beyond.

Distribution within Britain

Barn owls are widely distributed throughout much of England, Wales, southern, central and now northernmost Scotland, as well as much of Ireland. They tend to live in low-lying areas such as the river valleys and coastal areas where the

Forest clearance allowed the barn owl to colonise much of Europe.

land is often free from snow in winter but, more significantly perhaps, also free from large-scale disturbance, such as roads, large towns, cities and industry.

They were once reasonably common on higher ground, such as some of the low mountainous areas of northern England, Wales and Scotland, and until the end of the Second World War they even bred in a cottage high up at 'Brown Willy' on Bodmin Moor. Those birds continued to use their nest, which was in a cupboard within the derelict cottage, despite the use of that area as a battle-training ground prior to the D-Day landings. This demonstrates the tenacious manner in which barn owls may stay faithful to their nesting place in the face of adversity. The remains of that cottage were still visible in 2010, when I had the fortune to meet a man who lived there as a young boy just before the war.

High up on Bodmin Moor, lying in the shadow of Rough Tor, stands the remains of an ancient farmstead where barn owls once bred in a cupboard during the years 1942–4 (see Martin, 2008). Recent research (Batey, 2013) has found that, during the course of a study which ran from 1980–2011, the highest nesting barn owls in south-west England were on Dartmoor, at an altitude of 384 metres. It was considered that climate change was responsible for barn owls now nesting higher than previously. Rough Tor stands at 400 m above mean sea level.

Barn owls do nest in some of the low-lying areas of northern Scotland and those that live there are the most northerly to be found in the world, although a warming climate might encourage barn owls to breed more widely in Fennoscandia if the snow line continues to recede.

In recent decades they have suffered many problems due to the intensification of farming, and nowhere in Britain is this more of a problem than in the lowlands of Britain, a landscape that has, with a few exceptions, been largely overlooked in terms of barn owl studies, and where barn owls were once common.

Naming the barn owl

The naming of the birds by their vernacular, or common, names has been subject to change for many years. Montagu's harrier, for example, is named after the distinguished ornithologist George Montagu, but the origins of other names are less clear.

Scientifically the barn owl was once known as *Strix flammeus* (Linne.) by Linneaus, the eminent Swedish naturalist, but in 1769 it was reclassified and given the name *Strix alba* by Giovanni Scopoli, the Italian naturalist who originally described it. Later it was again reclassified as *Tyto alba*, following the cataloguing of the genus *Tyto* by Gustaf Billberg. Name changes affecting the barn owl took a long while to filter through and even in the later stages of the nineteenth century some naturalists still referred to it as *Strix flammeus*.

The name *Tyto alba* is derived from the Greek *tuto*, meaning night owl, and the Latin *albus* which means white. As for its vernacular name, it had to wait a further 114 years after Scopoli's description before a title was generally agreed on.

From the information available, it would seem the name 'barn owl' has its origins in the English county of Essex, a seemingly inappropriate part of England for the name to have arisen, so an explanation is necessary. Just to the south of the Essex town of Braintree lies the village of Black Notley where the famous naturalist John Ray grew up. He would have been familiar with barn owls as they were common in Essex at the time, and it is likely that he would have known it as the 'Church Owl', due to its predilection for occasionally nesting in church towers. He would, though, have been much more familiar with the local name 'White Owl', which was a common name for the barn owl in south-east England and especially Essex and Suffolk.

It was there, in Black Notley, that Ray studied natural history before going on to do research at the University of Cambridge where he became one of the greatest and most influential naturalists of his day. While he was at Cambridge he made friends with Francis Willughby, and together they formed a good and effective partnership touring Britain to study its fauna and flora. They spent a lot of time in northern Britain, including Scotland, but they also visited the West Country. In those northern and western areas there seems little doubt that these two naturalists would have observed many barn owls nesting in the rapidly growing number of stone barns that were being built in this period as a result of the enclosure acts.

Sadly, Willughby died at the young age of 37 but not before he and Ray had set out to write *The Ornithology*, which was the first serious attempt at classifying Britain's birds. Although known as Willughby's *Ornithology*, it was Ray who completed its three volumes and saw its eventual publication in 1676.

In this landmark work the barn owl is listed as the 'Barn Owl, White Owl or Church Owl', and the uncertainty as to what to call this bird was to linger on for much longer; in fact, even to the present day.

In Ray's time church towers were popular places for owls to nest. Later, church officials took to closing up the towers to exclude birds and especially pigeons, which were probably increasing due to the agricultural changes taking place. It is a habit for barn owls to nest in church towers throughout many parts of the world, and this is reflected in some local names that it has picked up over the years. For example, in Holland it is known as *kerkhuile*, or 'church owl', as it also used to be known in Somerset, a county with Dutch connections. In Sweden it is known as *torn uggla* or 'tower owl', as it is in Finland – *tornipöllö* or 'tower owl'.

Church towers were once favoured places for barn owls to nest in.

In many parts of mainland Europe, barn owls are still very reliant upon man-made structures for nesting, sometimes setting up home in the middle of villages and towns, as they used to do at the Smithsonian Institution building in Washington, D.C., USA.

The director of the Institution, Alexander Wetmore, described how 'after nightfall' he used to glimpse the white breasts of barn owls in the street lights as they set out from the Institution's towers to raid the sparrow and starling roosts in Pennsylvania Avenue. The owls nested in the Institution's towers until the buildings were closed off to them after the last war.

The common name by which we know it today was established in 1883, when the British Ornithologists' Union (BOU) officially adopted the title 'Barn Owl' and there seems little doubt that Willughby's *Ornithologiae* – to give it its Latin title – was an influence in that decision. However, it took some time for this new name to become universally accepted, and here I use an example from East Anglia to illustrate this point:

The distinguished Norfolk naturalists, the brothers James and Charles Paget, wrote of the natural history around Great Yarmouth and included an account of the 'White Owl'. Later, in 1884, the Suffolk naturalist Churchill Babington referred to it in his *Catalogue* as the 'White or Barn Owl', while later the Rev. Tuck continued to use the 'White Owl' in the *Victorian County History for Suffolk*. The reluctance to fully accept the new name continued into the 1930s and Claude Ticehurst sought a compromise by naming it the 'White-Breasted Barn-Owl', a name that was also used in the ground-breaking *Witherby's Handbook*. Certainly in Suffolk, where until recently most barn owls nested in trees, the name 'White Owl' hung on for many years and, even now, I occasionally hear it used by some of that county's older residents.

A 'White Owl'.

In neighbouring Essex the name 'White Owl' remained in use for some while. The late Alan Parker recounted the time he was carrying out a bird survey in 1968 at Gobions Farm near Collier Row, Romford. On informing the farmer that there were barn owls nesting on his farm, the farmer replied that his brother, who ran an adjoining farm just across the A12 road, also had a pair of 'White Owls'. Sadly, barn owls no longer nest in that area.

Even today, there is still confusion and indecision as to what vernacular name to give this bird, and the whole family of barn owls ensures that there will be further name changes in the future, but for the present I use the familiar name - 'Barn Owl'.

The barn door owl

In various parts of Europe the barn owl was sometimes referred to in the past as the 'Barn Door Owl', as it was once customary to nail a dead one to the door of a barn. It is not clear why this was done, but the practice might have had its origins in the Roman Empire, for in Rome it was once normal to nail a dead barn owl to the door of a child's nursery to ward off evil spirits. It is likely that this practice came north with the Romans as they set about conquering large parts of Europe. However, in northern Europe the reason might not have been to ward off evil spirits but to ward off bad weather. In other words, it was a good luck charm.

Many years ago the screech of a flying barn owl in England was believed to signify the onset of bad weather. Poor weather conditions during the spring may well have had a detrimental effect upon the coming harvest. Sometimes, a dead barn owl was nailed to the door of the barn that was destined to hold the harvested grain in an attempt to ward this off. The barn owl was often associated with superstition and bad luck in the old days, and this was a classic example.

This custom appears to have remained in use up until the nineteenth century when it seems the name faded into obscurity except in Suffolk where superstition linked with barn owls survived until at least the middle of the last century. Following the severe weather of 1947 the Reverend H. Copinger-Hill of Buxhall Rectory in Suffolk reported that, 'During the recent snowy weather, persisting from 28 Jan. to well into March, a barn door owl was picked up in a very emaciated condition in the garden'.

2: The barn owl described

The barn owl is undoubtedly one of the most attractive birds in the countryside. With its stunning plumage there are few other species that can compete with it, and yet this is only one feature of its make-up, for it certainly has other qualities that barn owl students find most interesting.

General description

A typical barn owl stands at around 300 mm and has an average wing length of 290 mm. The tail measures around 115 mm, although those of female dark-breasted barn owls are slightly shorter while the length of the tarsus on white-breasted birds is a little longer.

When seen from above, the overall impression is one of a contrasting beautiful golden honey-brown colour, interspersed with varying amounts of dark brown. A closer inspection, though, reveals that the colour is more buff than brown, with each of the honey-coloured body feathers having small flecks of grey and dark brown.

In flight, the birds appear to be white, hence the traditional name 'White Owl'; however, upon inspection, only the ventral or under parts are white, although some birds have varying amounts of dark flecking, which is usually more evident on females. With male birds the white of the breast usually extends up on to the sides of the neck, but on females those areas are light brown. This sexual dimorphism, or colour difference, can be a guide to gender identification in the field and is a feature that seems to be absent from all other owls apart from the snowy owl (Potapov and Sale, 2012). With that owl the colouring may change from bird to bird and appears to be responsive to environmental conditions, whereas with barn owls their colour differences are apparently sorted through genetics (Roulin et al., 1998). However, a word of caution is necessary here. Although females do tend to be darker on the neck, on occasion the brown is very light and the extent of the brown may also be asymmetrically unbalanced. Consequently, it would seem this is an unreliable method of separating the sexes and cannot be used as an absolute guide. (See Appendix.) However, this might only apply to birds in Britain. At present there does not appear to be any way that dark-breasted barn owls can be sexed in the field, whether close-up or not.

Turning to the individuals' plumages, for a number of years some ornithologists claimed that individual barn owls could be identified in the field due to patterning

The beauty of a barn owl's plumage caught in flight.

on the plumages, but such claims were discounted as imaginary. However, it was during a long-term study in Scotland, involving hundreds of birds, that the primary feather patterns on each bird were found to be different (Taylor, 1994). Each was found to have a unique pattern, or 'fingerprint', on their primaries which distinguished them from one another. As a consequence of this discovery it was found that the movements of individual birds could be tracked by collecting feathers at roost and nest sites, and then comparing them with those on birds that were caught at the nests. This scientific evidence thus tends to support the initial observation of Derek Bunn, that individual barn owls can be identified through field observations.

Wing shape is often useful in helping to inform us as to what type of habitat a bird lives in. For example, woodland birds, such as sparrowhawks and tawny owls, tend to have rounded ends to their wings, which helps them to manoeuvre through woodlands more easily, thus avoiding contact with trees and damage to their plumage.

Birds of the open countryside, such as kestrels and barn owls, have more tapered wings, which helps to provide them with greater lift and greater manoeuvrability. The statement is often made that the wings of a barn owl are rounded, but clearly this is not so.

The primary feathers of a barn owl Tyto alba. Beneath the 'top surface', the barn owl is indeed a 'white owl'.

It has been suggested that pointed wings are indicative of a northerly distribution, and indeed the northern hawk owl, a species of the circumpolar boreal forest taiga, and to some degree snowy owls, also have tapered wings. If this northern alignment is correct, the barn owl is indeed an enigmatic creature.

In flight, some barn owls can look quite large although this can be deceptive, for beneath the soft plumage the body is remarkably small, so small in fact that a

Top: The wing of a barn owl Tyto alba alba.
Bottom: The wing of a typical owl, the tawny owl Strix aluco sylvaticus.

full-grown adult will sit comfortably in the hand of most adult humans. It is true that females do weigh more than males, but there is very little difference in their wing and body measurements.

The live weights of adult barn owls may vary from location to location, and those that live in the higher northerly latitudes tend to be heavier than those further south. In Italy, for example, it was found that during the period October to March males weighed 271 g and females 298 g, but this was outside of the breeding season. In a live sample of 361 male birds in south-west Scotland (Taylor, 1994), the average weight was 330 g, and in a sample of 445 female birds from the same study, an average weight of 370 g was found. Female body weights can vary during the breeding season and this study found that at the time of laying the final egg they weighed an average of around 420 g.

From weights of dead birds that were either submitted for post-mortem examination or from information supplied by taxidermists, Shawyer (1998) found that the average weights of male barn owls was 288 g and for females 312 g. Like the one from Scotland, this research found that the weights of males tended to remain fairly constant throughout the year, but that the weights of females tended to be much higher during the laying and incubation period (March to May) than during the rest of the year. However, it is likely that dead birds will weigh less than live specimens due to the cause of death, such as starvation or ill-health, and the subsequent dehydration of the carcasses.

Barn owls ooze charm and good looks, and perhaps nowhere is this better captured than by the innocent allure of the heart-shaped facial disc. Indeed, they have one of the most developed facial discs in the owl world, equalled only by that of the great grey owl, a species of the northern holarctic forests. This species also has a heart-shape to its disc, although perhaps not quite so pronounced as that of the barn owl.

The eyes of a barn owl appear black from a distance, but on closer inspection it can be seen that they are a rich hazel brown. The horn-coloured bill appears small but underneath the facial feathers it is quite long, ranging from 32 mm on female white-breasted birds to just under 19 mm on male dark-breasted birds.

The heart-shaped facial disc of the 'cute and charming' barn owl is one of the key characteristics that sets the family of barn owls apart from other members of the Strigiformes. The great grey owl of the northern forests also has a heart-shaped facial disc though it is not quite so well formed. This 'heart-shape' has a key role to play in the hearing of these two unrelated species.

The moult in barn owls is not as simple as the shedding of feathers on an annual basis, and some individuals have been known to keep some of their primary feathers for up to three years. On a global scale, those barn owls that live in temperate climates, such as northern Europe, tend to begin their moult in the second year of their life and it is completed during a four-year period, after which the replacement of the feathers continues over a period of two years. In the tropics, however, they commence their moult in the first year, and complete the replacement of their wing and tail feathers over a period of approximately seven months. Feather replacement then continues on a yearly basis (Taylor, 1994).

In Britain, hen birds tend to moult during the incubation period when they are largely inactive. The males, on the other hand, keep their plumage in good condition at this time, as they provide most of the food for their mates and also for the owlets in the first few weeks of their lives. Consequently, they moult when the breeding season has finished, which may not be until September. In certain instances when the breeding season lengthens, either through bad weather or when two clutches are laid, some birds may not moult at all.

Camouflage, or cryptic plumage, is an important factor in the lives of many birds by helping to conceal them from their enemies. However, the barn owl is

A glance inside this big old oak tree would perhaps reveal nothing to the casual observer. Upon closer inspection, however, the white face betrays the presence of this owl.

a bit of an oddity, for how does a bird with a light golden-brown upper surface and white underparts avoid being noticed in the green landscape of the northern hemisphere?

Various examples have been discussed over the years where they appear to have chosen an environment in which they either unwittingly, or perhaps deliberately, use camouflage to escape detection. For example, many nest workers will have come across their habit of roosting and nesting in straw-stacks, and, while such an environment will provide a warm and secretive place in which to do this, is it coincidental that their plumage blends in quite well with their surroundings?

Limestone caves and crevices are other habitats that they have taken advantage of, and they still use these from time to time. Holes in old, large trees may also allow them to blend into the background.

The best example I have of cryptic plumage came to light in Norfolk in February 2011 when I observed a barn owl hunting in bright sunlight shortly after mid-day, and suddenly it seemed to disappear. But while looking at an alder tree that overhung a small stream nearby, I noticed a movement amongst the

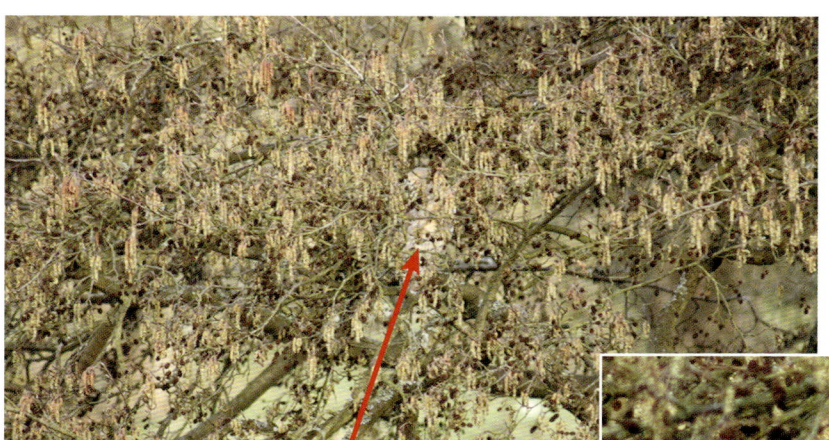

Spot the barn owl.
A camouflaged barn owl: deliberate or accidental?

This barn owl was observed in Norfolk in February 2011 where, from time to time, it would conceal itself beneath this alder tree, which was growing beside a stream. To the casual observers nearby it went unobserved. There were other types of trees in which it could have rested, so was it a deliberate attempt by the owl to hide itself beneath this tree's canopy, or was it just a coincidence?

leaves. By careful stalking I was able to confirm the owl's presence. Was this a deliberate use of camouflage, or just a suitable place for it to perch? Although barn owls have been recorded using alder trees for roosting, they did so when the tree was thickly clad in honeysuckle, which this one was not.

Silent flight

Barn owls are renowned for their silent flight but, just like so many aspects of their lifestyle, nothing is simple. I have closely witnessed adult birds flying in the field, and I have also watched them flying within a very quiet building that resonated sound very well. From these observations it seemed that they do fly silently. However, other observers have made alternative observations and these are worth looking at.

The naturalist Frank Gibson Phillips, who was studying barn owls in Hampshire before the Second World War, asserted that when they are flying to the nest with food they can be heard flying from some way off. He described the flight as being more ragged than was previously thought; he believed that they do not take any pains to fly quietly, but that they just flap along with larger and more decisive wing beats. He further stated that at the nest it was possible to hear a swishing noise from the wings as much as nine or ten feet away.

The Essex naturalist and bird photographer Alan Parker believed that their flight is not silent and that he could clearly hear the 'swish' of their wings when he was photographing at their nests. During the course of their studies in Lancashire and south Cumbria, Derek Bunn and his fellow workers pointed out the noises barn owls have to contend with when hunting, which included 'its own flight which is not quite as silent as one is usually led to believe'.

I once received a letter from someone who described the 'eerie experience' of a barn owl gliding silently over their head as they went to close a stable door late one night. Could this be a key feature of their silent flight? It is indeed silent, but is it only when gliding rather than when they are flapping their wings?

The late Eric Hosking described how he managed to get the first flashlight photograph of a barn owl with prey at its nest entrance. However, trying to see in the dark or anticipate when an owl would land at the entrance was impossible due to the silent approach of the owls, so he eventually decided to sit and listen for the bird's talons as it alighted at its tree hole.

In the search to discover how an owl flies silently, a great deal of investigation and experimentation has gone on. Amongst those investigations it has been found that on the leading edge of the flight feathers and in particular the outer primaries there is a fringe of stiff hairs which cut through the air and help to smooth the air-flow over the wings.

In addition to this, owls have a carpet of extended barbules on the upper surface of their primary feathers as well as on some of the vaned feathers. It appears that this carpet, which extends along the top of the vane, tends to dampen the flapping noise of the vanes touching each other and is a unique feature to owls, nightjars and herons.

Supplementing this, the primary and secondary feathers, but especially the wing coverts, have a soft downy upper surface that allows air to pass through the wings on the downbeat, and this helps soften the impact of the feathers on the air. As the air flows over the upper and lower surfaces of the wing, the trailing edges, which have very soft hair-like fringes, further reduce the air turbulence at the point where the two air-flows meet.

The wing coverts of a barn owl allow air to pass through them, so reducing further the wind resistance and helping to soften the flight.

We therefore have some dispute as to whether barn owls fly silently or not. It seems likely that at certain times they do indeed fly silently, whilst at others they are not so quiet. Gibson Phillips (as he preferred to be called) made the rather startling claim that barn owls have the ability to switch to silent flight or otherwise, as the need arises. This aspect of their flight does not appear to have been investigated to date. Could it be, for example, that they are able to manipulate their flight feathers much in the way that we are able to move our fingers? Probably not, but with this species nothing should be ruled out until disproven.

It may also be that the flight of the barn owl is inaudible to some humans due to the sound frequencies of their flight, so that some observers are able to hear their sound while others cannot; this would explain why there is some controversy over whether or not barn owls possess silent flight. It might also be that, as the nesting season drags on, the feathers become more ragged due to the continuous abrasion they receive as the owls enter and leave the nest site, as well as the extra hunting efforts required as they continually dive into vegetation for food to feed the young.

The possibility that the wings suffer from abrasion is demonstrated by the lack of melanistic keratin which is generally present on the wing-tips of many birds with white wings, such as many gulls and the northern gannet for example, and which prevents such wear. The reason snowy owls fly slowly, with a soft and easy flight, is possibly to prevent heavy wing beating and feather abrasion, and it seems likely that this may be the same for barn owls.

Effortless flight

In contrast with the size of the barn owl's body, its wings are large, which in aeronautical terms means that very little demand is put upon them to support the body when in flight. The barn owl's low wing loading allows them to fly very slowly so that they can scrutinise the ground for prey.

The wing loading is calculated by dividing the weight of the body by the area of the wing. The larger the wings are in relation to the size of the body the lower the wing loading will be, and the easier it will be for the wings to lift the body into the air. As a consequence of this, those birds that have a low wing loading can land, take off and fly at much slower speeds than birds with a high wing loading.

The barn owl *Tyto alba* appears to have the lowest wing loading (0.21 gms/cm^2) of all the world's owls (Mikkola, 2013), comparing favourably, for example, to that of the American barn owl, *Tyto furcata* (0.32 gms/cm^2) and the tawny owl (0.40 gms/cm^2). No one who has watched a barn owl fly moth-like over a meadow, hovering here, almost stalling there, could fail to have been impressed by the sheer buoyancy of its magnificent flight – and this is the reason. The lateral wing profile is also important in controlling the lift and air-flow over the wings; some of the earlier aeroplanes, such as the Hawker Hurricane, have a similar-shaped wing.

In recent years, the barn owl's flight has been the subject of considerable research. Some scientists in Germany are of the opinion that the unique construction of their wings may well have applications in physical science outside of the natural world. Specific research is proceeding on investigating the construction of the feathers and assessing the lateral shape and design of its wing, in the hope that those features will eventually be applied to a revolutionary type of aeroplane wing. Researchers are also looking into whether the principles involved could be functional to any surfaces that are subject to air or other flows, and might assist with noise reduction.

Scientific research on this subject is also under way at Cambridge University, England, involving a similar study. Scientists are investigating how the silent flight of owls might strengthen our understanding of how specialised feathering lessens noise. There is hope that the information from this project might find a use in the future design of conventional jet aircraft.

Voice and calls

Vocal contact is an important part of the owls' everyday life, and for most species there is still much to be learnt because owl vocalisations are now important in helping to determine their taxonomy. Many owls that were once thought to be subspecies of other owls have now been given full species status in their own right because we can separate owls through sonar sound recordings. Owl calls are inherited, not learnt, so a species that might look like another and be considered a subspecies may well be classed as a different species because its call is different when their sonograms are compared.

Although sonogram analysis does not appear to have been carried out on the barn owls in Britain, their voices have been studied and to date 15 different calls have had a meaning placed against them, while a further two non-vocal sounds have also been identified (Bunn, 1974).

The call that is best known is the screech, which is best heard when a bird is on the wing. It is not only emitted by the male, the female also gives this call, but hers is not as perfect as the male's and it has a different tone. This call can be heard in most months of the year but it is particularly noticeable in the autumn, when winter territories are being established, and in early spring, prior to the onset of the breeding cycle. Snoring, which is perhaps more readily identified as hissing, is another important call and is usually associated with hungry nestlings, although variants of this will be used by adults also.

Apart from these, there is an additional call which is not unlike the 'cuk cuk' call made by a moorhen. It has usually been heard when an adult is approaching the nest, which suggests that it may be some form of contact call to alert the nest inhabitants that the adult is about to alight at the nest entrance. Some other hole-nesting birds, such as great tits, also give a subdued call to their young before entering the nest, so this seems a logical explanation. Where barn owls are nesting in buildings, the need to use this call may not arise because the chicks can usually see the parent standing at the entrance hole before it approaches the nest, as they also can with nesting boxes that have platforms. Where trees are used for nesting this may not be the case and an unexpected visitor to a nest hole could in fact be a predator. By the parents announcing themselves as they approach the nest, the chicks can then come safely to the entrance hole to receive food. In 1925 a call resembling 'ick-ick-ick-ick' was recorded from an adult barn owl in the USA. It was thought that the call signified the bringing of food, and it is a call I once heard some years ago when observing a pair that were nesting in an old elm tree on the Essex/Suffolk border.

The possibility that this call could be echolocation has been raised by ornithologists working in South Africa, who stated that a 'double clicking' note is occasionally produced on dark nights. This type of call is more in line with echolocation rather than a distinct call but evidence is lacking that this is used systematically by owls. Even so, the case for barn owls using echolocation is growing, and both the Curaçao and Lesser Antilles barn owls have been recorded uttering clicking notes in flight. The debate on this has been widened as it has also been reported that the American barn owl utters metallic clicking calls. However, it has been pointed out that these are not in the same frequency range as those used by bats, in other words they are not the ultrasonic sounds generally used in echolocation. In the early 1970s, groundbreaking work was carried out on the voice of the barn owl. This seems to have been the first attempt to interpret the meanings of their calls, but further research may come up with other fields of interest.

For example, it appears that owls do not exhibit much variation in dialect and that there is little difference in the vocalisations between individuals. As far as British barn owls are concerned, this claim might be worthy of investigation for the possibility of dialects within the British population might be genetically important. Indeed, further research might reveal that there could be some interesting comparisons between those on mainland Europe and their British counterparts.

It is of considerable interest to see that the RSPB have launched a project to investigate the different accents that yellowhammers may use. They hypothesise that because yellowhammers do not tend to move out of their own area they tend to have 'thick' accents. This research appears to have been initiated by scientists at the Charles University in Prague, Czech Republic, who found that yellowhammers have ten basic dialects. Apart from the study being introduced into Britain, it is also being expanded into New Zealand, where these birds were introduced in the nineteenth century. The barn owls of Britain are also noted for their sedentary tendencies and might be a suitable subject for investigation in this matter.

Sight

Owls are credited with an ability to see in the dark, but this is a very oversimplified explanation of how they find their way around. Although they can no more see in total darkness than we can, it is true that their sight is quite extraordinary and some species, such as the tawny owl, do have an exceptional ability to see in very, very low light conditions.

A great deal of work has been carried out on the sight of animals who do not see light as we see it. Experiments at Bristol University have shown that ultraviolet (UV) wavelengths which are undetected by human eyes are utilised by birds when they are hunting and when they are seeking mates, and this may be a common factor with most bird species, but not for the owls.

Due to their nocturnal lifestyle, owls have evolved so that they can see when there is very little light available. The cornea – the transparent coating on the front of the eye – is the first stage in accomplishing this, and in the owl it is very large. The pupil, which is at the centre of the eye and the means by which light enters the eye, must be able to expand to allow sufficient light to enter when it is dark. The size of the pupil is controlled by the iris, the coloured membrane between the cornea and the lens. The iris is controlled by the creation of adrenalin within the body which relaxes the eye muscles and allows the pupil to expand. The larger the pupil, the more light passes through the lens allowing images to be captured on the retina, which contains the light sensitive cells at the back of the eye.

It has traditionally been thought that one-eyed barn owls could not survive, but clearly this Portuguese bird has no trouble in finding food, as the rear portion and tail of this disappearing mouse show. The owl is suffering from purulent conjunctivitis of the right eye, an injury that may later give rise to the appearance of cataract and synechiae, which are adhesions between the lens, iris and cornea.

The retina contains two types of photoreceptive cells called rods and cones. The rods are highly responsive to light, and a barn owl's eye, like those of other owl species, contains a great many of these. However, the abundance of rods is achieved at the expense of the number of cones, so the sensitivity to light is only gained by losing the ability to see objects in good colour, as well as the facility to see things in detail. In summary, therefore, barn owls can see in very low light conditions but their capacity to pick out detail is poor.

Like other owls, the eyes of a barn owl are tubular in shape and each is set within a socket of bony plates which surround the eye. This socket is known as the sclerotic ring and holds the eyes in a fixed position (the eyes can't swivel). A supposed benefit

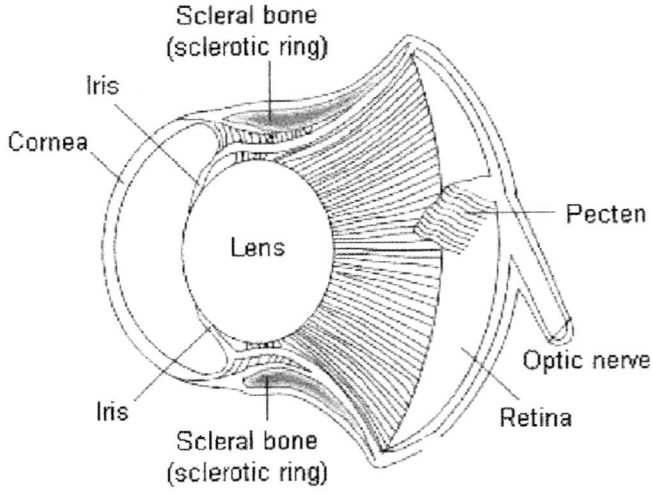

Cross section of an eye.

of having forward-facing eyes is that it provides the owl with binocular vision, allowing it to judge distances more accurately than if its eyes were on either side of the head. This would be of great benefit when trying to catch prey, but one drawback with binocular vision is that it restricts the field of view. This means that an owl can only see around 70 per cent of its field of vision through both eyes at once, and the total range of its field of view is only 110 degrees.

The long-held view that forward-facing eyes for owls are beneficial in terms of binocular vision has been challenged, however, for it has recently been proposed that the main reason why owls have forward facing eyes is to accommodate their large ears within the skull and that as a consequence of the ears' asymmetry an owl's eyes are also asymmetric.

The eyes themselves have three lids, the first of which is the upper one for blinking normally. There is a lower one, which is drawn up when sleeping, and a third, known as the nictitating membrane, is a layer of tissue which is drawn across the eye from the inside to the outside. The purpose of this lid is to clean and protect the eye, and it is particularly useful when an owl is feeding its young because boisterous owlets, in their eagerness to get at the food, could unwittingly damage the parents' eyes.

The ability of owls to rotate their heads in an extraordinary manner is gained by having a great number of vertebrae in their necks, for while humans have seven owls have twice as many. Not all owls can rotate their heads to the same degree as barn owls, though, who can turn theirs by up to 180 degrees in either direction. Besides the ability to rotate their heads so that they can see behind, they can also move their heads with an intriguing circular motion, but only when facing forward. For example, if they are interested in a particular object, they can tilt their head sideways so that one eye sits above the other. While these movements might seem comical, it suggests that they have difficulty in discerning what objects are. So by obtaining a number of sightings on an object from different angles they may gain a better idea of what they are looking at.

Unlike humans, owls are able to cope with these sudden twists and turns of their heads without causing damage to their circulatory systems because of the large cavities within their neck vertebrae, which allow the blood to flow freely without clotting. Sudden twists and turns in the human circulatory system can cause a stroke, but not so with the owls.

Ornithologists have for some time been puzzled as to why barn owls need to perform such contortions with their heads, but the general conclusion from field work strongly suggests that they are long-sighted. If they do have difficulty in discerning images that are close up this would explain why they need to twist and turn their heads in such a manner.

However, once again we have some contradiction as far as our barn owl is concerned, for like other owls they do sometimes fly into overhead wires, and occasionally they are killed, though I have found upon inspection that it is not through electrocution.

It is of some considerable interest, therefore, to know that at night they can land and perch on narrow overhead wires when there is little light, and five occurrences of this have been recorded. One such event took place on 22 October 1987 when we watched a barn owl by torchlight from our car for several minutes at Great Horkesley in Essex (Martin and Martin, 1990).

We witnessed the same behaviour the very next night, but on this occasion the owl flew off and alighted quite easily on the wire some 50 metres away. We then followed it and again it flew off only to perch on the wire further down the road, and this was repeated several times. There were plenty of trees and other seemingly suitable perches nearby, but the owl never used one of those. Despite follow up visits to this location, we never saw this owl again behaving in this manner, but clearly barn owls have no difficulty in seeing, and landing on, overhead cables in near darkness, so it is unclear why they sometimes succumb to collision with them. There is no doubt that the sight quality of some birds is questionable, and this may leave them vulnerable to collisions with objects such as overhead wires. Taylor (1994) found that the optimum height at which barn owls hunt for prey is around 3 metres so it is unlikely that, when hunting, they would collide with overhead wires, which are usually much higher.

The development of the eyes in young barn owls has been observed, though not beyond the nesting period. When the owlets hatch out they are blind until they are 12 days old, when the eyes start to open for short periods. At this stage the eyes have a blue blind-looking appearance, and this stays with them until around day 17. By day 24 the eyes begin to lose the blue appearance, so that by the time they are 27 days old, their eyes begin to take on the normal hazel-brown colouring of adult birds. It is not clear why this change takes place although it is likely to be due to the maturing of the pigment cells. It is not known whether a barn owl's eyes continue to develop with age but that is possible. Changes in eye colour throughout the lifespan have been noted in sparrowhawks, for example, so a subtle change in eye colour, which might be difficult to observe in the wild, may occur.

Why they have dark hazel eyes is not clear, but it should be noted that it is the only European owl that has such a coloured iris. It is interesting to observe that the eyes of many people who originate from the tropics are dark brown, and this may be to protect them against the effects of strong sunlight. It is believed that barn owls have strong links with the tropics so perhaps their eye colouration is for the same purpose.

This, however, leads to another contradiction with this fascinating owl, for it was not very long ago that it was unusual for barn owls to be reported as being out in daylight, but now we know that some barn owls are active during the day and in bright sunshine, so they might not be so shy of sunlight as originally thought.

In summary, therefore, we know that the sight of barn owls might not be as good as some other owl species. We also know that they have the ability to fly silently, at least some of the time, and that their effortless, buoyant flight allows them to fly very slowly over the ground. The question that arises, of course, is, why do they need to fly silently at all?

Hearing

Any inadequacies that the barn owl might have with its sight is more than made up for by its superb hearing, which it uses extensively when hunting. This was established during the 1960s, when at Cornell University in the USA considerable research was carried out into their hearing (Payne, 1971). From this it was revealed that a barn owl could catch its prey simply from hearing it rustling in the undergrowth.

This investigation revealed that the finely-feathered facial disc picks up sounds which are then filtered through those feathers to two crescent-shaped rows of stiff feathers located one on either side of the head, just behind the facial ruff. These curved rows of feathers grow just behind the ear openings and they differ in direction. Those on the left side of the head direct slightly downwards, while those on the right direct slightly upwards. The sounds collected by these feathers are then concentrated into the square-shaped ear openings; these not only differ in size, but are at different levels, the left aperture being higher than the right.

This arrangement means that sounds will be gathered and formulated in a variety of ways, which enables the owl to pinpoint the source of the sound. If necessary, it can bob, weave and tilt its head so that several fixes on the source of the sound are obtained. This, together with any visual contact it may have, provides it with enough information to decipher the location of its prey with remarkable accuracy.

It was also found during the course of this study that barn owls can hunt very efficiently in extremely low light conditions, although when they were placed in total darkness, their hunting efficiency was reduced to 60 per cent. A later study confirmed these findings, but it also discovered that when one ear was blocked, they were unable to establish the precise location of any sound source, thus confirming that barn owls need both ears to be operating efficiently otherwise they would probably starve. Furthermore, it was discovered that they can hear sound frequencies that are inaudible to humans, while conversely they are unable to hear some that humans can.

The ears of a barn owl are situated on either side of its head behind the feathers that are at the edge of the facial disc. When pulled back, as they are with this dead barn owl on the right, a half-moon row of stiff feathers can be seen. These collect the sounds that have been filtered through the disc's fine feathering and direct them into the ear openings. To some degree we can gain an idea of the effectiveness of this by cupping our hands to our ears.

This research was carried out using American barn owls, and it was an important milestone in helping us to understand how barn owls catch their prey. Whether all members of the genus *Tyto* have the same quality of hearing is a matter for further research, however, for to date no such study appears to have been undertaken.

Additional research has shown that the feathering on the facial disc is vital in delivering sounds to the ears and that, when most of the facial feathers were removed, an owl tended to make great errors in catching its prey and fell well short of its intended victim. The conclusion was reached, therefore, that the efficiency of these feathers is paramount to an owl's survival. We can now see the importance of the serrated edge on the middle talon which is used to comb the feathering on the facial disc to keep it in good working order.

Barn owls are able to twist and turn their heads in a most remarkable manner.

Although experiments have been conducted on the efficiency of their hearing, there do not appear to have been any precise studies seeking to establish the effects of background noise upon their hunting efficiency. The fact that barn owls tend to avoid disturbance suggests that this is a problem.

A study carried out in Devon found that barn owls no longer bred within 0.5 km of either side of the major roads in that county and that their populations were greatly reduced in a band stretching 0.5 km to 2.5 km from those roads. Beyond that measure their numbers fell up to a distance of 8 km, though not so significantly. This research concluded that barn owls were affected in some way up to 25 km beyond the initial measure. The general conclusion was that major roads were helping to keep barn owl numbers down in Britain and that road mortality was a key factor in this. There must be considerable agreement with that, though to what degree traffic noise plays a part in this we do not know, though it may be significant.

It is believed that barn owls are reasonably tolerant of day-to-day noises, and certainly owls that are born into a safe environment, even if it is a little noisy, soon get used to it, just like those humans who are born and raised in towns or cities. From time to time traffic noise does appear to influence their pattern of hunting, however, for, although they may not live in close proximity to a main road, at certain times traffic noise can be quite severe, even from over a mile away. At such times they do appear to be uncomfortable with this, judging by the apparent lack of concentration in their hunting efforts. This, however, is speculative observation. Even so, there is growing evidence that many wildlife species actively avoid areas where noise disturbance is great. It therefore seems logical that a creature that relies heavily upon its hearing for food will avoid such environments.

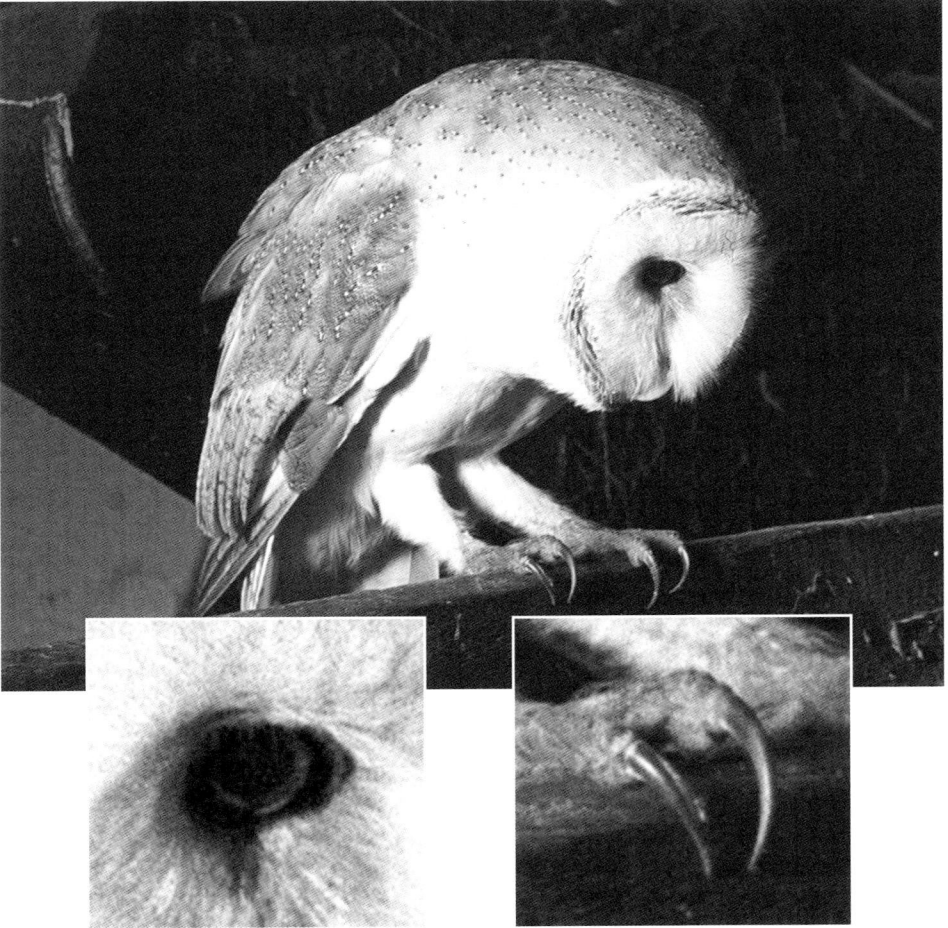

One can almost feel the intensity of concentration as this barn owl watches, and listens, for a mouse rummaging around on the floor below. Note the erect rectal bristles around the eyes and beak, waiting to catch any sound that the mouse makes. Note also the way that the talons are being used for grasping the top of this perch; two in front and two behind. It is also possible to see the serrated edge on the talon nearest the camera. The whole bird seems to be alive with expectancy. The inset shows the wide pupil, as the eye gathers in all available light.

Part 2
At home with the barn owl

3: The farmland owl
  The first agricultural revolution • The importance of pellet analysis • Opportunity knocks • Not just mice and voles • Review and conclusions

4: Prey and habitat diversity
  Hedgerows • Hedgerow diversity • Slow runs the river • Grassland: the weakest link?

5: Aspects of behaviour
  Establishing a territory • Diurnal behaviour • Hunting • Relationships with other owls and birds • Roosts

6: Roosting and nesting habitats
  Nightmare with elm trees • Buildings • Nest boxes • Thinking outside the box

7: Nesting
  Courtship • Gambling barn owls • Incubation • Captive breeding

8: The owlets
  A star is born • New kids on the nest • Chick survival • A matter of life and death

9: Dispersal and migration
  With this ring • Dispersal • Irruptions

3: The farmland owl

> 'He who controls the past controls the future.
> He who controls the present controls the past.'
> George Orwell, *Nineteen Eighty-Four*

If there is one thing that barn owls lack, it is a specific habitat category into which they can fit. Although they do have a woodland background, and they can often be seen hunting the coastal marshes, wherever you look around the world they are essentially farmland birds, and it is this that is the key to their success. If a piece of woodland or forest is cleared for farmland, it usually won't be long before a barn owl turns up to hunt the small mammals that have moved in to feed on the crops.

Those farmlands that provide a range of habitats will usually attract a wide range of small mammals, and in turn these will usually attract barn owls, as long as they have somewhere to roost and nest. Up until the Second World War that is what the vast majority of British farms provided: plenty of food and nest sites, as a consequence of which barn owls were quite common on most farms.

One of Britain's top ornithological scientists Dr Iain Taylor points out that, although we do not have precise and detailed information regarding the former status of the barn owl, there is sufficient anecdotal evidence to place this matter beyond any doubt. In Suffolk, where I carried out a survey of that county's barn owls in the 1980s, the written accounts of past authorities left me in no doubt that before the Second World War there once existed a considerable population of barn owls in that most rural of counties.

Largely from nest-box studies, the latest estimate suggests that Suffolk has around 300 or so breeding pairs on average, but I cautiously estimate that in the 1930s there were around 1,000 pairs living in that county and perhaps 1,500 pairs would not be an exaggeration, but we will never know for sure.

In his 1932 survey of England and Wales George Blaker proposed that there were around 12,000 breeding pairs of barn owls at that time, with a further 1,000 additional, or floating, birds. Most authorities now agree that, although the survey was a tremendous effort for its time, the actual population was likely to have been very much higher. To help try and explain why this conclusion has been agreed, it is necessary to go back a little over 300 years in time to gain an understanding of why the countryside was once a haven for barn owls.

It may be argued that to dwell on history is to dwell in the past, but it may also be argued that to use history as a learning tool is to dwell in the future, as we seek to secure the future of this bird, and indeed many other farmland species.

The first agricultural revolution

It was in the early part of the seventeenth century that work started on draining the vast East Anglian Fens for agriculture. Work on this extensive low-lying area to the south of the Wash heralded the start of the First Agricultural Revolution, a period that was to have a marked and positive effect on Britain's barn owls. The draining of the Fens continued into the nineteenth century and the maintenance of the water levels continues to the present day, for without it they would flood once again. This was only the start, though, as other low-lying places such as Romney Marsh in Kent, the Lincolnshire and Yorkshire wetlands and the Somerset Levels were also drained and brought under agriculture.

The Mildenhall Fens.

Draining these large areas was highly beneficial and brought great benefits for agriculture as the exposed peat rich soil proved to be highly fertile. In the Fens a network of minor drains was constructed by numerous drainage ditches, along which grew lush grassy verges that even today are the homes of voles.

Elsewhere, on these lands that were gained from the sea, cereal and other crops were grown and these would have provided food for mice and shrews.

Like the present day, natural nest sites were uncommon but here and there barns would have been constructed, as a consequence of which, by the end of the nineteenth century, barn owls were reasonably common fenland birds.

It was shortly after the start of the fen drainage projects that the first Act of Enclosure was passed by Parliament. It was this that ensured that for the next 200 or so years Britain's barn owl population thrived, as large parts of the countryside were transformed in ways that would very much suit their lifestyle.

The reason for these enclosures was to produce food. By this time Britain had become largely dependent upon overseas supplies, but the Napoleonic and other wars of the period meant that food security was compromised and supplies had become quite scarce, as a consequence of which prices rose sharply. These factors brought about the risk of human starvation and civil unrest, so it was decided that more home-grown produce was required. To reach that objective, drastic measures were needed.

For a variety of reasons the Enclosure Acts were controversial and very unpopular, but for barn owls there were positive outcomes. During the course of enclosure nearly all of the wide, open fields that had existed in Middle England since the clearing of the wildwood were enclosed by thousands of miles of hedgerows. Often these were composed of fast-growing species such as hawthorn (also once referred to as quick thorn) that were planted to separate properties and to enclose cattle, but they also had a side benefit.

Hedge-cutting was a manual task that was often carried out on a piecemeal basis by hedge-layers. They were able to construct a strong stock-proof barrier, which also proved to be a rich source of food for people. The usefulness of the fruits that grew on the hedges and elsewhere in the countryside is demonstrated by the number of old country recipes that are still to be found in many of the present-day cookbooks.

For example, rose hips are packed full of vitamin C; during the Second World War they were used to produce rose hip syrup to counteract the deficiency in children's diets brought about by a scarcity of green vegetables. Vitamin C is an important factor in the growth of mammals, whether they be humans or small ones!

Considering this, it would not be too adventurous to suppose that, as a result of the enclosure period, these hedgerows had a huge benefit for wildlife. The flowers and subsequent fruits would have been advantageous to a sequential myriad of wildlife species, including shrews, mice and voles. In a number of places dry stone walling and other man-made barriers, such as the drains on the Somerset Levels, would have played an important role in all of this as well. This is, of course, conjecture, but we do have enough circumstantial evidence to indicate that this may well have been the case.

It was around the year 1716 that a new arrival made its way onto the farmlands of Britain: the brown rat. This omnivorous rodent arrived on ships from mainland Europe and spread rapidly throughout Britain, using the newly created hedgerows and ditches as super-highways. It thrived on the food that was to be found amongst those hedgerows, as well as in the unkempt farmyards that existed at that time, and there can be no doubt that other small mammals followed in the footsteps of the new invader.

The production of food in the absence of closed grain silos would have created an abundance of food for rats and other small mammals, in the form of spilt grain and other foodstuffs, while warm dry homes would have been available in haystacks and farm buildings.

The anecdotal evidence to indicate that small mammals were abundant on our farmlands is so strong that it cannot be ignored. Farmworkers, for example, would often tie string around their trouser legs to prevent small mammals from running up the inside of the legs. Terriers were brought in to catch rats, and children would be employed with sticks to kill mice and rats when they ran from the wheat as it was being thrashed. Ridding the farmyard of rats and mice at harvest time was a major event in the farming calendar. Enter the barn owl – and by the beginning of the nineteenth century the ornithologists of the day were recording that it was a very common species.

With an abundance of food and nesting places in the form of trees and farm buildings, the countryside of Britain must have been a haven for barn owls. Tradition has it that barn owls were encouraged by farmers to take up residence by the creation of special 'owl windows' that were built in the gable ends of barns and other buildings. These can sometimes still be seen on those farm buildings that have not been demolished or converted for domestic use.

However, this was not to last, for just as the Farming Revolution was to have a positive and influential role in increasing the barn owl population so the Industrial Revolution heralded the start of its decline. The effects of persecution by gamekeepers on barn owls and other predatory birds was to dominate much of that century, and there can be no doubts that this was the cause of many barn owl deaths. However, the barn owl is an emotive species, and the sight of dead barn owls hung up on 'keepers' trees' aroused great anger.

A factor that has been overlooked is that, at the same time as they were being persecuted by gamekeepers, the return of the 'Little Ice Age' would have undoubtedly killed many barn owls, as we shall see later. Unable to find food beneath the snow, and therefore unable to withstand the cold, many barn owls would have perished as a result of that weather. It would be many years before the link between severe weather and barn owls deaths would be forged.

As the last vestiges of the Arctic weather were lost at the start of the twentieth century through the onset of a warming climate, not surprisingly barn owl numbers picked up. The present thinking is that much of the recovery was due to many gamekeepers being away during the Great War of 1914–18, and that was undoubtedly a contributing factor; but a turn for the better weather-wise would also have been beneficial as the climate warmed.

It was not long, though, before a fall in the number of barn owls was again noticed, and in 1932 a survey of England and Wales was organised on behalf of the RSPB. It was launched as a result of what was perceived as a declining barn owl population though there were no comparison figures to work with. Even so, there seems little doubt that a decline had occurred, and today we can see that a combination of factors had come together to bring this about, although they were not blatantly obvious at the time. Various reasons were given for the fall in numbers, including a loss of nest sites and agricultural poisons, but no conclusions as to the precise reasons for a sudden fall in numbers could be reached. Looking back we can see more clearly the likely reasons for the undoubted decline, and some 80 years later they have a resonance with the present day.

From late Victorian times up until the early 1930s a great amount of land had been taken out of production due to large quantities of cheap imported grain coming in from North America. This put many British farmers out of business and made their farms redundant, although it undoubtedly had positive results for barn owls as the land would have been ideal for small mammals. However, trends in farming had begun to change in the mid-1920s, and in 1932 the Wheat Act was introduced. As a result of this, British farmers were paid guaranteed incomes to bring land back into cultivation. Consequently, prime habitats for small mammals, such as grasslands, were destroyed as the land was ploughed up.

Alongside this, a huge building programme was launched in the mid 1920s as Britain sought to recover from the damaging effects of the First World War. In consequence, 65,000 acres of farmland were taken for building purposes in each of the years between 1925 and the outbreak of the Second World War in 1939. Combined with an annual destruction of 1,000 miles of hedgerow affecting Britain's small mammal population, and the loss of large numbers of trees and farm buildings, this would have dealt a devastating blow to Britain's barn owls. This time in Britain's history remains the era when the greatest amount of land was taken for building.

In conclusion, the severe winter of 1929 and the loss of small mammal habitat were, unfortunately, overlooked in the 1932 survey. A sudden drop in numbers brought about by bad weather is likely to have been the spark that ignited this survey, while in some quarters the subject of diet had aroused interest.

The importance of pellet analysis

It was the ornithologist Claude Ticehurst who carried out the first meaningful examination of pellets in 1935, drawing on a number of samples from across southern England for his study. He linked the availability of small mammals to the abundance of barn owls and drew the conclusion that 'opportunity makes the meal'. In other words, barn owls do not selectively seek out a particular prey species upon which to feed, they just catch what is available.

The results from Ticehurst's study showed that, in percentage terms, voles, and especially field voles, accounted for a large part of the overall diet. The proportions of shrews and mice that were taken were not that far behind, while other species, notably rats, helped to form a diet that was more diverse than it is today.

No further studies appear to have been published until, in the midst of significant farming changes that were taking place at that time, the late David Glue published a survey in 1967 which encompassed pellet results from 14 various locations in England and Wales. These involved a variety of habitats including rough grassland, areas of mixed farming, wet pastureland, water meadows and parkland. Most of the locations included in this study were again in the southern counties of England.

Altogether the remains of 3,657 small mammals and birds were analysed of which the three most frequently taken were field vole (45.3%), common shrew (21.1%) and then wood mouse (10.8%). The diet was dominated by field voles and common shrew, in an environment that was already changing in the wake of the farming revolution taking place at that time, with rodents forming only a small part of the diet. Later, Glue was to follow this up with a much wider survey of the whole of Britain (Glue, 1974), but, before we get there, it is worth mentioning some other events that provide us with a further insight into what Britain's barn owls ate in the past.

It was during the late 1980s that enough pellets to fill three sacks were recovered from a house chimney in Hampshire. A search of the building records revealed that the chimney had been capped in 1913, although before that event one or more barn owls had been using it as a roost and had deposited a large number of pellets there. Due to the warmth of an adjacent chimney, which had been in constant use during the intervening period, the pellets had dried and, as a consequence, they were perfectly preserved. Upon examination it was found those pellets contained the remains of no less than 813 prey items which together formed a diet that was strikingly different from that of today (Glue and Jordan, 1990).

They revealed that field vole, common shrew, wood mouse, bank vole and pygmy shrew each comprised ten per cent or more of an evenly balanced diet when they were deposited. Altogether the remains of some 14 prey species were found in this analysis. An inspection of some old maps and literature suggested that this was due to the varied landscape that surrounded the cottage at the time the chimney was capped. This contained a greater abundance of hedgerows, pastures and other landscape features which provided a greater diversity of small mammal habitats which in turn provided a wider range of prey.

Cough up

Unlike the diurnal raptors, owls do not have a crop in which to store their food, so after prey is swallowed (usually head first) it goes straight to the stomach where it is dissolved and the nutrients absorbed. As they are unable to digest bone, fur and feather matter, these are bound into a pellet at the end of the digestion process and are regurgitated via the mouth when the owl finds it convenient to do so. Bird prey is usually treated a little differently in that usually they are first decapitated and only the head may be eaten. Small birds such as sparrows may be eaten whole, while larger prey may be eaten piecemeal.

Barn owls usually swallow their prey whole, and head first.

Compared to those of other owls, barn owl pellets tend to be glossy in appearance and can vary in size. Measuring the length and width of each pellet might not be so important if you just wish to obtain a snapshot of what barn owls are eating in the area, but, if you are intending to use the pellet information on a more scientific basis and make your information widely known, then this might be worthy of consideration.

The formation and subsequent regurgitation of pellets has been studied in some detail on species such as great horned owls, but there does not appear to have been any such study carried out on barn owls.

However, it does appear that the ejection of pellets by barn owls is a voluntary action and that it can be encouraged by the sight or expectation of food. A roost site, therefore, that contains an abundance of pellets may suggest that an owl is depositing its pellet there in the expectation that it will shortly be catching food. The conclusion we may wish to draw from this is that a roost that regularly accumulates an abundance of pellets is used by an owl (or owls) used to catching food on a regular and reliable basis. Contrary to this, a roost that contains few pellets on an irregular basis may suggest that the hunting is not so reliable in that area and might only be used as food becomes available.

Barn owls often deposit their pellets in exactly the same place and at the same spot. This means that large piles of pellets can accumulate at some roosts. It is this habit that allows conservationists to collect the pellets on a regular basis in order to find out what they eating. This may provide a picture of how diverse and prey-rich their habitats are, which can be useful in helping to construct a conservation programme. Now, with the disappearance of many traditional old buildings for roosting, it is important to check nest boxes and clear them out from time to time.

If a dietary study is being carried out, pellet samples should be collected on a regular basis, say once every four weeks, so that seasonal comparisons can be made, and also to establish how regularly the box is used.

Unless nest boxes are periodically cleared out, the build up of pellets might eventually make a box uninhabitable.

Once pellets have been collected they need to be teased apart to examine the contents, and for this a good working surface is required, and water if the pellets are to be soaked prior to dissection. Some workers prefer to dissect the pellets when they are dry. Whichever method is chosen, forceps, dissecting needles or perhaps tweezers will be needed to tease the pellets apart. A good identification guide and a jeweller's eye glass or a magnifying glass will be needed to identify many of the remains, and a note book will be needed to log the results. Both the Field Studies Council and the Mammal Society produce good guides to help with pellet analysis.

When analysing pellets some guides stress that rubber gloves should be worn. If, like me, you do not wear rubber gloves, it is very important to wash your hands thoroughly afterwards.

Taking pellets apart may be great fun, but analysing the contents and making that information available is of great conservation value.

What are you likely to find in pellets? The most common finds will be the skulls of voles, mice and shrews, but keep a look out for any unusual finds such as frog remains, butterfly or moth wings, and bird skulls. While it doesn't happen that frequently, surprising finds like the skulls from such species as redshank and dunlin do sometimes turn up. Bearing in mind the size and shape of those skulls, it is quite remarkable to find that barn owls can swallow such prey without damaging themselves internally. Occasionally bird rings will be found, in which case they should be reported to the BTO. Whatever you find, you should always report your results to either your local natural history society or to your local Biological Records Centre (BRC).

The most common finds will be the skulls of voles, mice and shrews, but with barn owls very little is off the menu, provided they can swallow it. Occasionally bird skulls will turn up, as can be seen here.

In a report from 1939 that until recently remained unpublished (see Martin, 2008), the Hampshire naturalist Frank Gibson Phillips commented upon the hunting success of some barn owls he was studying. Through direct observation, and the examination of both nest and pellet contents, he estimated that 60 per cent of the diet was made up of rats, with mice, voles and a variety of other species, including two stoats and one weasel, making up the rest.

A further example of the diversity of prey that was taken in this period comes from some photographic evidence produced by the wildlife photographer Eric Hosking shortly after the Second World War. From the examination of a remarkable set of photographs taken in Suffolk, it was revealed that a pair of barn owls he was photographing at the time were feeding their young on a wider variety of prey than might be expected towards the end of the twentieth century.

There is considerable evidence to support that there was a greater diversity of habitats before and shortly after WWII, for it was in 1930 that L. Dudley Stamp organised the Land Utilisation Survey. This was a vast survey to determine what landscapes existed in Britain at that time as an aid for future planning, with the final report being published just after the War. It was probably the greatest field survey of its kind to have taken place in Britain since Domesday.

An important fact to emerge from this was that much of lowland Britain was devoted to mixed farming and that the landscape was largely composed of small fields bordered by hedgerows. Dudley Stamp's survey results were later brought together in a more concise form (Stamp, 1955), which is still available and worth reading.

This changed during the Second World War, when there existed an urgency to produce home-grown food. Despite the emergency measures that were taken (even the hallowed Wimbledon tennis courts were cultivated), demand outstripped supply, and Britain was heavily dependent on food imports. After the war, the 1947 Agricultural Act was passed to ensure the nation became less reliant upon imports in the future.

During the process of implementing the Act, the mixed farming practices that were in operation on a great number of Britain's farms were destroyed and those practices separated so that sheep and cattle farming dominated in the north and west of Britain while arable farming was concentrated in the south and east. This process continues, although now there is very little left to transform. In a number of instances it had a traumatic effect upon farming communities, while in wildlife terms it has had a dramatic effect upon the fortunes of barn owls, and perhaps a great many other wildlife forms besides birds.

In addition to these changes, grants were provided for hedgerow removal and for the renovation or replacement of farm buildings. Over the next forty or so years the eastern farmlands of Britain were transformed from a mosaic of differing habitats to a landscape that was largely devoid of habitats for small mammals. One of the most significant results of these changes was the wholescale destruction of hedgerows. We can gain some idea of loss by the farming returns from 1947 to 1970. In that period, the rate of hedgerow removal in Eastern England alone was more than 3,000 km (approximately 2,000 miles) per year. Of course, hedgerow removal continued after this period, but as time progressed the amount of hedging that was available for destruction grew less and less, while public anger increased.

It has been estimated that between 1950 and 1995

Rates of hedgerow removal in Eastern England, 1947–1970		
Dates	Period (years)	Miles per annum
1946–1954	8	800
1954–1962	8	2,400
1962–1966	4	3,500
1966–1970	4	2,000

From: Pollard, E., Hooper, M. D., and Moore, N. W., *Hedges* (Collins, 1974)

approximately half of the hedgerows throughout Britain were grubbed out (Pollard *et al.*, 1974), and this amounted to around 160,000 km; so, along with the pre-war destruction, vast amounts of hedgerow were lost in a little over 60 years. When the destruction from 1950 to 1995 is compared to the rate of destruction between 1947 and 1970 (approximately 116,000 km), we can see that around 75 per cent of those hedgerows were removed at a time when there were fewer naturalists, either amateur or professional, to witness and assess what was going on. It was this shocking transformation of the countryside that was to see the rise of the wildlife conservation movement.

It was in the wake of concern for the barn owl that the outcome of the first national enquiry into their diet was published (Glue, 1974) the consequences of which were to have a lasting impact upon the way that habitats for barn owls were managed in the future. Compared with some later studies, it was a relatively straightforward and uncomplicated presentation, but it well served a purpose.

The results were compiled from a total of 47,865 prey items extracted from 88 different sites around Britain which were then collated. The results showed that Britain's barn owls were being sustained on a relatively low spectrum of prey species, with field voles being the most common prey, accounting for nearly 50 per cent of all prey taken. They were closely followed by the shrews, which accounted for a further 32 per cent, with the common shrew comprising 25.6 per cent. This meant that Britain's barn owls were basically being sustained on just two small mammal species, which together totalled three-quarters of all prey at that time.

It was some 15 years later that Environmentally Sensitive Areas (ESAs) were introduced in various parts of Britain, and many of these were aimed at protecting grassland in the river valleys. Later, other environmentally friendly agricultural schemes were introduced, one of which was 'set-aside'. Initially this was a voluntary scheme where farmers were paid to take part of their land out of food production, but later all farmers were compelled to put 10 per cent of their land into set-aside, so that by 1990 the amount of land in this scheme stood at 71,890 hectares. This increased to 544,005 hectares during the next five years and continued on so that by 2003 a further 43,079 hectares had been included.

During this period another survey of the barn owl's diet took place and this one involved pellet samples from all of the main regions, although, apart from Eastern England and Wales, the total number of samples were fewer (81) than in the 1974 survey (143). This study tended to concentrate on the arable farmlands of Eastern England where 32 pellet samples were collected, as opposed to the eight collected in the 1974 study.

The authors of this survey (Love et al., 2000) found that there was a significant increase in the number of wood mice that were being taken and they believed that this was due to an increase in the amount of land that was in set-aside at that time. There may, however, have been additional reasons for these findings. In much of Eastern England livestock farming was continuing to decline, and so was the grassland that went with it. On top of that there had been some severe periods of drought during the survey period and this would probably have been more beneficial to wood mice and other rodents than to field voles. Although there is some imbalance between the surveys with regard to the number of pellet samples collected and the locations they came from, the conclusion to arise from this report was that the diversity of prey had slightly increased since 1974. Wood mouse had shown a distinct increase, with yellow-necked mouse, pygmy shrew and bank vole all showing slight increases, and only the common shrew showing a decrease. The view of this report was that, although other species of

Analysis of 188 pellet samples collected in Britain and Ireland

Prey species	Nos of diet	%
Common shrew	12,229	25.6
Pygmy shrew	2,567	5.4
Water shrew	574	1.2
Field vole	21,906	45.8
Bank Vole	1,876	3.9
Water vole	85	0.2
Wood mouse	5,640	11.8
Harvest mouse	248	0.5
House mouse	648	1.4
Brown rat	944	2.0
Mole	88	0.2
Birds	958	2.0
Totals	47,865	100.00

From: Glue, 1974

Glue's survey.

Mechanised farming has brought about huge changes in the way the countryside is now managed. This is especially significant in the south and east of England, but very few farmlands throughout the British Isles, including Ireland where barn owls are also declining, have escaped the effects of this.

small mammal were playing a greater role in the diet of Britain's barn owls, the diversity of prey was still lower than it had been earlier that century.

The latest results from the Mammal Society's barn owl pellet survey (Love *et al.*, 2000) show that in percentage terms field vole remains the most important prey item. In line with David Glue's survey of the 1970s it makes up around 45 per cent of all prey taken, and accounts for 60 per cent of its nutrition. Common shrew continues to contribute just over 20 per cent – slightly less than Glue's figure – which nutritionally makes it the third most important prey species. Wood mouse is showing some slight increase and now accounts for around 15 per cent of all prey taken and in nutritional terms its importance ranks second to field vole at around 17 per cent, with bank vole marginally increasing.

The continued dependence on field voles was demonstrated throughout this study by the fact that in all years the contribution of this species, as a percentage of prey taken, was more than that of the combined total of wood mouse and

The Barn Owl
3: The farmland owl

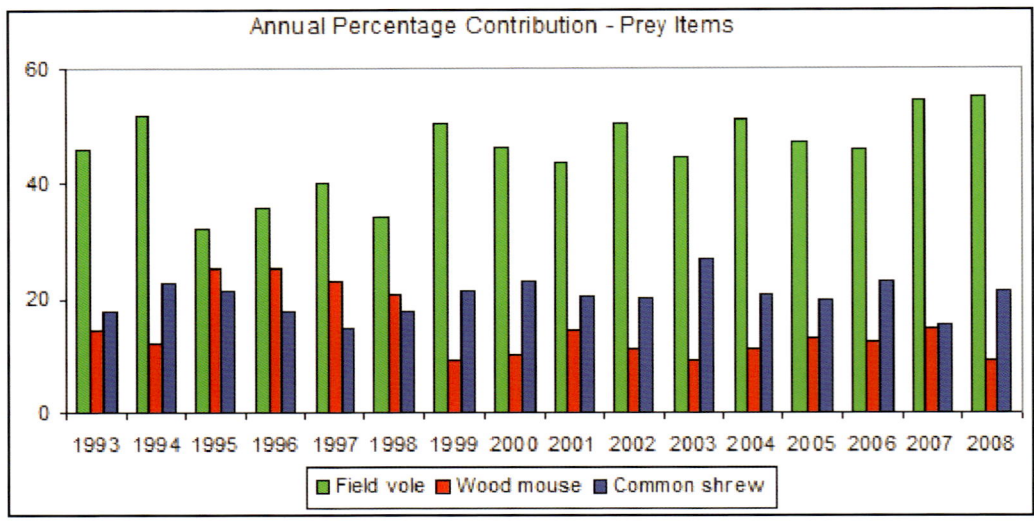

The annual percentage contribution of the three main prey species to barn owl diets across Britain 1993–2008. The importance of wood mouse during the main period of set-aside (1995–1998) is shown. (Source: The Mammal Society barn owl pellet survey).

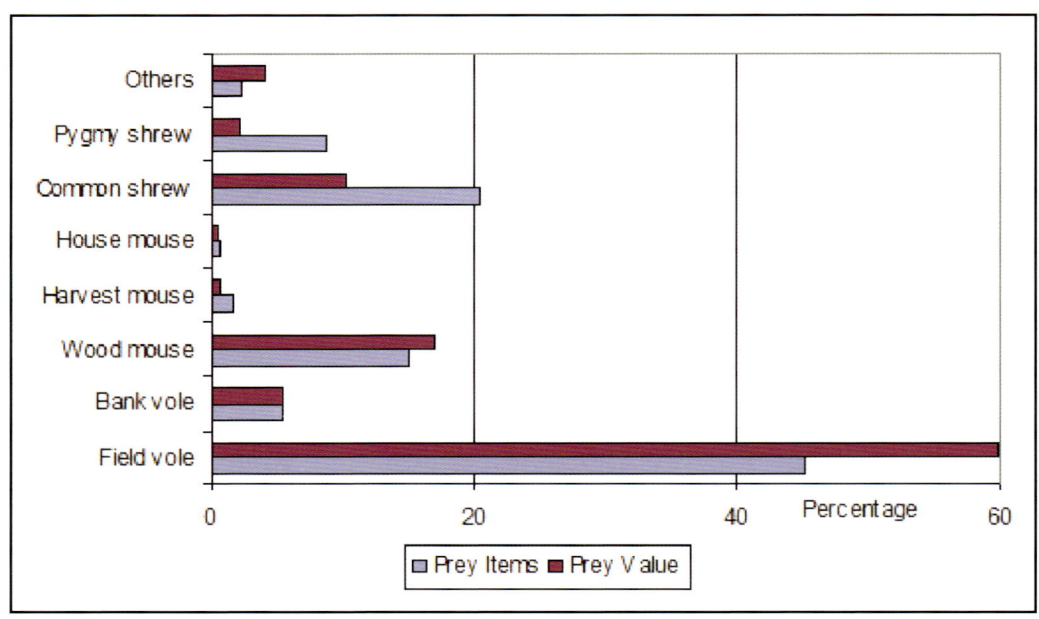

The importance of the main prey species to barn owls in Britain in relation to their relative nutritional value. (Source: The Mammal Society barn owl pellet survey).

common shrew. However, in the years 1995, 1996 and 1998, the importance of wood mouse grew to such an extent that it nearly vied with field vole as the most commonly taken prey species. It is interesting to note that this was during the period when the set-aside scheme was in operation. The Mammal Society's review pointed out that barn owls are now reliant upon just seven species of small mammal, with the aforementioned three species, plus pygmy shrew, accounting for just over 80 per cent of all prey taken.

Opportunity knocks

The view that 'opportunity makes the meal' has been overlooked in recent decades in favour of the view that barn owls selectively seek out field voles. It is a view that has had a profound effect on the way that habitats have been managed for barn owls, despite the evidence which points to the contrary.

It was in Ohio, USA, where the hypothesis involving prey selection appears to have been first challenged. During the course of research into barn owl diet during late summer and early fall (autumn), the examiners found that red-winged blackbirds accounted for 37 per cent of the prey, which surprised them because they were expecting to find the diet dominated by *Microtus* voles. Upon investigation they discovered that red-winged blackbirds congregated nearby in large concentrations and that the owls took advantage of those and preyed upon whatever food was readily available, regardless of any preference.

However, the view that opportunity makes the meal continued to find little support in Britain until 2012, when the results from a centrally based long-term study in England argued that barn owls will take what they can, when they can. Working on pellet analysis and habitat availability, they found that barn owls took whatever they could and whenever it was available. The authors of this report (Meek *et al.*, 2012) were of the firm opinion that it was time that the 'simplistic notion that barn owls in Britain preferentially target field voles was laid to rest'.

Clearly, barn owls are opportunists in their feeding habitats, because in many places around the world barn owls are not dependent upon voles since they do not exist there. In the tropics many feed on mice, rats, seabirds, reptiles, insects, grasshoppers and other small prey, as we saw earlier. These food items are eaten not because they are preferred, or because the habit is learned, but because food-wise that is what is available.

What conclusions, then, can be drawn from this? It would seem that if you provide lots of lightly grazed moist grassland, you will have lots of vole prey which, as we shall see later, has a profound effect upon the owls' breeding success. Contrary to this, if a diverse range of habitats is provided that will encourage a wide range of small mammals, the prey spectrum for barn owls will be wider and more reliable in the event of one small mammal species becoming temporarily, or permanently, scarce.

Not just mice and voles

Apart from small mammals, barn owls also eat a wide variety of other prey. From time to time young rabbits feature in their diets as well as weasels and stoats. The presence, or absence, of these two predators may also provide a guide as to the relative abundance of small mammals in a particular area. In places where their numbers are controlled, the abundance of prey available to barn owls is likely to be higher than in those places where *Mustelid* numbers are not controlled.

Although bats might seem unlikely food, greater horseshoe, noctule, grey long-eared and Natterer's bats, amongst others, have all fallen prey to barn owls in the British Isles. In Ireland it was found that some barn owls turn to eating Daubenton's bats when rivers are in flood and other small mammals are not available. Looking further afield, the remains of a number of bat species were found amongst pellets in a study carried out in Poland (Ruprecht, 1979), and there are many other instances of bats being taken by barn owls. While they do not feature highly in their diets, locally this can be a problem and care should be exercised when erecting nest boxes for barn owls, as local populations of bats could be plundered.

From time to time, birds are taken, although there does not appear to be an instance where game birds have been killed. This is usually because most game chicks are reared in pens within woodland.

Surprisingly, barn owls do take large birds such as redshank and dunlin, and even moorhen and water rail are not immune from their attentions, but these species are open-country inhabitants. However, they usually confine themselves to smaller bird species such as blackbirds, and over the years I have found headless corpses at barn owl roosts; no doubt they are attracted to blackbirds because of the noise they make at dusk as they go to roost. Starlings may also be taken at their roosts, as well as house sparrows, chaffinches and many other species of small bird.

There have been several instances where fish have been recorded as prey. The most recent account concerns the taking of 'a good sized roach' from the River Anholme in Lincolnshire (Bunn *et al.*, 1982). Lizards, frogs and toads are also taken but usually in small quantities, although lizards are commonly taken in drier climates, such as in Tenerife and the Balearic Islands, Spain, where reptiles make up approximately 5 and 7 per cent of the diet respectively (Roulin and Dunbay, 2012).

Although insects might not seem to be a typical food, barn owls will sometimes hunt them, especially moths and butterflies. Well-managed hedgerows will often provide good numbers of these as long as the weather is not too inclement; it is not unknown for barn owls to fly in front of cars at night, perhaps looking for any moths that might fly into the headlights. Bill Weber, a friend of the late Roger Tory Peterson, remembers watching migrant birds with him on 27 October 1935 underneath the lighthouse at Cape May Point, New Jersey, USA, with the sight of barn owls hawking moths around the town's lamp posts rounding off 'the magical night'.

Closer to home, evidence that barn owls will take moths and other insects comes from the days when it was not illegal to shoot barn owls. In his *Birds of Essex*, which was published in 1890, the Essex naturalist Miller Christy points to an instance where a barn owl was flying up and down a field 'and now and then catching at the grass'. He told his son to shoot the bird, and when they dissected it they found 'several of the White Grass-moths and other insects'.

Review and conclusions

Looking back over the years, it would seem that prior to, and perhaps immediately after, the Second World War, Britain's barn owls thrived in the era of mixed farming due to a rich and varied landscape that supported a wide variety of small mammals.

It was the 1947 Agricultural Act that determined the present-day farming set-up that now exists on the mainland of Britain, in which cattle and sheep tend to dominate in the west and the north, with arable and other crops dominating the south and east.

With wildlife in mind, let alone the damage it has done to farming communities and farmed produce, this may eventually prove to be one of the biggest disasters in recent history ever to have been inflicted on Britain's farmlands, with a subsequent negative effect for many lowland farm species.

The northward shift in the distributions of many farmland birds, for example, may be due to the effects of climate change but, equally so, they may also be the result of this farming trend which started nearly 70 years ago but which is only becoming apparent through better mapping techniques (Balmer *et al.*, 2013). The sweeping changes that devastated Britain's mixed farming community are now being inflicted upon those countries that are emerging on to the European stage, and this does not bode well for many of Europe's barn owls.

In conclusion, it appears that the diets of Britain's barn owls have narrowed considerably in the past 40 years but this process may have been gradually going on for much longer. The field vole remains the most important prey for barn owls and, indeed, they can be expected to remain an integral part of their diet in Britain, but whether this should be attained at the expense of a wider range of rich habitats that will provide a wider range of prey is a matter of conjecture.

There is a multitude of problems facing barn owls, not only in Britain but right across the northern hemisphere, as the world's barn owls continue to decline as a result of habitat loss. As an expanding human population makes demands upon the Earth's resources, so it is impossible to provide protection for them all. Even so, it seems there is much that could be done in Britain, and indeed across Western Europe, if we want to try and minimise the effects of future demands in the face of a growth in the human population.

4: Prey and habitat diversity

'But linking oneself so closely to a restricted diet is a risky thing to do. If for some reason that food disappears, an animal may be so specialised that it cannot switch to a different food and therefore starves.'
David Attenborough, *The Life of Mammals*, BBC Books, 2002

Catch us if you can – a bank vole.

Over the years a great deal has been written about the conservation of the barn owl but, quite remarkably, little of that has focused on their prey. Thankfully this is now changing as the attention increasingly highlights the role that small mammals play in the fate of owls. For example, an excellent publication on the snowy owl devoted a whole chapter to the prey of those attractive owls, and the authors took great pains to point out that, because lemming habitat was declining, so were the owls.

It was Derek Bunn and his fellow authors who were the first to highlight the influence that field voles have on the lives of barn owls in north-west England and that was reinforced by Iain Taylor's study in south-west Scotland. Both of those studies took place where grass was the dominant habitat. However, little attention has been placed on barn owls in the arable farmlands of south and south-east England.

The Barn Owl Monitoring Project's final report covering the period 2000–2009 makes interesting and useful reading. The conclusions of this lengthy report state that, while the usage of nest sites during the period of this study had significantly declined, the trends reported from the Breeding Birds Survey and provisional atlas results indicated that the population had actually increased over the same period. It was considered that this had been largely brought about by an increase in occupancy rates and brood sizes in areas of rough grassland, rather than in areas of pastoral or arable areas. In other words, barn owls were successfully nesting in areas of concentrated rough grassland while tending to vacate typical arable farmland habitats, nest occupancy and nesting success in the latter being far lower. This trend is reflected in the status of other farmland bird species during a period when a great deal of resources have been put into promoting agri-environment schemes. So, even though this book is about barn owls, one cannot help but wonder if there is there a common link here.

At a time when the UK is continually failing to meet its biodiversity targets and many farmland birds are in decline, the quality of our farmlands in terms of biological diversity must come in for scrutiny, especially in the light of comments made by such well-respected naturalists as the late Derek Ratcliffe (2007). He commented that there were a number of environmentally friendly farming schemes in place which were designed to pay farmers for improving the wildlife and the landscape, but his opinion was that, to date, the results had been 'unimpressive', despite the enthusiasm from some quarters. There must surely be substance in his comments judging by the publication of some recent studies and surveys, all of which have highlighted the continuing declines of farmland bird species, which is likely to have common ground with other wildlife species upon which they depend.

Britain's farmlands have a wide range of habitats which, put together, have the potential to form an attractive landscape for barn owls, and indeed for many other forms of wildlife. The results from the latest *Bird Atlas 2007–11* show that the present approach to creating a greater diversity of wildlife on lowland farms is falling short of expectations, and that it is those of southern England that are having the toughest time since the results of the previous atlas just 20 years ago.

This situation was further confirmed in the recent report *The State of the Nation's Birds 2013* which demonstrates that, whilst most groups of birds have shown a slight decline since the mid-1970s, the numbers of breeding farmland birds have plummeted. The fact that during a large part of this period barn owl

Make no bones...

There is little in the record that tells us much about Britain's barn owls until around the sixteenth century. Every now and then, though, something turns up in archaeological digs that provides us with an insight.

Most of the discoveries involve pellet remains found at Roman digs. These can provide valuable insights to the composition of the countryside during such periods, and what crops the Romans, and other civilizations, were eating.

For example, it was during the excavation of a Roman granary at South Shields near Newcastle in the early 1990s that a large number of small mammal bones were discovered. From their variety and concentration it was considered that this was the result of one or more barn owls depositing their pellets there. Perhaps the owls were using the building as a roost or, more interestingly, perhaps they were using it as a nest site.

During the excavation of a Roman villa at Gatehampton, South Oxfordshire in 2002 an assemblage of small mammal bones was discovered. Additional finds of small mammal bones were made at this site in 2008 and 2010, and from those it was deduced that they were the remains of prey that had been eaten by one or more barn owls. Carbon dating suggested that the bones had probably been deposited between the years 340 and 380 AD, and that research

Excavations of a Roman villa at Gatehampton in Oxfordshire. Digs such as this are slowly revealing in more detail what barn owls ate in the past.

has suggested that after this later date the roof collapsed and the building then probably became unsuitable for roosting or nesting purposes. Looking at the dates it seems probable that a number of owls had used this site and that, judging by the distributions of the pellets within that building, male and female birds had been using it, thus suggesting that formerly it was a nesting place.

numbers have shown an increase suggests that there may well be a connection here. Are we, for instance, forsaking our farmland wildlife in favour of promoting the attractive barn owl, as Iain Taylor (1994) warned us? And if we are, then the key question that arises is: can we increase our farmland wildlife whilst not harming our barn owls?

Hedgerows

There is little documented evidence to indicate that the loss of hedgerows has brought about a loss of small mammals on farmland. However, about the loss of hedgerows there is no doubt, and to assume that this has not affected small mammal populations is unrealistic. For example, from Suffolk comes the evidence that small mammals can thrive in arable farmland with drainage ditches and hedgerows.

Around the area of St Margaret, South Elmham, in north Suffolk a study was carried out a few years ago by a team led by Dr Martin Perrow of Norwich University (East Anglia). At the time of this survey it was a good area for barn owls and even today north Suffolk, together with south Norfolk, is one of the better places for barn owls in southern England.

Altogether five small mammal species were live-trapped during the course of their research ranging from common shrew, pygmy shrew, bank vole, field vole through to wood mouse. One of the interesting discoveries that was made during the course of this research was that in the absence of field voles their niche in the landscape was taken by bank voles, which appeared to thrive quite well.

My own studies have shown that small mammals will inhabit well-structured hedgerows and that in areas of the East Anglian countryside such as north Essex, where Ancient Countryside prevails, yellow-necked mice may also be found, suggesting that this species is largely dependent upon ancient habitats but not necessarily on woodland. Clearly hedgerows act as reservoirs for small mammals, allowing them to feed and breed in a tunnel system that may be constructed at the base of a hedge within a hedgerow bank. There is no doubt that hedgerows, if they are managed sympathetically for wildlife, are capable of supporting a wide range of small mammals; as a consequence of this they have great potential for increasing the abundance and variety of prey in the diets of many barn owls. At present, however, there is little evidence to suggest that hedgerows are being managed in a way that benefits small mammals, or indeed wildlife in general, according to the various reports that are regularly published, for example those concerning our moths and butterflies.

Sadly, it is abundantly clear that the ideology and vision of farmland biodiversity has failed to live up to expectations, but it must not be allowed to do so. Thus it would appear that there is a need for a new outlook in the way that we devise and implement sustainable environmentally friendly farming schemes that are right for farmers and for barn owls, while encompassing all other forms of wildlife.

Apart from devoting whole fields to grass, there is at present a fashion for leaving wide margins of grassland around field edges in the hope that they will provide a good habitat for wildlife and especially for voles and other small mammals, and some of those margins I have seen are extraordinarily wide. At this precise time it seems that we can afford to do this but whether these field edges have a long-term future is debatable. There may well come a time when under-utilised farmland will need to be brought back into production, so perhaps it is time to turn our attention to creating field borders which incorporate not only grassland fringes, but also species-rich hedgerows. Together with modest grassland margins, they have the potential to increase the diversity of small mammals in barn owl diets, offering a more reliable and sustainable food source from one year to the next. They would also create habitats for a wide and diverse range of other species, which would undoubtedly increase the numbers of many farmland bird species.

There are various forms of 'hedgerow' around the British Isles, each

Wide grassy borders, such as this, may enhance the countryside and provide feeding habitats for small mammals. With the prospect of future food demands, are such margins a realistic long-term proposition?

playing its own part within the habitat that suits the location where it is found. For example, in many parts of western and northern Britain dry-stone walls are the main 'hedgerows'. In parts of south-west Britain, such as Devon and Cornwall, dry-stone walling forms the basis of many hedge-banked walls. Devon is a somewhat different county from many others, in that it has a rich mix of banked dry-stone walls and a good blend of hedges; and, historically, this is a good county for barn owls. In general, the dry-stone walls of northern Britain tend to be somewhat featureless in terms of plant growth, although there are many nooks and crannies within them in which small mammals and other creatures may live. Plants may also survive there, even in the bleakest of areas, so perhaps there are opportunities to increase the diversity of small mammals and other wildlife there by allowing plants to become established in them – especially in the face of climate change.

In those walls, wood mice and perhaps bank voles may live and feed as well as common and perhaps pygmy shrews. It all depends upon wall structure and fabric. In many northern walls, it may be difficult to establish plant and animal communities, so, where that occurs, grassland is likely to be the dominant habitat. In the west and south-west of Britain, however, the walls sometimes form banks with earth in which there may be a vigorous and varied plant community. These offer homes for a wide variety of small mammals, especially mice, bank voles and shrews.

Do the dry-stone walls of western and northern Britain offer an opportunity for encouraging a range of small mammals?

Dry-stone walling is now increasing in popularity across many parts of Britain, and perhaps formation or renovation of these walls might be carried out with wildlife in mind.

Turning to hedgerows, at present many – but by no means all – farmers operate under the Higher Level of Environmental Stewardship in which they are encouraged to cut their hedges on a three-year basis, as this is deemed the preferred method for raising the levels of farmland biodiversity. This suggests that every three years a farmer should cut most, if not all, of his hedges. Alternatively, under the minimum level of farm subsidy, hedge cutting is done on an annual basis but this is considered to be the least preferred method for biodiversity. We should also be clear that some farmers are not conforming to the rules of these agri-environment schemes.

The problem here is getting the wildlife to conform to these regimes, because wildlife tends to plough its own furrow. For example, a particular wildlife species (and not necessarily a bird or mammal one) may be largely dependent upon hedgerows for its life-cycle, and it might have two poor breeding seasons in succession. On the third year the conditions might then just be right for it, only to find that, under the present rules, the hedgerow upon which it lives is cut. If this is carried out on a blanket basis, and that species is not very mobile, it may well become extinct from that locality, either temporarily or permanently.

Ideally, rotational cutting on a piecemeal basis, involving sections of perhaps about 10 metres, may be the best way of meeting the needs of nature.

This comparison example of hedge and verge management demonstrates different approaches. The hedge on the right was cut at a time when young barn owls should be just leaving the nest. The section of hedge on the left has been left uncut, at an important time for fledgling owlets. (Essex, July 2013)

This can incorporate one, two, three and even four year regimes with perhaps some even being left longer, as certain species may require such an interval. Rigid cutting regimes, while working within the scheme guidelines, do not allow for diverse management of hedgerows, and so they reduce the opportunities for biodiversity.

As for the hedges themselves, to increase species diversity within these there is a need for them to be cut in a manner that is attractive for wildlife. In spring this means leaving many to bud and then flower, thus encouraging a myriad of different insects to feed on the subsequent nectar. These include bees, butterflies and a whole host of smaller ones that may be preyed upon by shrews, wood mice, bank voles and, of course, insectivorous birds, especially the summer migrants. The flowers that are produced in the hedges will in the autumn turn into fruits, such as haws, hips and other berries. These in turn will be fed upon by birds, such as thrushes, and small mammals. That is assuming that the hedgerows aren't cut again, as many are, when the 'non-hedge-cutting season' has finished. Some restraint on cutting needs to be implemented in the autumn if this habitat is to be enriched for the coming winter. What species of small mammal can we expect to find within a well-managed hedgerow?

Once used to enrich the diets of humans, delicious countryside fruits such as wild plums, hazel nuts and berries can also enrich the diets of small mammals.

Bank voles are largely herbivorous and feed on a variety of foods including fungi, moss and grass, but they will also eat insects and worms. Fleshy fruits and seeds are readily eaten, as well as beech mast, acorns and hazel nuts. They are agile climbers and will often climb bushes and hedges to feed on the buds and berries. During the summer months they are active throughout the 24-hour period, with peaks of activity in the mornings and early evenings, but in winter they tend to be more active by night rather than by day. They are an increasingly important part of barn owl diets in Ireland where their recent introduction is being closely monitored. On the Continental mainland this attractive vole has a similar distribution to that of the field vole, although in general bank voles are restricted to woods, forests and covered clearings, rather than open areas. They are important prey items for some of the northern forest owls such as the boreal owl, northern hawk owl and great grey owl, but they are also important prey items for barn owls in Italy, where field voles are absent.

In the absence of field voles, bank voles can also be an important prey item for barn and other owls, as they are in many parts of the wider Europe.

Rodents are our most widespread and numerous group of small mammals in the British Isles, and amongst these are the wood, or long-tailed field, mice which are the most abundant. They are found in a variety of habitats including deciduous and conifer woodlands, hedgerows, arable fields, urban and rural gardens, roadside verges, grassland, hillsides and other open spaces. They feed largely upon seeds but they will also eat buds, fruit, snails, insects, fungi, moss and tree bark. When food-rich habitats are available for them, they can form an important part of barn owl diets. Wood mice are similar in behaviour to other rodents, with the exception of rats, in that they are usually nocturnal.

The ubiquitous wood mouse can be an important prey species in barn owl diets.

Yellow-necked mice are attractive creatures which are closely related to wood mice. In general they are found in the ancient countryside of southern England, where they tend to be more confined to woodland than the slightly smaller but ubiquitous wood mouse, although their remains do sometimes turn up in pellets. It is likely that they inhabit hedgerows more frequently than is at presently thought, where they tend to feed on a wide variety of food including insects, seedlings, buds, fruit and insect larvae.

The attractive yellow-necked mouse. An indicator of ancient woodland habitats.

Hazel, or common, dormice are interesting prey, for although they are usually inhabitants of woodland, they were once frequently found in hedgerows, where their 'snoring' during the spring and summer would sometimes reveal their presence to the hedge-layers.

The discovery of their bones in a barn owl pellet in Cumbria not long ago revealed the presence of a remote and unsuspected population, thus emphasising the importance of pellet analysis and, just as importantly, recording the contents. They have a fairly broad taste in foodstuffs, although they prefer flowers and pollen in spring and fruits and nuts – especially hazelnuts, sweet chestnuts and beech mast – in autumn. They will also feed on small insects. Dormice regularly feature in the diets of barn owls in Greece, albeit in small numbers, but they are more regularly taken by barn owls in the Middle East. This is another species in Great Britain which may fare better in the face of climate change, along with sympathetic hedgerow and woodland management.

Once common throughout much of Britain, the house mouse is now an infrequent creature of the countryside, but might its numbers increase as a result of climate change?

In Britain hazel dormice rarely feature in the diets of barn owls, but in parts of the Balkans and the Middle East they are taken a little more frequently.

Brown rats were once common and widespread in the British countryside, and they were important prey for barn owls. However, over the years great efforts have been made to eradicate them from farmland and so – like many foxes – they are now more likely to be found in cities, towns and villages rather than in the countryside. Consequently, they are now a very small component in the diets of barn owls. Brown rats feed on a wide variety of food but it is their liking for grain and root crops which has led to their persecution though they will also feed on meat, fish, bones, fruit and invertebrates.

Hedgerow diversity

While there is not the wealth of hedges that were once around, it is clear that we still have a considerable amount of this valuable resource available to wildlife, with new plantings taking place here and there. By the time autumn arrives, those hedges that have escaped the attentions of the hedge cutters in spring, do not usually escape their attentions in autumn. Increasing the food availability for small mammals will often increase the food availability for birds. It is little use for birds, and indeed small mammals, if farmers refrain from cutting the hedges in spring, only for them to denude the hedges of fruits in the early autumn.

New hedgerows not only produce a fine countryside feature, well-nurtured hedges may produce a wide diversity of wildlife. Sensitive cutting regimes will do this. New plantings, such as this, need to be protected in their early stages against browsing by deer, rabbits and even voles, but once the hedgerow has become established the guards should be removed to allow the hedge to develop into a robust feature, otherwise it may become spindly.

Over the years the management of hedgerows has gone from one extreme to the other. Once upon a time manual hedge cutting, which often included layering, was the usual practice. In that way workers could be more selective in what they cut in a hedge and how they cut it. Mechanical hedge cutters get the job done more quickly and cheaply but they are indiscriminate. They do have their uses but for the purposes of environmentally friendly farming they need to be used wisely.

To enrich the countryside, a different approach to the way that field margins are presently managed must be worthy of consideration. Perhaps some of the funds that are currently provided for environmentally friendly farming schemes should be channelled into providing labour for such management, rather than providing funds for land to stand idle? The countryside is a working environment and ideally should be treated as such, as many farmers believe. For many years machines have played a dominant role on our farmlands and that won't change, but the time might now be right to encourage manual workers back on to the land to work alongside them. It may also be a good time for manufacturers of hedge-cutting machines to take this subject on board, not only by providing environmentally friendly guidance to the operators, but also by providing machinery with more wildlife-friendly cutting possibilities incorporated into it. The technology is there.

Hedges do need to be cut back quite severely from time to time, thus allowing them to grow strongly from the base and to develop character, but many hedges are left spindly and lack substance. With some judicious coppicing, many may grow into strong and useful plants. It does not take an expert to gain some idea of how rich a hedgerow is in plant species. Even the most modest of fieldworkers, working with an appropriate field guide, can obtain a reasonable assessment of what common fruiting shrub species there are within a hedge.

Amongst the best shrubs for wildlife are wild cherry, wild plum, apple, rowan, white-beam and hawthorn. But there are many more flowering and fruiting species that could be encouraged in a simple manner. These include field rose, dog rose, bramble, elder, honeysuckle and many, many more.

During the course of their climb from bud in the spring to fruits in the autumn, they will encourage a myriad of wildlife to feed off them, which in turn will provide food for others. Hedgerows, managed with small mammals in mind, are potentially rich habitats for barn owls and all sorts of wildlife, and may well go towards helping the UK reach its farmland biodiversity targets.

In addition to hedgerows, headlands are sometimes to be found jutting out into the landscape. Often they are the remnants of what was once a much more robust habitat that was probably swept away in the post-war farming revolution. These unassuming places are often valuable wildlife reservoirs where ancient families of voles, mice and shrews may still be living.

While well-managed hedgerows are an excellent habitat for small mammals,

A bare hedgerow in winter is of no use to barn owls, but a hedgerow managed with wildlife in mind can enhance the countryside. The berry-laden bushes are surrounded by fruit-bearing brambles, which in turn are surrounded by a modest margin of rough grassland. These, together with other seeds and fruits that are available on the surrounding trees and bushes, ensure that this is a good habitat for small mammals. Not surprisingly barn owls are sometimes seen hunting this particular hedgerow.

Well-vegetated headlands have a role to play in barn owl conservation, especially if after the harvest some stubble can be retained through to the following July as a habitat for wood mice.

on a wider scale their linear features are excellent for bats which use them not only for feeding but also as guides when moving around their territories. Birds such as swallows also use them as guiding features when on migration. This is not always so obvious on the coast but such migration, when viewed inland, can be quite astonishing.

Slow runs the river...

Farmland forms part of river catchments and so well-managed banksides along with clean, unpolluted water also have a role to play in providing alternative hunting areas.

In the latter half of the twentieth century it emerged that rivers and other watercourses were the most important habitats for barn owls

Bank voles are an important prey species for many owls in Europe, and they are becoming an increasingly important prey species for barn owls in Ireland where they were introduced some years ago. With judicious management, is it possible that they could play a greater part in British barn owl diets than they do at present, thus offering alternative prey when field voles are scarce?

throughout much of Great Britain's lowlands because, as in the fens of East Anglia, their bank-side vegetation was an attractive habitat to field voles and some other species of small mammal.

Apart from field voles and shrews, the river valleys and their catchments may also hold populations of water voles; these feed on lush vegetation, such as reeds, sedges, grasses and fruit, but occasionally they will also take insects and other invertebrates. They inhabit the grassy banks of slow-moving rivers, ponds, lakes and marshes, but their numbers have been declining for some years now.

'Old Ratty'. The water vole is now a specially protected species in Britain. The historical records tell us that in the past they were once common in the wider countryside and a favoured prey for barn owls.

It is clear from the literature that they were once more common, and the discoveries from archaeological excavations suggest that they were once abundant in some barn owl diets, even though the nearest rivers were a few miles away. So clearly they are not totally dependent upon rivers and other waterways for their survival. Lush vegetation usually grows along the banks and margins of slow-running rivers in the summer but this is often cut back in the winter, thus denying water voles vital food at an important time.

Although mink are often blamed for the demise of the water vole, there is a view that this species is often used as a scapegoat whereas adverse river management may have a strong influence on this. The pellet analysis that David Glue carried out in the late 1960s and early 1970s strongly suggests that water vole

Water shrews live in clean unpolluted water and feed on a wide variety of aquatic foods, including caddis larvae, crustaceans, frogs and fish.

numbers had plummeted long before mink were common in the countryside and subsequently implicated in the water vole's decline.

Of course, intensive riverside bank management takes place in autumn to allow rivers to flow easily and to prevent flooding. In years past there were flood plains that temporarily took a great deal of floodwater out of rivers thus easing flood pressure on domestic and industrial buildings. It wasn't always the answer, but in many cases it was.

Amongst the skulls and bones that are to be found in owl pellets, the remains of the uncommon water shrew will sometimes be found. These robust and attractive shrews live not only on the banks of rivers and lakes, but also in reed-beds, fens and marshes; on occasion they can also be found in woodland and other habitats that are well away from water.

They have a wide-ranging diet which includes spiders, beetles, millipedes, centipedes, molluscs and earthworms, and in water they will sometimes tackle freshwater crustaceans and cased caddis fly larvae. On occasion they will sometimes tackle much larger prey such as frogs, newts and even small fish. It is a species that is vulnerable to water pollution and, although water quality is

In 1932 Claude Ticehurst wrote of the harvest mouse in Suffolk, 'Beyond noticing its pretty woven nest in corn-stalks and tall herbage, the best way of finding its presence is when corn-stacks are thrashed: then six or eight of these very handsome mice are not uncommonly discovered in one stack.'

better in many places than it was many years ago, it remains a declining species.

In this section I also include harvest mice, which are Europe's smallest rodents. They are omnivorous and will eat a wide range of fruits and insects, as well as grain. As the name suggests, these endearing creatures were called after their once familiar habit of nesting in the growing wheat, and they were often found in the stooks at harvest time.

With the advent of mechanised farming their numbers have declined sharply, as a consequence of which they are now absent from large parts of the countryside. Most are now found in reed beds, ditches, and other wetland areas where they sometimes fall prey to barn owls.

Away from riparian habitats they may be found in areas of long, rank and undisturbed grassland which may sometimes hold substantial numbers of their round grassy nests. In Britain, the harvest mouse is at the furthest north of its European range, while being absent from the whole of Ireland, most of Scotland and parts of northern England.

Grassland: the weakest link?

Earlier we saw that rough, lightly grazed grassland is now considered to be the prime habitat for barn owls. It is a habitat which has been declining, and is continuing to decline, for a variety of reasons. These include replacement by arable crops or through the sowing of improved grass seed, which is often excessively fertilised to increase growth to feed cattle. Now they are at risk through progressive afforestation and subject to inland and coastal flooding. In addition to this there has been a serious decline in hay meadows.

With this in mind, grassland in general is an important habitat for field voles, which in turn is an important prey species not only for barn owls but for a number of other creatures such as buzzards, kestrels, short-eared owls, long-eared owls, foxes, stoats and weasels, to name but a few. It is the one species of small mammal upon which virtually all barn owl conservation efforts in Great Britain are presently directed, so we'll look at this creature, and its habitat, in a little more detail.

Field voles are distributed throughout much of Britain but they are absent from the whole of Ireland. They tend to be active during the hours of daylight, especially in winter time. Their dietary requirements are narrow in that they feed predominantly on palatable vegetation, so they may be especially plentiful where there are suitable areas of rough grassland, including roadside verges, river valleys, woodland rides and young woodland plantations.

Within these the voles will construct a network of runs which they will fiercely defend against other voles. Amongst these territories the females will build their nests which they will also strongly defend. Of all the small mammals in the British Isles, this species provides the greatest interest in terms of population self-regulation, which in turn regulates the numbers of its predators.

Many populations of field voles are subject to cycles that fluctuate around every three to five years. In some southern areas these cycles may be less obvious or even absent but in northern Britain things are very different, as there is usually a marked three-year population cycle, and this has a pronounced effect upon the barn owls that live there.

Field voles are prolific breeders and, depending upon the weather, they may start their families as early as March. They have large litters, and the females become pregnant again before an existing litter has become fully independent. The young develop quickly, so that those born early in the year may themselves be breeding in a favourable autumn and, as a result of this, vole numbers can be quite high by the end of the year.

Provided that no catastrophe arises during the course of the oncoming winter, their numbers may be relatively high as winter falls away to give way to the emerging spring. Any large falls of snow that had occurred during the winter may well have prevented predation by barn owls and other predators, as the voles can live quite happily beneath a firm blanket of snow.

In a good spring, breeding may commence early but this time the number of breeding voles will be higher than the previous year. This means there will usually be a greater abundance of prey for barn owls, as a consequence of which the number of young barn owls that are successfully fledged is likely to increase.

Field voles require succulent vegetation to feed on and ungrazed grassland to live in where they create a territory composed of a network of runs which they defend against other field voles. Sometimes the entrance to these runs can be detected amongst the grass.

The whole process will be repeated during the next winter and into spring so that by the end of the third summer the number of voles may have reached very high proportions. This in turn may create an abundance of owls that will feast themselves on the available prey.

This continues until the cycle reaches a peak, and then suddenly the population crashes. Various theories have been put forward for this sudden fall in vole numbers, and trains of thought include severe weather and the effects of predation by the wide range of species that feed on them. The much favoured reason is that as vole numbers build up they become increasingly territorial and spend most of their time fighting amongst each other rather than breeding, while predation and normal mortality may also take its toll. In addition to this, the territorial females may kill any unrelated juveniles that they happen to chance upon ensuring that any young other than their own do not enter into their community.

While this process has been taking place the populations of their predators have also been building up, so that by the peak of the cycle the number of creatures that are feeding on them will have increased significantly. In the case of barn owls the increase may be quite dramatic as more young are successfully raised.

If, for whatever reason, the vole population declines suddenly, the populations of their predators follow suit as they progressively die through starvation. In the nesting season this may have a serious and dramatic effect on barn owls as they respond accordingly to the shortage of food. While the effects of this sudden fall in vole numbers can be quite dramatic, and particularly if this coincides with a bad winter, the positive side to this is that the cycle will usually start all over again in the spring.

When exceptional habitat and weather conditions exist, the vole populations may very occasionally reach 'plague' proportions, and when that happens they may number in their millions. At such times they can devastate the vegetation leaving the surrounding areas stripped bare. Death due to starvation, disease and predation, usually follows on from these plagues.

In Britain there have been some recorded vole plagues: one such plague occurred at Southminster, Essex, in 1580 followed by another there in 1660, and previously a further two were noted in Essex at Rochford and Foulness in 1648. In 1875–6, a vole plague was recorded in the Borders Region of northern England and southern Scotland, with animals 'swarming in their millions'. This was followed by even larger numbers in Dumfriesshire between the years 1889 and 1893 which appear to have been as a result of the sheep being removed from the area to allow for tree planting. The areas were fenced off to prevent the sheep from grazing the newly planted saplings and this allowed the grass to grow ungrazed in the manner which suits voles. In Galloway there was another vole plague in the 1930s for the same reason.

Vole plagues take place elsewhere: in 2007 one occurred in northern Spain, where an estimated 750 million common voles were present in an area north of Madrid. This species is normally confined to the higher meadows of the Pyrenees but the irrigation of what were formerly arid areas of Castilla y León encouraged the voles to feed lower down the hills and on to the resulting succulent vegetation. As a result of this, over 500,000 hectares of crops were destroyed by these creatures. This led to civil unrest as farmers saw their livings being literally eaten away; fields were set alight and large amounts of rodenticides were applied in efforts to try to kill them off. These measures, along with the possible starvation of the voles themselves as they ate themselves out of food, meant that their numbers eventually dropped back to normal levels.

Looking to the future, there exists the possibility that vole plagues will occur when farmers turn to irrigation as they strive to bring arid lands into production. In the face of climate change this is an important issue which may have consequences for human food supplies in years to come.

While the case for retaining and providing vole-rich habitats in the future might sound compelling, there are reasonable arguments against this strategy. This is because, once a creature narrows its diet and becomes dependent upon one foodstuff for its survival, it exists in a parlous state. For example, in 2011 two giant pandas were brought on loan from China to Edinburgh Zoo. When the representatives from the zoo were interviewed they stated that their priority was to ensure that there was a readily available and plentiful supply of bamboo shoots, for this is the only thing that pandas eat and without it the pandas would die.

David Attenborough (2002) has described the outlook for a species when it becomes mainly or wholly dependent upon one food for its survival as 'a high-wire act – spectacular when it is successful but catastrophic if there is one small failure'. Some would say that this aptly describes the ups and downs of Britain's barn owl population which has, for the last fifty years at least, been largely dependent upon one prey species for its sustenance. What happens when the wire breaks?

If we look at things on a wider scale, the implications for the grass itself may be important, for with climate change the succulent grasses which are so loved by field voles may dry up. If this occurs, over time some grasslands may be replaced by shrubs and small trees, which will ultimately result in woodland. For the barn owls there may also be a danger of becoming 'hooked' on field voles, as short-eared owls appear to be, and this presents other problems.

The short-eared owls of northern Europe, Scandinavia and Russia will travel thousands of kilometres in search of field voles; Mikkola (1983) has described those owls as 'veritable nomads'. While it seems unlikely that British barn owls will become international nomads searching for voles, some may lose their sedentary reputation and end up travelling further, and more often, than their predecessors once did. While this may well have benefits in terms of gene dispersal, it may also leave them vulnerable to dangers such as road traffic.

Shrews are also important, and common shrews often feature highly in the diets of many barn owls in Britain. This is especially true of common shrews which live in a wide range of habitats, including woodland, grassland

Are barn owls now following in the shadow of that veritable nomad the short-eared owl? Are they now losing their sedentary reputation by travelling further and further in search of voles?

and hedgerows where they feed upon a variety of prey including, spiders, earthworms, slugs, insect larvae, beetles and other invertebrates. They are most lively just before dawn and just after sunset, and are least active in daylight. Due to their low weight (5–14 grams) any barn owls which largely feed on these creatures will have to work a lot harder for their survival than if they were feeding on larger prey.

Even smaller is the pygmy shrew, which weighs between 2.4 and 6.1 grams. Pygmy shrews also live in grassland, deciduous woodland and hedgerows where they feed upon a range of invertebrate food including beetles, spiders, woodlice and flies, although, unlike common shrews, they do not eat earthworms. Like all shrews they live energetic lives and are active throughout the 24-hour period.

Where poisons and traps are not put down for them, moles occasionally fall prey to barn owls. In late spring especially, young animals may become vulnerable as they disperse above ground in search of their own territory.

Moles are inhabitants of woodland but their earthworks will often be seen in spring grassland so it is not surprising that they sometimes turn up in barn owl pellets. Even so, they are powerful and formidable creatures that can exert a sharp bite, so it must take a certain amount of expertise for a barn owl to catch and kill one.

In late spring especially, young moles sometimes disperse overland, where they may make a fine meal for a hungry barn owl.

In conclusion, if grass continues to be projected as the single most important habitat for barn owls, it seems likely that Britain's farmland birds will continue to decline. Simplistic and popular conservation measures often come at a price, and so it may prove to be with conserving grasslands for field voles. From time to time grass does need to be grazed, and recent research (Villar et al., 2013) suggests that heavily and regularly grazed grassland increases the amount of silicon dioxide in the soil. This then renders grass tough and inedible for voles to eat, with obvious implications for vole-dependent barn owls.

In addition to this, voles can be linked to disease in humans, such as cowpox. This can have horrific results if humans come into contact with infected voles, although it might not be a problem in Britain. In addition, there is a virus called *Mycobacterium microti*, which is a form of tuberculosis and may be found in voles. This disease was discovered many years ago; it does not appear to be easily transferable to humans, but it is to barn owls!

While it may be considered that these thoughts on vole dependency are scare mongering, a word of warning comes from the Kielder Forest in Northumberland where a 27-year study on tawny owls has revealed disturbing information which may well have serious long-term implications for barn owls (Millon *et al.*, 2014). In the Kielder, tawny owls atypically feed largely on field voles whereas those that live in broad-leaved woodland feed on a wider range of prey such as wood mice and bank voles, as well as field voles.

The survey found that, due to a changing climate, the 3–5 year cycle of the field vole has been upset and has flattened out, as it has in other places in Europe, with no obvious peaks and troughs in prey density. Consequently, vole numbers in spring are becoming progressively smaller, and this has negative implications for breeding owls. The report concluded with the strongly held belief that the tawny owl will eventually become extinct in the Kielder Forest and that, in the future, other field vole dependent species across Europe are also vulnerable, due to climate change, which is a view that I expressed some years before (Martin, 2008) and which has now been supported by scientific evidence.

5: Aspects of behaviour

A barn owl carries its prey off to feed its young. Daylight sightings like this are not such an uncommon sight in parts of the British countryside as they once were.

To ensure population continuity, the nesting period is the most important time of the year for barn owls. Before this can take place successfully, however, there are other matters which need attention.

Establishing a territory

The first step to breeding is the establishment, or re-establishment, of a territory that will be capable of providing adequate food for a family, and a suitable nest site in which to raise the young.

Once this is made the search will be for a mate, if one is not already available. Of course, finding an area that has adequate food does not necessarily mean that there will be adequate food for a pair, and this may well account for the number of 'floating' birds that exist. Even so, barn owls are quite tolerant of one another and are not territorial in the manner that some species are. Robins, for example, will fight to the death to defend their territory, but there are no known instances of such behaviour with barn owls. In fact they have been known to nest in close proximity to one another, and, while there is not usually any sign of aggression between them, they do become more vocal. As a consequence of this, birds that nest at low density are likely to be very quiet on their breeding grounds and may go undetected.

Diurnal behaviour

Historically, British barn owls have always been crepuscular or nocturnal in their behaviour and rarely have they ever been thought of as diurnally-active creatures. This is a fact that is supported by the omission of such behaviour from the accounts of many of the naturalists of the nineteenth and early twentieth

Hunger brought on by hunting in harsh weather was once thought to be the reason for barn owls to be out in daylight.

centuries. Some mentioned that, while daylight sightings did sometimes occur, they usually did so only in times of harsh weather or when the owls had young to feed – the conclusion being that these daylight observations were the results of hunger, forcing the owls to hunt longer. The Victorian naturalist Charles Waterton wrote that, if barn owls hunted by day instead of by night, those who persecuted them (gamekeepers) would witness that they only caught mice and not game birds.

The first recorded instance of regular daylight hunting by barn owls in Britain appears to have occurred in the early part of the twentieth century when Eric Dunlop stated that they could often be seen out in bright sunshine. Dunlop was born and raised in the Lake District where he learnt to study natural history. Sadly, he was killed in the First World War, but shortly before then he was attached to Carlisle Museum and therefore his observations were all made in the north-west of England. The same is true of F. Smalley who regarded daylight hunting in the winter as quite normal. He believed that this was also due to hunger because barn owls require more food than some other birds, such as hawks and falcons. His belief might have been founded on his observations that,

when food is readily available, they will gorge themselves. This is because they do not have a crop, and as a result they cannot store food for consumption later but need to feed as often as they can. Common starlings behave in the same 'greedy' manner, as they also do not have a crop.

In 1928 the noted Cheshire naturalist T. A. Coward was another to draw attention to the barn owl's daylight activity. 'Crepuscular and nocturnal in its habits, it eludes observation', he said, but then pointed out that, 'When the young are being fed, the barn owl will hunt in the daytime, but as a rule it does not set forth until after dark.'

By the middle part of the twentieth century daylight sightings remained uncommon, and when they occurred they usually raised comment. In August 1946 a letter to *The Field* remarked upon the fact that earlier in the year it had been quite common to see up to a dozen barn owls hunting for food at any time, even though the weather had not been unduly hard. Yet, by the end of that century daylight activity, at all times of the year and at all times of the day, was considered to be quite normal in some places.

It was Derek Bunn (1972) who first grasped the reality of this when he started his study in the 1960s. He was somewhat surprised to find that – contrary to what he had expected – many of the barn owls he was studying were active during the hours of daylight. He also found that some of the birds he was watching were diurnally active at all times of the year, while others were less so. In addition to this, some birds suddenly stopped hunting in daylight and reverted to being nocturnal. Clearly something was happening which was sparking this behaviour.

Basing his thoughts upon the records he had built up, he discounted the once-held view that barn owls could foresee the onset of bad weather and that consequently they would hunt more actively before it arrived. While barn owls might not be able to anticipate bad weather, field vole activity appears to increase in overcast and rainy conditions. Contrary to this, the onset of rainy weather, accompanied by cold conditions, has the reverse effect. Therefore, those barn owls which are dependent upon field voles may be active in overcast and wet conditions but will be less active in cold weather, with potentially fatal consequences. Studies have shown that high daytime temperatures also lead to more nocturnal behaviour in summer but cold winter nights lead to greater diurnal activity. Radio tracking has demonstrated that field voles are more active throughout the day than was once thought, and that light levels may be instrumental in this.

Working with the information he had, Bunn was of the view that field vole activity was largely responsible for the daylight activity of the barn owls he was studying. He highlighted the voles' two- to four-hour peaks of activity, which were after sunrise and after sunset, with a higher level of activity at night. He found that these peaks tied in with his observations, except for those birds

Until the Second World War, regular diurnal behaviour was uncommon. Towards the end of the twentieth century, however, barn owls were often to be seen hunting by day.

which emerged from their day roosts at least one to two hours before sunset and occasionally before that.

It was because of this he reached the conclusion that it was the relatively poor sight of barn owls that was responsible for daylight hunting because in daylight their hunting efficiency was improved; but of course, hunting would only have taken place in the expectation of food.

More than 40 years later the information that is now available is much greater than was available to Derek Bunn when he brought this to the attention of the wider world. It may be that the hunting efficiency of barn owls is heightened through daylight hunting, but it may also be that this ties in with the life patterns of field voles as well as those of the summer peaks of wood mouse thus inducing the peaks of daylight activity.

Not all of Bunn's birds behaved in this manner. Sometimes only one of a pair was involved, while other pairs remained nocturnal, suggesting perhaps that they were feeding on species other than voles or perhaps they were feeding on different vole populations with different patterns of activity? His observations were considered to be so unusual, at that time, that there was no hesitancy in publishing them. This was followed by a number of letters from birdwatchers and ornithologists around Britain some of whom considered this behaviour quite normal whilst others expressed their surprise. As a consequence of this he reached the conclusion that there were barn owls all over the country that were habitually hunting by day but that others were hunting only by night, the proportions of which he did not know.

An important factor surrounding Bunn's research was that his study took

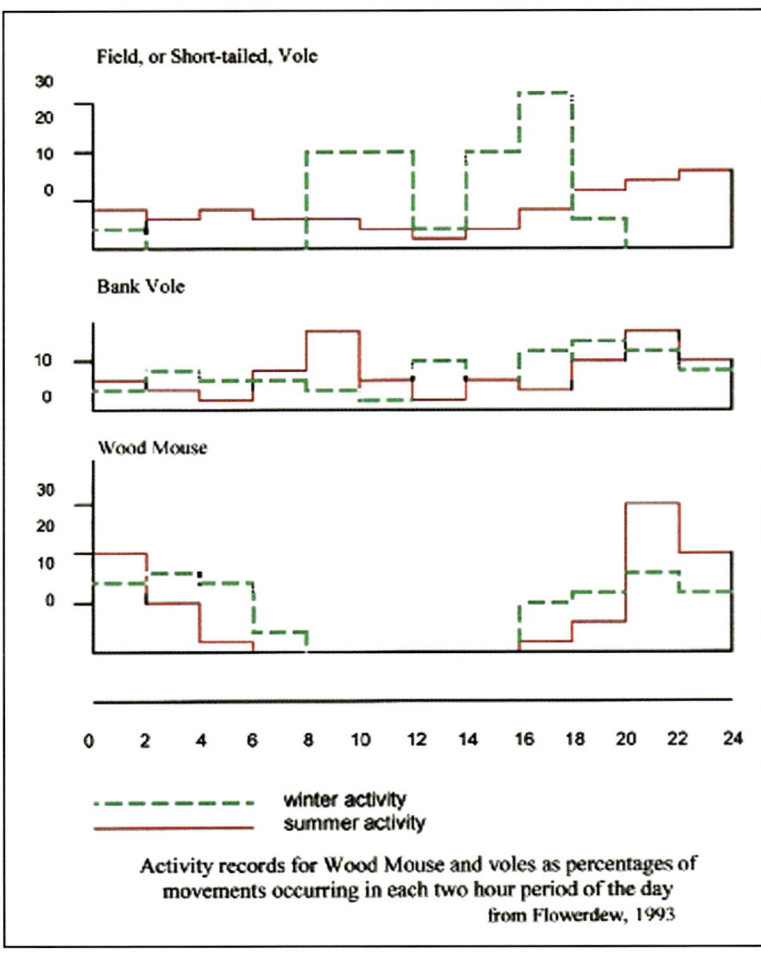

Patterns of activity of three small mammal species.

place in an area which was largely, but by no means totally, comprised of young conifers. This is the prime habitat for field voles, and an examination of pellets suggested that they accounted for well over three-quarters of the diet.

Field voles are also the main prey in south-west Scotland where regular daylight hunting by barn owls was similarly observed during the course of a lengthy study (Taylor, 1994). One conclusion from this research was that daytime hunting only occurs with the barn owls in northern Europe and that it is a rare event elsewhere in the world. The likelihood arises, therefore, that the activity of field voles correspondingly influences the hunting patterns of many of Britain's barn owls and not just in north-west England and south-west Scotland, although that is unlikely to be the complete answer.

The reality of daylight activity in the British Isles was recently brought up to date (Martin, 2008), and Palmer (2013) has drawn fresh attention to this subject by pointing out that daylight activity by barn owls only appears to be common in Britain and nowhere else in Europe or, indeed, elsewhere in the world, as Iain Taylor had noted around 25 years earlier.

Attention was drawn to the possibility that, because common buzzards were formerly absent from many parts of Britain, barn owls have taken advantage of that to utilise the daylight hours to hunt in times of food shortage or when feeding young.

Buzzards do kill barn owls, and an incident was observed in Wales which involved a buzzard attacking a barn owl and chasing it into a wood. Subsequently, the remains of a barn owl were found and the conclusion was that the buzzard had killed it. It was thought to be a 'remarkable incident' because buzzards are normally non-aggressive.

It seems possible that, in Britain, aggression by buzzards towards barn owls is on the increase; however, there is no evidence from the two major studies mentioned above that predation by buzzards on barn owls is a problem. It is important to stress that these two studies took place in what might be described as buzzard strongholds before their recent spread across Britain, so perhaps the buzzard and barn owl relationship should be looked at in a different light. Why are buzzards now attacking barn owls is perhaps the pertinent question.

The top predator will always try to remove competitors for food and it seems likely that it is the food factor which holds the key as to why buzzards are killing barn owls in various parts of Britain. If only barn owls behaved in the manner they did a hundred years ago, this problem would have been unlikely to arise.

Elsewhere, in drier climates where voles are absent or less common, barn owls turn to other prey. In Spain and Greece, for example, they feed largely upon mice (Bontzorlus et al., 2005) and it is rare for them to be diurnally active. A similar situation exists in Pakistan (Mushtaq-Ul-Hassan et al., 2007) and southern Syria, where mice and other small prey apart from voles are important: here daylight activity appears to be rare, though not completely unheard of.

Barn owls around the world must suffer from a shortage of food from time to time and yet none of those appears to have taken up the habit.

Perhaps one of the most interesting facts to emerge from this how a piece of atypical behaviour can develop into a regular and accepted way of life, without questions being asked. Barn owls have evolved over millions of years to be supreme night-time hunters and yet, despite Derek Bunn and then Iain Taylor drawing attention to this unusual behaviour, the reasons for it have never been explained in detail. Many people, even now, believe that it is quite normal for an owl to be abroad in the middle of the day, often in bright sunshine, but Bunn and Taylor, quite rightly, didn't think so.

However, there may be more to this behaviour than the activity patterns of field voles, for while it may have been their activities that originally sparked daylight behaviour it does not explain why sometimes barn owls may be seen in daylight either sitting out in the open, or in flight, without the slightest indication that they are looking for something to eat. In the light of recent research on tawny owls (Martin and Mikkola, 2014) it may be that these day-flying barn owls may be doing nothing more than signalling to conspecifics.

Hunting

Some of the more dramatic birds of prey, such as peregrines and sparrowhawks, rely upon speed to catch their prey, but not so the barn owls, who rely upon patience, stealth and surprise. They use two methods of hunting, the most obvious of which is carried out on the wing and is known as quartering. The second, dubbed post-hopping, is more efficient and saves energy. This technique is frequently used in the winter when the need to conserve resources is most important, but it may also be that because most barn owls hunt at night when they may not be observed it is the most frequently used method of all.

When post-hopping, barn owls will sit on top of a post

Post-hopping in daylight is a common feature in some parts of the countryside, but are those owls hunting or signalling to conspecifics?

patiently watching, and listening, for any small mammals that may be scurrying around in the undergrowth below. If, after a while, they do not detect anything, they will move on to the next post, and so on, until they are successful.

For effective hunting to take place, the conditions need to be relatively undisturbed and quiet so that their eyes, but especially their ears, can be used without hindrance. It was stated earlier that road traffic and other background noise is likely to affect their hunting efficiency, and barn owls do avoid hunting in windy and rainy conditions. Both will negatively affect their hearing and consequently their ability to catch prey. The sound of rain will certainly disguise the noise of small mammals in the vegetation, while wind noise may leave them vulnerable to predators. In windy conditions it is possible to move to within a very short distance of roosting barn owls without causing them alarm. The fact that it is possible to watch them by torchlight is an added bonus.

Another reason barn owls avoid hunting in the rain is to avoid getting their plumage wet. They lack sufficient oil in their feathers that many other species have, and getting saturated could lead to hyperthermia and subsequent death. They also tend to avoid adverse weather because their feathers are thematically suited to warm environments and they may lose body heat very quickly.

Quartering is used to catch prey, but a quartering owl may not just be hunting, it may also be patrolling and familiarising itself with its territory, as previously mentioned. It needs to establish where the best places are for hunting; at the same time, it is advertising its presence to other barn owls –

Post-hopping comes with its dangers.

Barn owls will hunt reluctantly in the rain. Not only can the sound of the rain affect their hearing, their feathers are not able to withstand saturation, and this can lead to hyperthermia and death.

When wing hunting, barn owls have an amazing ability to hover over a piece of ground, scrutinising it for prey.

both male and female. Spot observations of day-flying barn owls suggest that male birds may be more active during the day, though more research is needed on this.

When they are wing hunting, barn owls will fly slowly above the ground at a height of between one and three metres and their ability to fly silently will greatly assist them. The methods they use to catch their prey are basically the same as when post-hopping.

A perched barn owl will usually locate its prey by sound, but it will also use its eyes. When it is satisfied that it has located prey it will usually launch itself silently in that direction. As it glides towards its victim, it keeps its 'face' looking directly at the source of the sound, obtaining precise sound fixes as it does so. Then, just as it is almost upon its victim, it will swing its talons up in front of its face, while at the same time throwing its head back to avoid injury. In other words, its talons occupy the position where its head was.

If the owl has got it right, and more often than not it has, the owl will grasp the prey with its talons and squeeze it to death. If the prey continues to wriggle after a short while, it will usually be dispatched with a nip to the back of the head. This explains why, when analysing owl pellets, some of the skulls are found to have holes in them: the owl has delivered the *coup-de-grâce*.

Should the food be for the owl itself, it will usually eat it there and then, but if it is taking food to its young or its mate it will grasp it with one of its talons and head off towards the nest. It now depends upon where the nest is located. If it is in a barn, or a box with a ledge for perching, the owl will usually alight at the entrance and transfer the prey from its foot to its bill before entering. If it is in a tree or a box without a perch, the parent will transfer the prey from the foot to the bill in flight, thus allowing the bird the freedom to grasp the entrance hole with both feet. Sometimes a nearby branch comes in handy, so the bird can land there first before transferring the prey. Whether a barn owl is hunting from a perch or quartering a field, the method of catching the prey and carrying it to the nest is usually the same.

When carrying prey to its nest, a barn owl will usually carry it in its talons. No one has yet discovered whether barn owls are selectively right- or left-footed.

Sometimes the owl that catches the food is not the one that takes it to the nest. On 3 July 1987 a remarkable piece of behaviour was observed at Sudbourne in Suffolk when a mid-air food-pass was observed between two barn owls. Food-passing has been observed in diurnal raptors, such as marsh harriers and kestrels, but this appears to be the first occasion it has ever been observed in barn owls. The remarkable thing is that this unusual activity was seen in the same area some two years later, suggesting that the same pair was involved.

If both feet are needed to land safely at the entrance to the nest, the prey is usually transferred to the bill in flight.

Relationships with other owls and birds

From time to time conflict arises between different bird species and this is known as inter-specific, or inter-guild, aggression. On the other hand, *intra*-specific, or *intra*-guild, aggression is conflict between two or more birds of the same species. From the records it appears that intra-specific aggression does not take place between barn owls, though they do chase one another from their territories. However, in general they carry out their daily lives without any serious aggression towards one another.

Barn owls show little aggression towards other owl species except for the little owl; there have been at least seven instances of barn owls killing little owls, of which three occurred in England. Aggression by barn owls towards little owls has also been noted elsewhere in Europe including Spain and Portugal (Zuberogoitia *et al.*, 2005).

There appears to be little in the way of aggression by barn owls towards the day-flying birds of prey except for kestrels, and there are a number of instances where they have been observed stealing food from barn owls and where they have also been observed trying to steal food from short-eared owls, albeit with little success. Although kestrels will attempt, and sometimes succeed, in robbing barn owls of food, there do not appear to be any instances of kestrels killing barn owls. Not so the other way round, however, for in Europe there have been three reported examples of kestrels being killed by barn owls. Although there have been no confirmed instances of this in Britain that I know of, I once found a dead young kestrel in the vicinity of a straw-stack in which barn owls were nesting. The kestrel had been decapitated so it is possible that it had been killed by a barn owl. Yet despite the potential for conflict, there are several instances where both species have nested in close proximity to one another in apparent harmony.

Perhaps the greatest threat that now faces barn owls in the UK comes from the northern goshawk because, in recent decades, this formidable and powerful raptor has been increasing in range and numbers.

In the absence of a top predator (for example, the eagle owl) to control its population, the northern goshawk is the main predator of owls, with 13 barn owls amongst its 573 owl victims

Kestrel with water vole. Kestrels often share the same habitats and the same food as barn owls, and from time to time aggression breaks out between the two.

(Mikkola, 1983). However, before thoughts turn to introducing eagle owls to the UK, the same survey revealed that, although eagle owls had killed 55 goshawks out of a total of 705 diurnal raptors, they had killed 1,288 owls amongst which were 46 barn owls. That figure will now be much higher, though, as others have also been killed in southern Spain (Penteriani, 2012), and more will have gone unreported.

As far as other owls are concerned, tawny owls have been accused in the past of causing the decline of barn owls, and there are records of tawny owls predating barn owls, but none of barn owls killing tawny owls. In northern Spain, where tawny owls are very common, they displaced barn owls on six occasions, and each time this occurred during the egg-hatching period.

However, it may be that dominance by one species over another may not necessarily be measured by who kills whom but who can shout the loudest. Intense calling, or the presence in numbers of one species, may be a factor by which one owl species dominates the presence of another. It may be, for example, that a colony of calling little owls may well preclude a pair of barn owls from establishing a territory, but this requires investigation.

Natural aggression between species occurs, and, whilst it may appear that a collection of tame owls at a country fair are all getting on well with each other, in

Tawny owls are amongst the most aggressive of European owls, although there is no evidence to suggest that their presence has contributed to the decline of Britain's barn owls.

the wild nothing is likely to be further from the truth. Such thoughts on predator behaviour and other considerations should be applied when constructing a nest-box scheme.

The issue of erecting nest boxes without giving thought as to what other species may already be present in the area has been raised in the past, and each species of European owl has now been given an 'Inter-specific Aggression Index' (Mikkola, 2013), in which, not surprisingly, the Eurasian eagle owl topped the list, followed by the tawny owl. A number of owls on this list do not breed in Britain but both long-eared and short-eared owls, which were listed as positive aggressors, are resident with barn and little owls listed as less aggressive.

In Finland the near relative of the tawny owl, the Ural owl, which is third on the list of positive owl aggressors, is thought to be responsible for an annual 2 per cent decline in the numbers of boreal, or Tengmalm's, owls. This, it seems, is largely due to a corresponding 1.6 per cent annual increase in the number of Ural owls brought about by the large numbers of nest boxes that have been provided for them.

Apart from the barn owl, all of the UK's rodent-eating bird predators, such as the short-eared (left) and long-eared owls, appear to be in decline.

In the *State of the UK Birds 2013* report it was pointed out that, according to the Breeding Birds Survey, there had been an increase of 279 per cent in the barn owl population from 1995 to 2011 but that kestrels had declined by 30 per cent and tawny owls by 18 per cent over the same period. There may be a connection here. Especially with the kestrel, which also hunts small mammals over farmland, and it might be that the 'angelic' barn owl may not be quite as white as presently thought.

Roosts

In a barn owl's life cycle the availability of roosts is an important factor as they will be visited by owls on their nightly rounds, while during the nesting period they offer male and female individual owls a place to rest and spend some 'leisure' time alone, away from the confines of the nest and the demands of the young.

Although many roost sites are in tree holes and now boxes, those that are found in old farm outbuildings are favoured 'overnight' roosts. These are useful places, as they provide nice quiet shelters where owls can stop off and perform a variety of activities, such as regurgitating pellets, grooming or shedding feathers. It is interesting to note that most barn owls regularly use not only the same beam within the roost but also the same place on that beam, as a consequence of which the build-up of pellets below can sometimes be considerable.

Where barn owls are nesting in trees and there may be a shortage of alternative roost sites, a discreetly placed nest box may well be useful during the course of the breeding cycle.

Roosts are also invaluable for birds that are dispersing from their natal site, and this may explain why a bird may be seen at a roost for a while but then disappears because it has been unable to establish a territory.

Both males and females will use roosts although, as the build up to the nesting season begins early in the year, females will spend more and more time at the nest. Sometimes two or more females will roost together and, on occasion, males will also roost together, but only outside of the breeding season. When the breeding period commences the male will not tolerate another at its roost.

Good roosts also provide shelter from the weather. On their nightly rounds barn owls will spend much of their time just loafing around, and to have an undisturbed, sheltered quiet place is ideal for them. Outbuildings can also play a vital role in the winter, when they remain snow free, and there, owls may sit on their perches, ready for any

Valuable roost sites, such as this remote farm building, are fast disappearing from the countryside.

unwary mouse that may be scurrying around on the uncovered ground below.

For the owl student these roosts can provide opportunities for study due to the pellets that can be collected from them. As mentioned above, roosts may be used by more than one bird, and this event may be detected by an examination of the feathers that the owls might cast there. They are also great places to observe barn owls if you are prepared to sit very still and quiet, but you have

Roost sites such as this are ideal places to collect pellets and moulted feathers. They are also useful for sitting quietly and patiently to watch roosting barn owls by torchlight.

to take up your position well before the owls arrive. There you can watch your owls by torchlight, which they will ignore provided that you switch your torch on silently.

Today many of these outbuildings have either been demolished, fallen into disrepair, or have been converted for another use, and their absence has now taken some of the fun and interest out of owl study, as well as denying some owls safety, relaxation, the occasional meal, and some variety in their lifestyle.

6: Roosting and nesting habitats

'Nowadays, nest boxes are widely used as a conservation tool. But I have to point out explicitly that the provision of artificial nesting sites is not an appropriate long term conservation strategy. In the longer term, natural breeding sites have to be re-established, e.g. through the planting of orchards and willows.'
Dr Klaus-Michael Exo, Institut für Vogelforschung, Wilhelmshaven, Germany. From his foreword to *The Little Owl*, Nieuwenhuyse, *et al.*, 2008, Cambridge University Press

The conservation of wildlife can be difficult and complicated, but every now and then one or two simple acts can produce spectacular results and reverse the downward fortunes of a particular species. This, it would seem, is the story of Britain's barn owls. It was just a few decades ago that some people in the British Isles feared that barn owls were on the verge of extinction, but now they are found in places where they had not been seen for many years. Some, such as those in parts of Cambridgeshire and the Lincolnshire Fens, for example, are relatively new arrivals, for it is likely that they have never nested there with any great success due to a general lack of nest sites.

Elsewhere, there can be no doubt that since the Second World War there has been, in many places, a severe decline in nesting opportunities due to the effects of elm disease, while other trees were felled in their thousands, perhaps millions, to make way for farming. We don't know the exact number because, unlike the elms, it appears that nobody counted them. In addition, large numbers of old barns – the type so loved by barn owls – have been replaced by modern constructions, or they have fallen into disrepair or been converted for domestic use. These losses have all played their part in reducing the availability of nest sites.

The loss of nest sites, both natural and man-made, is a widespread problem that affects much of Europe, and not just Britain. Here, it seems likely that the loss of buildings as a nesting habitat is more of a widespread problem in the west and north than the loss of trees, the latter having affected large parts of central and eastern Britain.

In this section I look at the various types of nest sites that barn owls use

Volunteer putting up a nest box.

and discuss their merits and drawbacks. I also look at various matters with regard to the present trend concerning barn owls and nest boxes. At a time when we are constantly being told that Britain, and indeed Europe, is missing its 'biodiversity targets', is it at all possible that through an alternative approach which complements the present nest box strategy barn owls could help meet those targets? We should bear in mind that one leading authority has stated that around 75 per cent of Britain's barn owls now live in nest boxes.

Nightmare with elm trees

It is difficult for anyone born after the late 1960s to appreciate just how common elm trees once were in the countryside up until the mid-1970s. While they were found in virtually all parts of the British Isles, they were most common in central and southern England. They were particularly abundant in some of the eastern counties such as Essex, for example, where there were so many that their former presence has been likened, by the late John Hunter (1999) of the Essex County Records Office, to that 'of a monoculture'. The loss of elms is an important part of the barn owl story and requires looking at in the light of present-day developments.

Elms are a complex group of trees which, when mature, have an ability to unexpectedly shed large boughs – sometimes with fatal results for any humans below. For barn owls, though, the shedding of those large boughs is a welcome event, for where they detach themselves from the trunk a cavity usually develops which in time provides a suitable hole for nesting. Until the 1970s there were around 23 million medium-to-large elms in the British countryside, and without doubt they were a significant component of barn owl nesting habitat (Osborne, 1982), especially in southern and south-east England. However, elms have been subject to disease for thousands of years, and throughout that time barn owls have survived those losses, so there is no reason not to expect their numbers to rise naturally when the elms return, as they seemingly will do. Unfortunately, in these days of instant conservation, perhaps one of the biggest long-term dangers that barn owls face is human impatience and a failure to nurture the natural habitats.

It was in the 1920s that an outbreak of elm disease was noted on the European mainland which then spread to Britain, where an estimated 20 per cent of all trees were killed during the 1920s and early 1930s. The infection was called Dutch elm disease (DED) due to the research that was carried out by Dutch scientists. The disease then faded away only for it to re-emerge in the late 1960s when another outbreak occurred which spread rapidly throughout the British Isles and eventually into mainland Europe.

The virus is invasive and is caused by the fungus *Ophiostoma novo-ulmi*, a disease that blocks the water-conducting vessels. This then affects the elm's growth by impeding the flow of sap, and the tree wilts as if killed by drought. Of significance is the fact that the disease is usually transmitted from infected trees to healthy trees by the elm bark beetles, *Scolytus scolytus* and *Scolytus multistriatus*.

As a result of this disease, virtually all of the tall elms have now gone from Britain and Europe, and all that we are left with in a number of places are elm hedges. These consist of the suckers which are still growing from the stumps left in place after the tree itself was felled. These suckers will continue to grow, although any which develop at present into a reasonably sized sapling will eventually succumb to the disease. However, when the disease has finally run its course then some of those suckers will eventually grow into large trees which will once again grace the European countryside. All that is needed is patience and some sympathetic hedge-trimming.

From this it may be thought that the loss of elms has been the main cause of barn owl decline in Britain, and there can be no doubt that this has been one factor that has contributed towards its decline. The remedy for this problem has been a relatively simple matter to put in place, though.

The shortfall of nest sites has been met to some degree by the provision of nest boxes. However, we should be very clear that when the elms graced the countryside, farmland habitats were likely to have been more prey-rich than they are at present. This is probably why the take-up of nesting boxes has not been as good in some places as it has in others.

Buildings

It seems distinctly possible that, in the fullness of time, the object that provided the name for the barn owl – the barn – will have all but vanished in its agricultural form from the British countryside. What shall we call it then? The box owl? Probably not, but it is a sad fact that many of the thousands of barns that once existed across Britain, and which were once home for barn owls, have now either been converted into houses or become ruins, and it seems that more are likely to follow.

Old barns, such as this one to the south of Ipswich in Suffolk, are ideal places for barn owls. Close inspection of the 'owl window' reveals traces of white which are indicative of use by barn owls. Brick-built barns are uncommon in eastern England.

Due to a perceived housing shortage there is growing pressure on farmers to allow redundant farm buildings to be pulled down and the site rebuilt for housing, or for the existing buildings to be converted for the same purpose. This is an ongoing problem from which there is no protection for any barn owls that may roost or nest there. It is against the law to disturb barn owls when they are nesting; any building that is being considered for development should be thoroughly checked to ensure that there are no barn owls present, bearing in mind that they can be very secretive. However, once the nesting season has finished in the autumn, then conversion can start, irrespective of whether owls have nested there for many years and whether they may do so the coming year.

In the move towards tackling the problem of barn owls and barn conversion, the Barn Owl Trust in Devon has to some degree been successful in encouraging

This industrial unit on the outskirts of Colchester, Essex, is an example of how barn owls may take up residence in unlikely places if they are left alone and if there is food nearby.

The owls have been observed flying into the building through this passageway.

The copious droppings and presence of pellets indicate that at least one barn owl roosts on a beam in the roof space and also on the top of a door to the right of the picture. The fact that there are two different roost spots suggest that more than one owl may be using this building.

the owners to make nesting space available in the loft area of any new conversions. The presence of barn owls using inhabited buildings is not new in Britain, for there are records of owls being ousted from their nest sites many years ago because residents were kept awake at night due to their 'snoring'.

In Essex the records of barn owls using buildings are few, and so it was of some considerable interest when, in October 2014, I became aware of barn owls frequenting an active industrial building on the outskirts of Colchester, Essex. Due to the complexity of the structure, it is not presently known whether the owls are using the building for nesting or whether they nest in the trees to the rear of the premises and use the building as a roost. But the potential for barn owls to use such premises is something to be explored because there are many commercial properties on the edges of towns that, with a little thought, could well provide a haunt for barn owls, as long as there are quality habitats nearby for small mammals.

The loss of buildings for nesting is not a problem that is confined to Britain; it is a widespread issue that extends across Europe and beyond due to the thousands of barns and other rural buildings that have been converted for domestic use in recent decades. In the wake of those building conversions there is no indication at present of the size of Europe's barn owl population. In the

Throughout Europe, barn owls are losing man-made nest and roost sites through demolition or – as with this barn in East Anglia – conversion.

European Breeding Bird Atlas (Hagemeier and Blair, 1997), Osieck and Shawyer estimated that there was a total European population of between 110,000 and 230,000 breeding pairs, of which 90 per cent were estimated to live in the west of Europe. One wonders what the barn owl population will look like by 2020 when the European Bird Census Council plan to publish their new bird atlas (see www.ebcc.info/new-atlas.html).

There seems little that can be done about this problem. Farmers and landowners are sometimes co-operative in helping to prevent barn conversions in favour of barn owls, and occasionally, through some understanding and tolerance, a converted farm building can retain its barn owls, but these instances are in the minority. There is, however, one form of building that could help stem the flow: churches.

We saw earlier that one of the names that the barn owl was once called was the 'church owl' due to it choosing to nest in churches across Britain, Europe and elsewhere. However, access to these was closed up to prevent pigeons and the like from entering and creating a mess. Although most of the entrances have been closed off, there remains the possibility that church towers could once again be used by barn owls if provision is made for them.

One of the shutter-type panels could be removed and fitted with an entrance hole, just big enough to allow barn owls to enter; behind that a nest box could be placed with its entrance firmly against the shutter entrance so that pigeons cannot

Known throughout Europe as the 'tower owl', the barn owl was known in John Ray's time as the 'church owl'. Here lies an opportunity, surely, for a community barn owl project.

enter the church tower (C. Durdin pers. comm.). Large boxes would be ideal, but on no account should an external ledge be provided which might allow access for pigeons or any other non-target species. It was pointed out earlier that barn owls can enter very small entrances quite easily and they do not need a ledge to perch on. This could make an ideal project that, if monitored on a regular basis, could involve volunteer ornithologists as well as professionals – though not on Sundays!

Barns are not always ideal for nesting. In eastern and southern Britain, many are made of wood, and while they have beams on which owls can roost they

Barn owls are opportunists in their selection of a nesting place, and straw stacks are sometimes used. Occasionally this can end in tragedy as straw is moved and a nest is accidentally destroyed: usually to the distress of the farmer.

Barn owls will use whatever nest site is available. In places where brick or stone barns exist they will often take advantage of any ledges inside them.

This nest was in the ventilation shaft of an old Second World War gun emplacement. One chick is partly hidden in the shaft to the right, and there is at least one other of its siblings hidden completely.

Timber-framed barns make poor nesting places unless a box is provided. However, they do make excellent roost sites.

do not have ledges suitable for nesting. There still are, though, many old pollard trees with wonderful holes just right for this purpose. This did not mean that barn owls chose barns in the west and trees in the east on an exclusive basis, as once thought; it was just their availability. Now, across Britain, they use nest boxes inside buildings, outside on buildings and on trees, demonstrating quite clearly that it is nest site availability that determines which sites are used and not climate. The decision has very little to do with the weather conditions, as Iain Taylor (1994) proved in south-west Scotland. There are no reliable figures as to the proportion of barn owls that actually nest in boxes at present as opposed to those that continue to use barns and tree sites, but estimates that three-quarters of the population now depend upon nest boxes for their survival is an interesting scenario. It may be that a significant proportion of Britain's barn owls once nested in other man-made structures, namely barns, many years ago – long before nest boxes were thought of – when Ray and Willughby made their grand tour.

Nest boxes

For many years conservationists have put up nest boxes for birds. For barn owls this appears to have been first advocated on a general basis in 1945, while the first scientifically monitored scheme to use nest boxes for owls in Britain was applied shortly after the Second World War in a study on tawny owls in Wytham Woods, Oxfordshire (Southern, 1954). The reason for using boxes in this instance was to allow easy monitoring of the nests and their contents for scientific purposes. Nest boxes are usually fitted with a small door which allows easy access for any eggs to be counted and any chicks to be weighed and ringed. They also enable pellets to be collected for analysis. Used in the right manner the nest box is a powerful aid to owl science and conservation.

The first large-scale nest-box scheme for barn owls in Britain would appear to have been that of the South-West Lancashire Ringing Group. Iain Taylor's (1994) intensive study in south-west Scotland followed on from this and during the course of his investigation, which ran from 1978 until 1992, well over 100 nest boxes were used to monitor the owls regularly.

However, it is largely since the mid-1990s that the wildlife conservation movement has been gripped by the fashion for erecting large numbers of nest boxes for barn owls. According to the BTO's website, there were around 25,000 boxes in place by the middle of the 1990s but some 15 years later that number is very much greater and the figure of 50,000 which has been quoted by one authority does not seem outrageous. This seems rather grand conservation indeed, so let's look at the merits of nesting boxes.

Most boxes are of a sturdy construction that will probably last for many years and may provide a quick and simple nest or roost site. In a long-term study of boreal owls in Finland it was found that the occupancy of nest boxes declined with the age of the boxes (Korpormäki and Hakkarainen, 2012). They discovered that those boxes that were between one and four years of age had a take-up greater than 20 per cent but then this declined to 10–18 per cent when the boxes were between five and ten years old, falling to less than 10 per cent for those boxes that were between 11 and 18 years of age.

They then compared nest boxes to natural cavities and found that the decline increased significantly with the age of the hole, and that the decline in usage was steepest with natural cavities rather than those of nest boxes. Their conclusion was that boreal owls preferred to nest in new cavities and nest boxes because the quality was better, and they lowered the risk of predation by species of marten.

They considered that martens have a long-term memory of their home range and that after a while they got to know where nest contents could be plundered. The locations of new boxes would have to be learnt by the martens, while moving old boxes also had a positive and similar affect. It would appear there is no such study that has investigated, or is investigating, the quality and usage of nest boxes for barn or any other owl species in Britain. With a recovering pine marten population in Britain, this is a subject for long-term monitoring; with a large number of owl boxes now in place, it seems possible that these boxes will help assist this species to spread south from its northern retreats by providing places to live, and food to eat!

This study in Finland has special interest because there are records in the literature where British barn owls have nested in ancient trees for many years and, while boreal and barn owls are two different species, their lifestyles make an interesting comparison. In Iain Taylor's study in south-west Scotland many of his barn owls used the same box over the whole period of his study from 1978 to 1992.

Looking at the downside of nest boxes, most are made of wood. Most are placed outside and are thus exposed to the elements in both cold winters and hot summers even though their construction may be sturdy. In Spain it has been found that, although warmer and drier springs encouraged lesser kestrels to breed earlier, the benefits of this were lost due to chicks suffering high mortality rate in the chick-rearing stage because of dehydration within wooden nest boxes, as the temperatures rose to 55 °C. Those involved with this study considered that with 100 per cent of all lesser kestrels occupying nest boxes in their study area, there was the probability that the population would suffer an annual loss of 7 per cent in the face of climate change; this highlighted the need for a different approach to the conservation of these kestrels to take account of that.

In addition to this, nest boxes need regular long-term maintenance, and there can be no doubt that most of them will need to be replaced eventually. In reviewing the management of nest sites across much of the northern hemisphere, Iain Taylor was of the opinion that conservation programmes for most barn owls will involve the long-term provision of new sites and the maintenance of existing ones, with the implication that nest boxes were the future. This seems a sound

According to recent estimates, there are now more than 50,000 such boxes dotted around the country. Used wisely, well-designed boxes are a valuable conservation tool, but is this the ultimate destination for all of Britain's barn owls, and, if so, is it sustainable?

assessment with regard to scientific monitoring, but it also seems likely that many other boxes, such as those in areas that are not scientifically monitored, will fall by the wayside.

One of Germany's top ornithologists, Dr Michael Exo, is of the view that nest boxes are 'something like a bridge technology', providing nest sites until natural sites have been developed and nurtured *(in litt.)*. It seems likely that for the long-term conservation of barn owls in Britain this will eventually be the way forward, although it may take some while before agreement is reached on this. In parts of the countryside nest boxes do have a role to play, not only in the wider conservation, but as a convenient and effective way of monitoring their populations. As a living part of the environment, and as an aid in helping biodiversity, however, they have no role: they are sterile habitats.

The provision of nest boxes is, at present, playing an important role in helping to stabilise and increase the numbers of barn owls in some places, but whether they are the ultimate solution for providing nest sites for the long term is perhaps questionable. Admittedly the take-up of boxes is often quick and dramatic, but that should not automatically be looked upon as an instantaneous conservation success.

Our standpoint as to how we view nature conservation takes on many twists and facets, for during the 1980s and 90s the act of breeding and releasing barn owls was frowned upon by the conservation movement. Ultimately this led to the barn owl being

Taking barn owl conservation to the extreme. This oak timber-framed demonstration model at 8.8 metres tall and 3.66 metres square was seen on display at the Royal Show, Warwickshire in 1993. It was subsequently bought from the manufacturer by a Suffolk resident who had it dismantled and shipped to their south Suffolk home where it was erected in the grounds of their house. My advice was sought on making provision for barn owls, including the construction and sighting of an interior nesting box as well as specifying the dimensions for the owl window. Kestrels and stock doves have used the box, but, to date, barn owls have failed to use this 'des res'.

placed on Schedule 9 of the Wildlife and Countryside Act, which means that it is illegal to deliberately release a barn owl into the wild without the proper authorisation.

Apart from the welfare aspect, in that captive-bred released birds were found to be more vulnerable to traffic accidents and starvation through release into unsuitable habitats, the more pertinent view was that this diverted attention away from the burning issues of the day, which were the protection and promotion of good wildlife habitats. Are we not now in danger of doing exactly the same thing with nest boxes? Suppliers of nest boxes may feel threatened by these words, but surely here lies the opportunity for them to grasp the nettle and promote biodiversity.

Thinking outside the box

Looking at alternative nest sites, then, a natural one, such as may be found in an oak tree for example, is a living organism that cannot only provide a nest site, it can provide a habitat for a whole raft of species. Some of these long-lived trees have had a succession of nesting barn owls stretching back many years. There are oaks in the British countryside which are well over four or five hundred years old, some even older. During its life an oak may provide a habitat for a wealth of insect life, each of which plays its part within the natural history framework of providing biological diversity. If the tree is left to mature, along the way it is likely to lose a bough or two. Later, a wound may develop into a cavity and this may eventually provide a home for a wide range of species, including barn owls. By that time the tree will have built a place for itself within the surrounding landscape, and then an even greater diversity of species may follow, especially if the tree has been pollarded.

Pollarding is the ancient craft of taking the tops off trees at a height of around 4–5 metres, to allow the resulting shoots that follow to grow into poles for tool handles and other uses. Oak trees which have been pollarded usually have a much longer life than those which have not and they also tend to be more stable in wind blow. On their way to maturity, those that have been pollarded usually develop small holes, and these may be used by a succession of species as the trees develop.

Bees, wasps and hornets may first nest in oaks; later bats may roost or breed in them, while bird species such as redstart, nuthatch, tits and woodpeckers may all use them. In addition the foliage will provide a rich source of food for growing nestling birds, from the thousands upon thousands of insects that inhabit this most iconic of all British trees.

As the trees grow, and the holes develop into cavities, stock doves, kestrels, jackdaws and other hole-nesting species, including tawny, little and barn owls, may also use them. Some of the old parklands that are liberally spread around many parts of Britain have a collection of wonderful pollarded oak trees.

This oak was pollarded in 2006, but already it has started to develop cavities. In the winter of 2010 a pair of blue tits took possession. In the fullness of time there is no reason why it shouldn't play host to a pair of barn owls.

Hedgerows can also play a role. In large parts of the countryside there are many hedgerow pollards. Often these may grow alongside lanes and roads, while others grace the open countryside away from any thoroughfare. Locations where road traffic is a problem are not ideal places to encourage owls, but there are many areas where the countryside remains quiet and where trees could be strongly promoted as nesting places, both now and in the future. On minor roads barn owls are at very low risk of being killed by traffic. When I carried out a survey in Suffolk during the 1980s, nearly all of the 32 road kills that were reported during a period of 15 months were of birds found dead on major roads.

There are problems to contend with. At the time of writing a 'new' tree disease called 'Sudden Oak Death' has appeared. Like elm disease, this one is also caused by a fungus and at present comparatively little is known about it and what the long-term effects are likely to be. However, the planting of oaks is continuing in new woodlands, so this might not be the problem that was first envisaged. Most trees are subject to fungal infections of one sort or another and the presence of fungus in old oak trees is not unusual. In some instances fungal activity is beneficial to a tree's longevity.

Of course, other species of tree will be used if they have suitable nesting cavities; across Europe beech is used as a pollard tree in a number of places. In Britain there are important woodlands such as the New Forest in Hampshire, Burnham Beeches in Buckinghamshire and Epping Forest in Essex where pollard beeches are significant places for tawny owls. Beech is used on the Continent as a hedgerow and avenue tree, but its use as a hedgerow tree in Britain appears to be limited. Whilst it might not have quite the same attraction to invertebrates as oak, it is a valuable wildlife tree that can live for 500 years or more if pollarded, and it is a species of tree that barn owls will most certainly use. In the face of climate change, then, beech, a species which is not favoured by many conservationists, may offer a suitable nesting opportunity in the future.

Nesting cavities for owls in the countryside are no longer common. Each tree, such as this, should be treasured.

Pollarded hornbeams could also become popular in time, although at

Pollarded beech trees at Urkiola and Berlitz, Basque Country, northern Spain. In view of climate change, the use of pollarded beech trees may be a long-term initiative in providing nest sites for barn owls.

present there does not appear to be any research into this subject. They are quite numerous in Epping Forest, Essex, where they are used by tawny owls, and they are also used as a staple nest site in the Kozłowka Forest near Lubartow in eastern Poland. However, it appears that their use by barn owls anywhere is yet to be explored. Hornbeams prefer a mild climate and respond well to pollarding, so if the climate continues to warm, it may be another tree that could have nesting potential.

With large trees there are factors that need to be addressed. For example, many people are either fearful of large trees or consider them a nuisance, and trees are often removed at the slightest excuse. Sadly, falling boughs and trees do occasionally kill people and there is a tremendous outcry when this happens, yet in the UK more people are killed on average *each day* by motor cars than are killed by falling trees *in a year*. We must surely learn to live with trees and respect them for what they are, just as we have learnt to live with the motor car. In addition to the cause of wildlife, trees are valuable components in the environment which help to reduce the amounts of greenhouse gases in the atmosphere by absorbing carbon dioxide and giving off oxygen. Large trees are especially valuable for this.

It is perfectly understandable that farmers and landowners are concerned in case a falling branch or tree injures or kills someone, because they may be held legally responsible. They surely must have some form of protection against litigation, while there is a need for greater public awareness with regards to countryside matters. This is something that is sadly lacking at present, and countryside education may well have its place in the classroom or the home.

In addition the suppliers of electricity and other such services are concerned when their lines are brought down by falling trees or branches. The power suppliers have not yet widely introduced methods to reduce or remove this problem, as the telephone service has, although there are signs that this is changing.

There are, of course, practical reasons why nest boxes are preferred to trees in conservation plans. From the view of gathering nest record information they allow easy access to the nest contents, and their value for gathering useful information has been demonstrated in many studies. Trees, on the other hand, can often present a challenge. Nest information is important, but might it be that an integrated approach involving natural nest sites and nest boxes could be the long way forward in terms of science and conservation?

Today many trees are planted in 'new' woodlands, and, whilst the planting of such trees is commendable, these trees will be unsuitable even when they are mature because barn owls avoid enclosed woodland. With considerate planting and a suitable regime, however, they may help to provide an integrated approach to managing Britain's barn owls and woodlands.

Looking at things on a wider scale, we know little if anything about the

The state of our present-day pollards must not be overlooked. Many are in need of re-pollarding, although this should be addressed skillfully.

ecological impact that the sudden appearance of large numbers of nest boxes might have on other species. For example, what is the effect of encouraging a sudden influx of barn owls into an area where they have either been absent for many years or never been present? Do the effects of their predations affect populations of kestrels, weasels, stoats, foxes and other creatures that also prey on small mammals, and what is the knock-on effect? All of these creatures add to the biological diversity of the countryside, and their needs should not be overlooked.

On mainland Europe the countryside is richer in woodland than Britain, but by comparison it has fewer large hedgerow trees. This means that many of Europe's barn owls are reliant upon man-made structures for nesting, which leaves them vulnerable. In Britain more barn owls nest in hedgerow trees than they do on the Continent but, just as in mainland Europe, British barn owls are becoming more dependent on nest boxes.

In conclusion, it is especially worth looking at the plight of non-woodland trees in the countryside of southern and eastern Britain, because traditionally that is where barn owls have nested. For many years these trees have suffered from neglect and many are now in need of attention. In many instances pollarding or re-pollarding is desirable for the long term, but this needs to be addressed by specialist tree surgeons. We ignore the role of these trees at our peril.

For example, as a plant, ivy is a double-edged sword for wildlife. On the positive side it provides nectar for countless insects in autumn when other nectar sources may be scarce, while its berries may provide food for thrushes and small mammals in winter. Its dense foliage can also provide roosting places for birds, including owls. On the negative side, if it is

This oak tree can provide food for hundreds of different species, as well as roosts for owls. It may be prematurely nearing the end of its life, though. When all of the branches are smothered in ivy it will no longer be able to photosynthesise and it will then be literally smothered to death. In autumn gales, instead of allowing the wind to pass through its branches, the ivy may act as a wind barrier which could cause the tree to be blown over.

left to run rampant it will eventually smother a tree, thus denying it the ability to photosynthesise, and if a tree cannot absorb light through its foliage it will die. Along with this, a tree that is heavily covered in ivy will be vulnerable to wind-blow through acting as a barrier to high winds. In a gale the tree may be blown down.

In lowland Britain tree sites once made up a sizeable proportion of nesting habitat for barn owls. Valuable trees such as this lovely Suffolk oak pollard, however, do pose problems if you want to check the nest contents and ring the young.

7: Nesting

For barn owls the breeding cycle can be a lengthy procedure which lasts from around February to August and sometimes longer. It all depends upon whether the start of egg-laying is delayed, whether a replacement clutch is laid for an earlier one that may have been lost, or whether there is the opportunity to raise a second brood.

Courtship

From around the end of August until early winter, a pair of barn owls may well spend much of their time apart, meeting up from time to time to commence, or re-affirm, the pair bond. Some pairs do remain together throughout the year and these perhaps may be perennial birds that have a long attachment. After

In the build-up to egg-laying, food will regularly be brought to the nest by the male to provide an indication of how abundant prey is. Sometimes the amount of food brought to the nest exceeds the needs of the female, but this abundance of prey will determine how much weight she puts on, thus determining how many eggs will be laid.

the bond is cemented, the male will usually – though not always – spend time away in his own roost. By mid-winter he will begin to visit the female at the future nest site on a more regular basis, and when he does he will usually bring food; the abundance of this will help her to put on weight and to bring her into breeding condition in the build-up to egg-laying. A greater intake of prey will also provide calcium, which will be needed for egg shell production.

By February the male begins visiting the hen more frequently, and from then on he will spend most of the time with her, only leaving the nest site to go out hunting or to patrol his territory with frequent screeching. The frequency and intensity of the screeching is likely to be determined by the proximity of other barn owls that may be breeding nearby. It is at this time that many males become more visible as they begin the build-up to the breeding season. Sometimes they will be joined by the females, and there will be frequent and hectic chases in the nesting area, with the male closely following the female. During the course of my Suffolk survey (Martin, 1984) I recorded the monthly sightings of barn owls, and they tended to fit the general trend of barn owl activity prior to breeding.

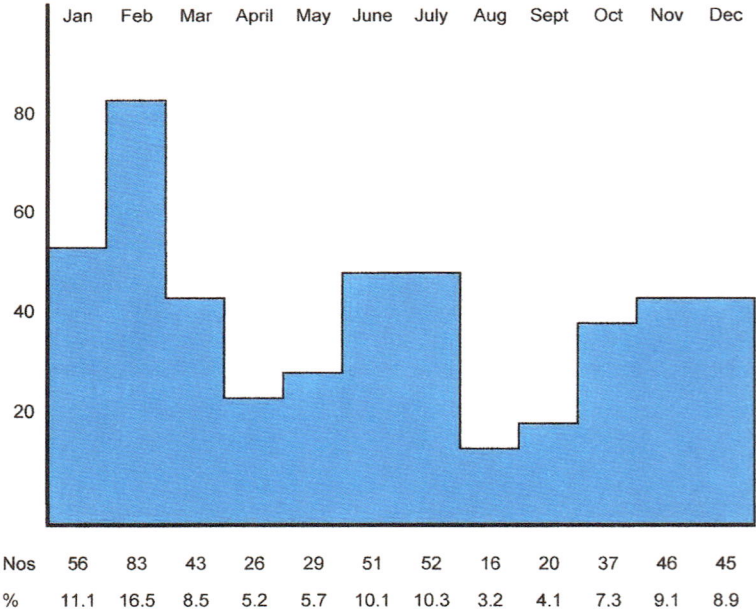

Casual sightings of 504 barn owls recorded in Suffolk, 1983–6

In March and April the males become even more territorial as they frequently screech both in and around the nest site. By April a behavioural change occurs with the females who now rarely leave the nest, exiting only for exercise and perhaps bathing. Based on the number of casual sightings in Suffolk, I found that April and May were months when barn owls were less frequently observed; this suggests that hens were tending to stay within the confines of the nest site and that incubation was in progress during that period.

Each time the male brings food to the female he will copulate with her, and the number of times he does this generally increases up until the time of egg-laying, which usually occurs around late April to early May. Regular copulation throughout this period will also take place irrespective of whether he has brought food to her or not. In their description of the courtship procedures, Bunn *et al*. (1982) provide the impression that barn owls actually enjoy sex and indulge in it quite frequently in the build-up to egg-laying. The report on a study of snowy owls (Potapov and Sale, 2012) was more forthright in suggesting that snowy owls indulge in 'recreational sex', and the authors strongly implied that those owls actually appeared to enjoy it, while acknowledging that their comments could be classed as anthropomorphic.

A poor breeding season has often been attributed to the over-wintering body condition of female barn owls prior to breeding, although it was considered their fat reserves are not as important for breeding birds as they are for non-breeders. The general findings of this study suggested that the over-wintering condition of the female's body is not that important for starting a clutch, though the abundance of food that is brought to her during the immediate build-up to clutch formation is significant (Durant *et al*., 2000).

As the female's bodyweight starts to increase she becomes largely dependent upon the male for food. The more he brings, the more her bodyweight increases, until she is in condition to commence egg-laying. If food has not been very plentiful she will not gain much weight, so that only a few eggs will be laid. If food has been plentiful her weight will then increase accordingly, and the number of eggs may be great. It has been considered that snowy owls are 'spring lemming abundance gamblers' and that these owls lay clutches that are based upon the present abundance of one particular food, and because of this they are reliant upon its abundance later in the breeding season. If the subsequent supply of food dries up, the outlook for the brood is not good. It is a similar scenario with those barn owls that are largely reliant upon voles for their survival.

In times of real food shortage the hen may lay no eggs at all. Or if, through an abundance of food early in the breeding cycle, she lays a large clutch of eggs only to find that some catastrophe befalls the food supply, disaster may follow. She may then desert the eggs, or only a few, if any, of the young will survive. With extra feeding, captive barn owls can be induced to lay large numbers of eggs – a clutch of 26 has been recorded. In the wild this number decreases and the largest ever recorded in Europe was in 1953, when a hen laid 16 eggs. However, care should be exercised when assessing such numbers: in 2013, a 'brood' of 16 young barn owls was raised to fledging in Israel (Yosshi Leshem *in litt*.), only for it to be found that this was the result of two free-flying females being mated with one male.

Gambling barn owls

The timing of egg-laying and the subsequent availability of food is crucial to the success of the brood. If the clutch is laid in April or early May, then the timing of the brood will often coincide with a time of peak food. It largely depends upon whether they are being fed mainly on a diet of voles and, if so, at what stage the vole cycle is. If there is a delay in clutch production, perhaps due to inclement weather, then incubation might not start until late May or early June. In that case, the young will not hatch out until early July and their increasing demands for food in mid to late July will be crucial, just as field vole numbers start to fall away. If the brood is not dependent on field voles, the effects are unlikely to be so damaging, as bank vole, wood mouse and shrew populations start to pick up.

The late summer period, when second clutches are started, is usually a time of low vole abundance; this is likely to be the reason why second broods are fewer and smaller in Britain than they are on the continental mainland. There, barn owls are not so dependent upon field voles because the diversity of prey species is greater.

Most owl species do not make nests as such, but barn owls may be different in that regurgitated pellets often form a soft base upon which the female will lay her eggs. Very often the pellets – which would otherwise become quite hard when dry – are chewed to soften them. Contrary to most expectations, I once found a nest in which it appeared that the female had formed a slight depression in the pellet layer. Whether this was intentional or as a result of her body weighing down on the nest I cannot say, but it appears from a recent study that female snowy owls make a scrape 'in the peat or soil', and Iain Taylor thought that barn owls also made a scrape or shallow hollow.

Heimo Mikkola *(in litt.)* is of the view that most, if not all, owls make a scrape or hollow. He feels this is especially true of short-eared but also of great grey owls. It is the disturbance of the twigs in the nest which has led to false claims of nest building by great greys.

All owl eggs are dull white and most are almost round, but those of the barn owl are oval, or sub-elliptical. On average an egg measures 40 mm x 32 mm, although in Scotland it was found they measured 42.1 mm x 31.8 mm; however, egg size can depend upon the location and the race or species of barn owl involved.

Barn owl eggs are smaller in proportion to the female's bodyweight by comparison with other European owls. A typical bird using the same body reserves as a barn owl, but laying eggs of the predicted weight for an owl of that size, would normally lay fewer eggs. It is believed this strategy allows barn owl females to lay a greater number of eggs than females of other species, so that when food is plentiful a greater number of young can be raised.

The nest will usually be in a quiet corner of the nesting chamber.

Using examples of females from six species of owl, Fitzpatrick (1934) concluded that owls possessed a unilateral (single) ovary which restricted them to laying only one egg at a time, and at varying intervals. With barn owls the interval between egg-laying is usually two to three days, but this can vary depending upon such circumstances as weather or perhaps the experience of the female.

It appears that there are two (bilateral) ovaries in some of the diurnal raptors, such as the Eurasian sparrowhawk and common kestrel, as well as the rough-legged buzzard, a species which will occasionally lay two eggs in one day (see Potapov and Sale, 2012).

On average it takes 15.7 days for single egg production in snowy owls, and it is a similar time period for barn owls (Durant, 2004). The production of a clutch of snowy owls has been likened to that of an 'egg-production conveyer belt' (Potapov and Sale, 2012) with the eggs in a continual process of initial egg production, yolk development, fertilization, shell formation and the laying of the completed egg. A similar process exists for barn owls, which means that, with a typical clutch of five eggs, the actual time period for the production of such a clutch will be around 30 days.

Incubation

Incubation starts after the first egg has been laid, and the time taken for each one to hatch out is around 29 to 34 days. During this period the female will form an even stronger bond with the nest and its contents, and she will only leave it on rare occasions, being almost totally fed by the male who will invariably copulate with her each time he brings food even though she is incubating.

From time to time the hen will raise her body to turn the eggs with her bill before settling down to recommence incubation. As the time of the hatch of the first chick approaches, she begins to become more restless because she can hear the calls of the chick from within the egg, which she replies to with a soft twittering.

Although copulation continues each time the male brings food, this normally stops around a week after the first egg is hatched, although some birds will continue to copulate for longer.

While the female is incubating, the male is free to get on with life, and this might be the ideal time for him to find an additional mate. However, while it might be thought that the male abandons his first mate, nothing is further from the truth. Successful polygamous behaviour has been recorded in the Lake District as well as in southern Scotland where males were recorded as mated with two females on seven occasions out of a total of 419 nesting attempts; the above example from Israel provides further evidence of this. However, the males have to be careful, for while they are away other males may visit their nest site and copulate with their mate. It is perhaps for this reason that males tend to lie low at this time so that they do not draw attention to the presence of the nest. Barn owls do lead complicated and fascinating lives, which is one of the reasons why people find them interesting creatures to study.

In a study of boreal owls in Finland polygamous behaviour has also been recorded, even though 24 per cent of the male population were bachelors. In good vole years 10 per cent of the male population was polygamous and this was despite the fact that bachelor males possessed nest boxes nearby, to which they brought and stored food, but in which they did not breed.

Some owl species are able to manipulate the sex of their owlets so that more males are born in years when food is plentiful, as in the case of boreal owls and tawny owls. This is likely to have implications for barn owls, although this subject is yet to be explored.

In the case of tawny owls it appears that when food is plentiful the females may produce more male chicks. If this applies to barn owls, but only occurs every now and then, there might not be a problem. But if it occurred over a length of time and on a regular basis then ultimately there would be far more males than females.

Captive breeding

For many years uncommon species, such as the barn owl, have been kept in captivity for the purposes of breeding with a view to releasing the offspring into the wild. In some cases there have been remarkable successes, but in many instances environmental circumstances have prevented this.

In the 1980s there was a significant interest in breeding and releasing barn owls into the wild in the hope of increasing their numbers. However, this was brought to a halt in January 1993 when the barn owl was placed on Schedule 9 of the Wildlife and Countryside Act. This meant that barn owls could no longer be released into the wild without a special government licence. Since that time, though, there has been a significant rise in the number of birds that are kept in captivity, and these are often used for breeding purposes.

In reviewing the global challenges that evolutionary biology faces, Carroll et al. (2014) pointed out that, where captive breeding programmes are used to rebuild numbers of rare species, they usually experience a 50–90 per cent failure rate due to their inability to adapt to a change in the environmental wild landscape; thus bringing into question the issue of keeping barn owls in captivity if they do not have a role to play in replenishing wild stocks. But there are other issues.

These authors point to the fact that, for humans, a sedentary modern lifestyle, coupled with a diet based on high glycemic processed foods, is leading to obesity, diabetes and cardiovascular disease. While it would be difficult to accuse barn owls of having a high glycemic diet, one wonders what effects a caged environment consisting of a sedentary lifestyle coupled with very little exercise and a restricted diet, often consisting of day-old dead poultry chicks, is having on captive barn owls. This is apart from the psychological effects that solitary captivity may have on such creatures, with little or no chance of natural interaction with other barn owls (Korneliussen, 2015). It may be argued that the birds can be used for breeding, but for what purpose?

These aspects of barn owl conservation do not appear to have been studied, so perhaps this is a subject which requires investigation.

Of course, the question that tends to arise from this is what to do with an injured owl that cannot be released back into the environment. Here the finder has a dilemma: whether to consign the bird to a life of captivity, where it may possibly degenerate both physically and mentally, or whether to have a creature, which they emotionally find attractive, humanely destroyed. With seemingly abandoned owlets, then, surely the best course of action is to return the individual immediately to the area from whence it came; but that does not always happen (personal observation).

Eggs

Like those of most other bird species that nest in dark places, owl eggs are white and nearly round. Barn owl eggs are a little different in that the shape is more elliptical than round, and the eggs are smooth but not glossy. In his south-west Scottish study, Iain Taylor (1994) found a clutch of five eggs that were finely flecked with brown, but that is highly unusual.

From a sample of 100 eggs the size of *alba* eggs was 36–45 mm x 29–34 mm, with an average of 40 mm x 32 mm and an average weight of 21 grams (*BWP*). During the course of his Scottish study, Taylor found the average size was 42.1 mm x 31.8 mm, with an average laying weight of 17.9 grams.

As a percentage of egg weight against body weight, Taylor found that *alba* and *guttata* egg weights were 4.9 per cent of female body weight, and in the North American barn owl *Tyto furcata praticola* they weighed 4.8 per cent.

The conclusion he arrived at from his interesting study was that, if barn owls laid eggs that were equivalent in size to other owl species, they would weigh 24.6 grams rather than 17.9. The smaller eggs were a strategy that helped cave dwelling birds to produce large broods.

8: The owlets

From the time that the last egg is laid, the pair have a relatively quiet time, as the female spends nearly all of that time incubating while the male's role is to find food for them both. At the end of the incubation period, however, their lives are about to change as they prepare to enter their most hectic time of the year: the arrival of the chicks.

A star is born

Due to the asynchronous manner in which the eggs are laid, a clutch of five eggs will hatch out over a period of approximately 10–15 days. No two broods are likely to be the same, for there is a variation of individual birds within different broods. Some of this variation arises through the supply of food, which is often reliant upon the weather conditions, but it is also dependent upon the parents and their behaviour towards them.

The nest site itself also plays an important role in this: those young which are born in open nests, such as barns, for example, develop more quickly than those that are raised in such places as tree holes and walls, where the opportunity for exercise is less, although this might not be such a problem in very large trees with large cavities. The hatching of the chicks and their subsequent development has been well described (Bunn *et al.*, 1982), but a brief insight into the world of a new-born brood of barn owls from that description is always worth repeating.

The female is aware of the imminent hatching of the first egg by the calling of the chick from within it. This she replies to with a soft twittering note which is similar to the food-offering call. The start of the hatch begins near nightfall when a hole appears in the egg; the hole is made by the egg-tooth of the chick which appears on the front of the ivory-coloured bill. By the following morning the owlet has hatched out.

When hatching is complete the hen will remove the eggshell by either discarding it to one side or removing it from the nest site completely. Sometimes she will eat it, and this will enable her to replace some of the calcium she has lost during the course of egg-laying. In the first few days the young are nothing like the beautiful creatures that we see flying around the countryside; a writer once described them some years ago as 'proverbially ugly'.

When they are first hatched, the chicks are blind, pink skinned and covered on their upper parts with short greyish-white down known as the protoptyle plumage. The remaining skin is uncovered and they are markedly pot-bellied and large-headed. At this time they usually measure around 50 mm and weigh around 20 grams.

On the first day an owlet does not appear to take any food, but by the second day it is noticeably bigger and stronger. It begins to utter begging snores and gives off chittering noises which are answered from inside the egg by the next owlet due to hatch. These calls may help to maintain close contact with the clutch, as any owlets which stray as little a distance as 20–25 cm away from the clutch could be ignored by the female and are likely to starve. This is because all of the female's attention is focused on the nest contents, and any owlets which stray outside of the nest will not be fed. This might not be such a problem in tree nests, and perhaps in nest boxes, but, in unconfined roof spaces where there is plenty of room to roam, the dangers are obvious.

The nest and its contents are the hen's focus of attention. Any chicks that stray away from this concentration will usually be ignored. There are six chicks in this brood.

This young barn owl fell out of a nest box which was three metres above. It had been ignored by the parents and consequently would have starved to death if it had not been put back into the nest box. There is also the risk of predation from a fox or perhaps a farm cat.

An interesting instance of chick survival was noted in this context when it was observed that two chicks, one of which was only one day old and the other three days old, had unintentionally been displaced by the hen from the nest centre. They managed to regain the nest despite the fact that they were helpless and blind. It was believed that the chicks were able to accomplish this by listening to the calls of the chicks within the three unhatched eggs, which allowed them to home in on the nest. It was further considered that they were able to do this by differentiating between the distress calls of their sibling and the more contented calls of the unhatched young.

When she is feeding very young owlets, the hen will tear off small pieces of meat to feed to them, but it is not long before they are able to swallow whole prey. A young owlet of about four weeks old will require around three good-sized voles, or their equivalent, each day. That means that a healthy brood of five young barn owls, at around one month old, will require, between them, around 15 voles, or their equivalent, *per day*. In addition their parents will each require around five each per day. So every day, a family of five young barn owls and their parents will require a minimum of around 25 good-sized voles, or their equivalent – 175 per week or more – and that is when the owlets are just one month old; this number rises as the chicks get bigger, and the parents demand more energy in trying to feed them. The territory which surrounds a nest site must, therefore, be rich in prey if they are to meet these demands while countering the needs of other predators such as weasels, kestrels and so on.

New kids on the nest

If food is in sufficient supply, the weight of an owlet increases dramatically by around 12 grams per day. Towards the end of this period patches of bare skin are beginning to emerge until the original down filaments scarcely cover the body. Then, at around 13 days, tiny quills appear and these quickly open to form the long second (mesoptyle) plumage which, unlike the protoptyle plumage, is pure white and more dense. It is at this stage that the egg-tooth is lost. When the owlet is around three weeks old its approximate weight is 140 grams, which is around a third of the maximum body weight of a full-grown owlet. It is also around this time that there is a greater demand for food as the chicks begin to develop rapidly and the quill tips of the first primary feathers begin to show

At around three weeks old the quill tips of the first primary feathers begin to show.

through. At this point an owlet is usually capable of swallowing prey whole. It also begins to explore its surroundings and progressively begins to take on the appearance of its parents.

During this period a transition in eye coloration takes place. When an owlet's eyes first open, at approximately 12 days old, the pupil has a blue, almost blind-looking, appearance. This is a feature not just confined to barn owls as the eyes of tawny owls and some other creatures behave in a similar way. At day 17 the eyes still have a blue appearance, and it is not until day 24 that they begin to lose this 'blue' look; at day 27 the eyes begin to take on the hazel brown coloring of an adult. Whether changes in eye coloration continue on through a barn owl's life, as they do in other species such as sparrowhawks, we don't know; however, it seems possible that there is a gradual progression in the darkening of the eyes.

Although the facial disc is fairly well formed, the eyes of this chick have still not completely lost their blue appearance.

By this time the rate of prey being delivered to the nest has usually increased, and throughout this period it is the male that has been the sole provider of food for all the family, including himself, of course. During this time the hen keeps the nest clear of faeces by eating them, while brooding the young. At day 24 the facial disc of the young is taking shape, although it is not yet fully developed, while the quills of the primary feathers are just beginning to unfurl. At day 27 the facial discs of the ever-growing chicks are well formed and the hen no longer tends to them but instead helps the male with the hunting. This is the time when sightings of barn owls may become more frequent, with some birds opting to hunt in daylight if food is not readily available at night.

During the next four weeks the chicks rapidly develop so that by around day 57 they are so large and boisterous that both of the adult birds tend to roost elsewhere, only coming to the nest to bring food. Usually they roost independently of each other and this is an important factor to consider when constructing a nest-box scheme. By day 60 the owlets look very similar to their parents, and they begin to make short flights from the nesting area, and by the time they are around three months old they become independent.

The Barn Owl
8: The owlets

At around seven weeks this chick has lost nearly all of its mesoptyle plumage, and the primary feathers are developing.

The progression from hatching to independence is a very long time for a bird, and it is this timescale which will determine whether two broods are raised or not. A typical brood will take nearly five months to reach the fledging stage from the time that the first egg is laid to the time that the young become independent. However, second clutches would normally be started before the end of that time. This means that a new clutch of eggs is unlikely to be started until around late July, and the young from that brood are unlikely to fledge until around November. It was previously thought that there was not enough time in the year for two broods to be raised, but with egg-laying tending to take place a little earlier, perhaps due to climate change, this may now be happening more frequently. Successful second broods are heavily reliant upon the autumnal food supply.

It is not absolutely clear whether the parents encourage the young to fly, but I once observed a tree nest where the female arrived at the nest entrance with prey; she then flew off with it and was closely followed by a hungry chick. This certainly gave the impression that the owlet had been enticed from the nest by the adult.

Chick survival

There are three stages during which the chicks are subject to different risks: when they are in the nest, after they have fledged and their subsequent existence. Nest survival is almost entirely dependent upon the amount of food that the parents supply. If this dries up during the nestling period, the chances are that not all of the chicks will survive.

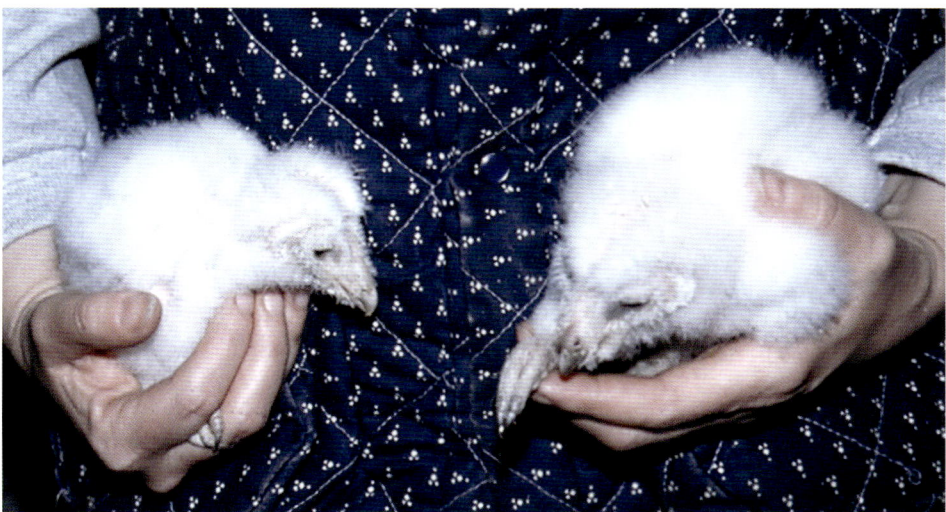

These two chicks from a brood of three serve to demonstrate the size differences within a brood.

Nest survival also depends upon whether the female survives until after the fledging stage. If she should die when the chicks are very young, the male will almost certainly not feed them, as he is incapable of tearing up the prey and feeding it to them in small pieces. However, should they reach the stage where they can swallow whole prey, he may decide to feed them and their chances of survival are much better, although it cannot be guaranteed.

Should the food supply dry up halfway through the nesting period, the resulting effect on the brood may be traumatic. This is where the asynchronous, or staggered, hatching comes into its own. Due to their impending starvation, the largest chicks may eat some of their smaller siblings; a sad but necessary survival mechanism if some are to survive.

Cannibalism amongst barn owls had long been suspected, but until recently there was no cast-iron proof that it occurred. Any doubt about this, however, was dispelled a few years ago when, during a scene captured by a nest-box camera on the BBC's *Springwatch* programme, an older chick made its way over to what appeared to be the youngest of the brood, picked it up by the head and promptly swallowed it!

Should progressive cannibalism not be sufficient to sustain the brood, all of the chicks will eventually die, either through cannibalism or starvation. In extreme circumstances it is very likely that one or other of the parent birds will also eat the chicks, whether they are alive or dead. During the course of a long-term study in south-west Scotland it was found that some chicks were discovered partly consumed at the nest sites, but sometimes their remains were found in the pellets of other chicks. It is because of this factor that it is vitally important to know how many owlets fledge from the nest and not just how many are present at the time of ringing. The number of eggs laid and the number of chicks ringed, therefore, might not necessarily reflect the success rate of a particular nest. It is this factor which makes estimating the success rate of any nest-box scheme so difficult unless it is closely monitored.

Cannibalism is a common feature amongst many predatory birds and is not confined to barn owls. A study in Finland (Mikkola, 1983) found that, in a sample of short-eared owl pellets containing the remains of 49,971 prey individuals, 85 of those were the remains of owlets. The main prey items from this study were either common or field voles, so the possibility arises that in some instances nest-site cannibalistic behaviour might be largely, or perhaps totally, confined to species that are mainly dependent upon voles. It might be that the cyclic lifestyle of voles, and the lack of alternative food when their populations peak in early summer, might trigger this behaviour.

Although much is written about the predation by hen harriers on grouse, it is often overlooked that these birds also feed on voles, and Watson (1997) recounted several instances of cannibalism amongst these skilful predators. It does not appear to be widespread behaviour with all harriers, so it does seem possible that this behaviour affects mainly those that feed largely on voles.

Although cannibalism has not been recorded in snowy owls, females are able to reduce the size of their clutches when necessary either before the egg-laying stage – when the follicles needed to produce the egg may be reabsorbed into the body before the egg is formed – or after the clutch has been formed. In the latter case, the hen chooses simply to roll eggs away from the nest, although it is not known how and why she decides to do this.

It may be that in barn owl nests the incidence of so-called unfertilised eggs might be a result of the same behaviour and that the females deliberately discard excess eggs in a similar manner when the food supply is suddenly reduced. Any further reduction in the food supply, after the chicks have hatched out, may then result in actual cannibalism.

One factor that does not appear to have been fully explored with regard to cannibalism is the possibility of stress. If there are no suitable alternative roosting sites nearby, and one or both parents are required to share the box with the nestlings, might overcrowding encourage this? In addition, could disturbance play a role? In their study of barn owls in north-west England, Bunn *et al.* (1982) pointed out that they were most careful not to disturb the nests in their study area. They were of the firm view that disturbance at the nest site plays a fundamental role in cannibalism.

Working in south-west Scotland, Iain Taylor (1994) pointed out that barn owls usually 'conduct their lives quietly and unobtrusively', and he stated that no one but himself visited his nests. It cannot be emphasised strongly enough how secretive these birds are, and it is this that makes them so difficult to observe and study in the wild, even when nest boxes are involved. When they are nesting, barn owls should be left alone as much as possible. It may seem to us that they are unaffected by our behaviour, but we cannot read their minds.

A good spring, therefore, may not always prove ideal for barn owls. If the weather is good, and prey appears plentiful, the hen may be encouraged to lay a number of eggs. If things go wrong, and the food supply dries up by the time the eggs hatch out, the amount of food may not be adequate to feed all of the brood. Here we see the advantages of having a wider range of prey: it might improve the fledging success of a brood of youngsters if they are not so dependent upon a narrow diet. If the range of available prey is narrow, and the supply fails, so do the young barn owls. In Taylor's Scottish study it was pointed out that the survival of the chicks was strongly aligned with vole abundance, because they were living off one main prey item.

The Mammal Society's ongoing pellet survey into the diets of Britain's barn owls indicates that, as spring merges into summer, the importance of field voles is not so great, and this is due to the population dynamics of that species. It is at that time that other species should become more important, before vole populations have built up once again for the onset of winter.

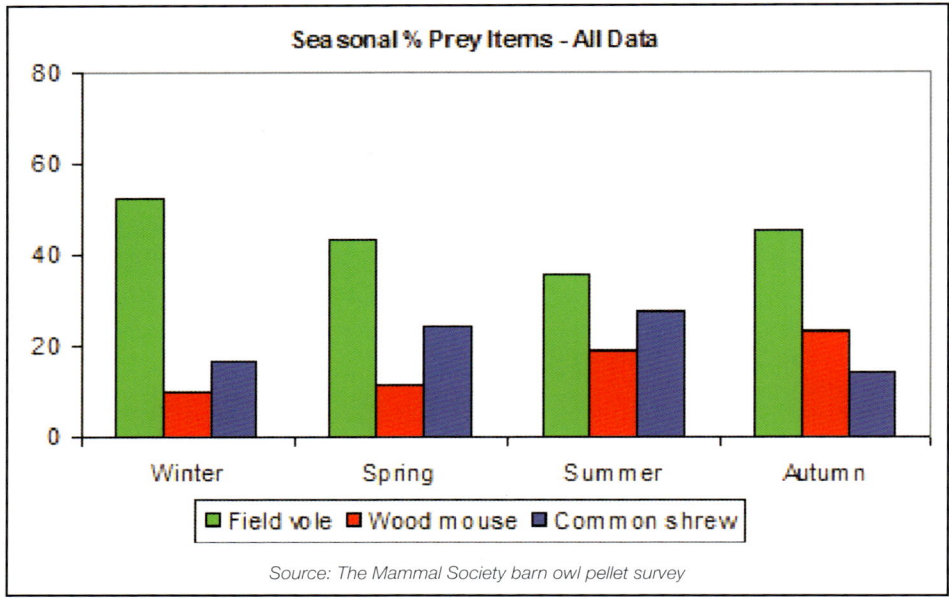

In the late-summer period, as young birds begin to disperse from their natal areas, other prey species become important rather than just field voles. During the winter and spring periods voles become important again, and any deficiency in prey abundance will create a second period of mortality in late winter.

On a national basis it is the critical period around October, before field voles are once again in good supply, that many barn owls die, although in Suffolk (see below), I found that the second winter period around January and February was the peak period when barn owls were found either injured or dead.

This might have reflected the mix of farming that was still in place here and there in the 1980s, thus providing a wider spectrum of prey, but there is no certainty about that.

A matter of life and death

The continued existence of a barn owl population, whether it be on a local, regional or national basis, is strongly reliant upon the survival rate of the young, so that they can take their place within the breeding community when any adult birds die or when a vacant territory becomes available. Following his long-term, detailed study of barn owls in south-west Scotland, Taylor (1994) reached the conclusion that, if a barn owl population of any size is to remain sustainable, an average of 3.2 young barn owls need to be produced per nest on a regular basis, otherwise that population is likely to go into a long-term decline.

It is encouraging to find a clutch of five or six eggs in a nest, but the outcome for this clutch needs to be closely monitored. The number of young that may be ringed may be a guide to the survival of a brood, but alternatively it does not provide the vital information as to how many young actually survive to fledging. After all, chick mortality may occur for a variety of reasons after ringing.

'Chick survival' also covers how long they survive once they have left the nest, and here I include mortality of all ages. Most chicks die within the first few months of fledging. Those which can find a suitable territory close to their natal area (the place where they were born) tend to stand the greatest chances of surviving to the following year, when they may also breed. Owlets that have to disperse the furthest distance in search of a suitable territory place themselves in the greatest danger of dying early. Even so, the survival of those long-distance travellers is most important, for they are vital in helping to maintain the gene flow between populations, while also assisting in the colonisation and recolonisation of suitable unoccupied territories.

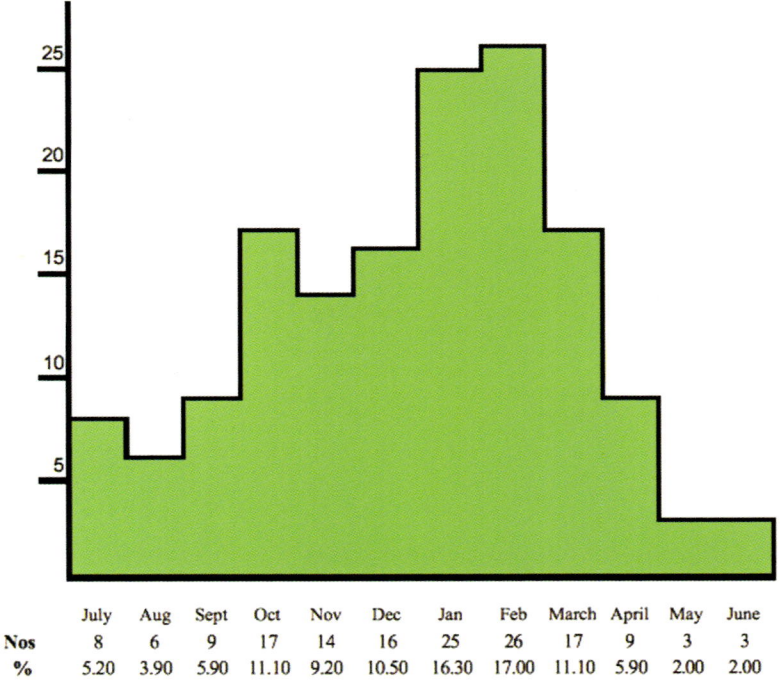

	July	Aug	Sept	Oct	Nov	Dec	Jan	Feb	March	April	May	June
Nos	8	6	9	17	14	16	25	26	17	9	3	3
%	5.20	3.90	5.90	11.10	9.20	10.50	16.30	17.00	11.10	5.90	2.00	2.00

Dead and injured barn owls from a survey in Suffolk.

The month of October is considered to be a peak time for mortality as young and dispersing birds seek a suitable territory. Many either die through starvation or are killed by road traffic. Throughout many parts of the world, including Britain, many studies of barn owl road casualty rates have found that those killed are either juveniles or females. During the course of my enquiries in Suffolk,

I found that January (16.3 per cent) and February (17 per cent) were the peak times when barn owls were found dead or seriously injured. On a national basis this is usually the second peak of mortality and occurs at a time when courtship begins and any unpaired birds try to seek a mate.

Contrary to the national picture, October (11.1 per cent) was the next most important month for barn owl mortality, and it may have been that the differing findings of my survey were the result of fewer fast roads. Even now there are fewer of those in Suffolk than there are in many other counties. It is one of the few counties in Britain that does not have a motorway running through any part of it, with only one major trunk road (A14) running through its entirety breadthwise, while another (A11) brushes the north-west of the county.

In the 1980s there was a view that, when any barn owls that lived in close proximity to busy roads were killed, replacement birds did not move in to take their place (Shawyer, 1987). In 2003 this was supported by a report from the Barn Owl Trust, which found that fewer nests are found near to major roads, and that, in general, there are no nests within half a kilometre either side of these roads. A likely reason why barn owls are not found dead on the roads so often now may be due to the relatively small numbers nesting in their vicinity. Even so, it is startling to find nest boxes provided for them alongside busy roads.

Many barn owls continue to be found dead at their roost or nest sites and this can lead to speculation as to the cause of death, although very often the reason is hyperthermia brought on by a lack of food. Young birds without a territory are particularly vulnerable to this, it seems. In conclusion, therefore, it is the period from October through to February which tends to be the time when British barn owls are most vulnerable to death and injury, and hunger and cold are largely responsible for this.

Up until 2011 the oldest known British barn owl living in the wild was a male bird which was a little over 15 years old. This bird was caught alive by a licensed ringer and was just 4 km from where it was ringed as a nestling (source: BTO website) and is further evidence of the sedentary nature of this bird. Up to 2010, the oldest known barn owl on the European mainland was one that was found dead in the Netherlands at the age of 17 years, 11 months. In captivity barn owls may live up to 34 years or more.

9: Dispersal and migration

With this ring...

The ringing of birds has been with us now for over a century, in which time the methods have changed very little. An adult wild bird may be ringed either by being caught at the nest or in the special mist-net of a qualified BTO-trained bird-ringer; nevertheless most barn owls are ringed as owlets while they are still in the nest.

These are ringed with an open, light alloy ring which is placed around the bird's leg and is then closed using a pair of special ringing pliers. All of these rings are supplied through the BTO, and each one is numbered and shows where to report it if found.

When a bird is ringed the details are entered in the ringer's log book and are subsequently forwarded to the BTO where they are entered onto their database. Consequently, if a ringed bird is later recovered, either dead or alive, the ring details should be sent to the BTO who can then tell how far it has travelled in its lifetime and how old it is, depending on whether it was ringed as a chick or an adult. The recovery circumstances may also provide some indication of how the bird died. The procedure for this may be found on the BTO website.

There are acknowledged problems with ring recoveries. For example, an owl which is found dead beside a road might not have been killed by a vehicle, even

Leg with ring.

though it may seem the most likely cause. In addition it might not have been killed where it was found, for barn owls have been known to be hit by road traffic and then carried on the vehicle that struck them before falling from it some considerable distance further on.

Yet, despite these drawbacks, the ringing of barn owls has an important role to play in conservation. Because of ringing, today we have a much greater knowledge than we once did of how long the birds live, how far they travel and in which directions they fly. In consequence, ringing is a vital conservation tool as well as a useful marking device.

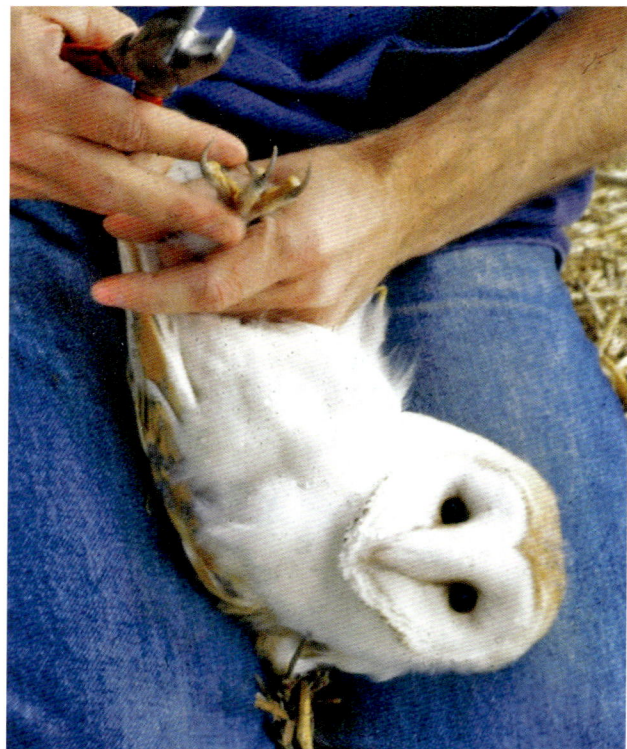

A well-grown owlet being ringed.

For example, it has long been suspected that individuals of the dark-breasted race *guttata* have visited Britain and bred with individuals of the indigenous race *alba*. This was first suspected in Sussex and Northumberland a number of years ago, but it was not confirmed until 2008 when a dark-breasted bird was found incubating three eggs. It had been ringed as one of a brood of six chicks the previous year near Doesberg, Overijssel, in the Netherlands. Without ringing, it would have been impossible to have proved this movement, unless perhaps by the evidence of DNA.

Dispersal

The dispersal and migration of barn owls is a very interesting subject for which many questions remain unanswered. It seems, for example, that young Continental birds tend to disperse longer distances than those in Britain and that they also tend to disperse, or perhaps even migrate, in a southerly or westerly direction during the autumn before winter sets in. In the face of climate change, this may change in the future. Irruptive migration sometimes occurs, and this usually happens after a good breeding season that is then followed by a shortage of food.

There is no evidence to suggest that British barn owls migrate in the true sense of the word. In other words, they do not fly from one area to another at the end of the breeding season and then return at the onset of the next; quite the contrary, so it seems. They are recognised for their site fidelity, which appears to be stronger in British barn owls than with those on mainland Europe.

Dispersal migration also takes place, and this usually involves young birds which tend to leave their natal site if they cannot find a suitable territory near to where they live. Ring recoveries suggest that young owls tend to disperse randomly in search of a territory of their own, although it may be that in Britain some tend to use certain routes when they are dispersing.

For example, there is some evidence to suggest that they travel along the chalk escarpment in southern England known as the Ridgeway, an ancient and historic route for human travellers. This long ridge of hills rises gently on the Wiltshire Downs and follows the route eastwards through Oxfordshire, the Berkshire Downs and the Chiltern Hills through to a point where the three counties of Suffolk, Cambridgeshire and Essex meet at its eastern extent. This area of convergence is sometimes referred to as the East Anglian Heights.

As long ago as 1949 this flyway was identified as a migration route, and many important observations were recorded at such places as Uffington camp and White Horse Hill in Oxfordshire. It is still an important overland migration route and it may well be of significance for barn owls, but it was not explored at its eastern extent until recently (Martin, 2010).

Using information from the relevant county bird reports and additional data from the BTO website (accessed 2014-05-04) I was interested to find that there has been some migration along this overland passageway, not only in the vicinity of the East Anglian Heights but also at its westerly extent in Wiltshire. In the table on the next page we can see that recoveries 1, 2 and 3 consists of birds that were ringed within Wiltshire and which were later recovered in Suffolk.

The bird that was ringed in Bedfordshire (11) was later caught by a bird ringer in a nest box at Great Bradley in south-west Suffolk, which is also suggestive of this route. There has been some interchange between Hertfordshire (4 and 5) and Wiltshire while ring 7 demonstrates interchange between Oxfordshire and Wiltshire. I include the ring recovery from Wales (6) as this is also of interest.

The ring recoveries 9 and 10 suggest a southerly movement to the Ridgeway by other young birds. Further evidence suggesting the possible attraction of this route came in 2008 when a female that had been ringed as a nestling at Tiptree Heath in Essex on 15 July 2005 was caught in a nest box 34 kilometres to the north-west at Kedington, in south-west Suffolk. This location stands against the rising backcloth of the East Anglian Heights.

These recoveries are not conclusive evidence that barn owls either disperse or migrate along this chalk escarpment, but they may pave the way for future research. Tracking by the use of radio telemetry has been in operation for a number of years now. Until recently it has been an expensive project, but improving technology means that costs are not as great as they once were. One wonders just how many other barn owls travel along the Ridgeway.

Some selected barn owl recoveries in southern England

	Place of ringing	Date of ringing		Place of finding	Date of finding	Dist. trav	Direct.	
1	Church Farm, Maiden Bradley, Wiltshire	12.05.2005	12	Ipswich, Suffolk	31.01.2006	261km	ENE	FD
2	Oxenwood, Wiltshire	01.07.2003	13	Cockfield, Suffolk	c20.11.2003	187km	ENE	FD
3	Knook Castle, Salisbury Plain, Wiltshire	30.11.2002	14	Bury St Edmunds, Suffolk	11.03.2004	225km	ENE	FD
4	Beech Farm, St Albans, Hertfordshire	30.06.2009	15	A303, Amesbury, Wiltshire	01.11.2009	127km	WSW	DOR
5	Beech Farm, St Albans, Hertfordshire	30.06.2009	16	A303, Amesbury, Wiltshire	19.11.2009	127km	WSW	DOR
6	Morfydd, Clwyd, Wales	14.07.2007	17	Langford, Bedfordshire	31.01.2008	235km	ESE	DOR
7	Lower Boddington, Oxfordshire	21.06.2000	18	Hankerton, Malmesbury, Wiltshire	01.11.2007	78km	SW	FD
8	Hen & Chickweed, Shilton, Oxfordshire	03.07.1999	19	Shotover, Oxfordshire	05.07.2007	34km	E	DOR
9	Ashwell Grange Lodge, Ashwell, Leics.	23.06.2007	20	Woodeaton, Oxfordshire	21.09.2007	106km	SSW	DOR
10	Sutton, Nottinghamshire	25.07.2009	21	Haverhill, Suffolk	17.01.2010	130km	SE	FD
11	Harold-Odell CP, Bedfordshire	24.06.2007	22	Great Bradley, Suffolk	25.06.2010	71km	E	CBR

CBR = Caught by ringer   DOR = Dead on road   FD = Found dead

Sources: BTO website and various bird reports

Selected ring recoveries.

Looking to the coastal areas, some interesting northerly movements have been recorded, including birds that have been ringed in Essex and Suffolk and have been found at such places as Salthouse in Norfolk, Greenabella Marsh in Cleveland and South Witham in Lincolnshire. Why this should be is not absolutely clear, but it is not unusual to see barn owls in the coastal regions of eastern England during winter time. Perhaps the white-breasted barn owl that was captured near the lighthouse on Fair Isle in Orkney, in February 1924, might have been one of the heralds of northward barn owl migration?

Up to the end of 2012 there had been four recoveries of birds ringed in Britain and recovered on the European mainland. These included one that was ringed at Little Clacton, Essex, on 10 July 2008 and which was subsequently found on 8 November of the same year 1,105 kilometres to the south, at Gerona in Spain. Apparently it had been predated. Of course, the recovery of ringed birds takes on an interesting aspect from time to time; one such instance concerns a bird which was ringed at Humberside on 27 June 1994 and which was found dead later that year at a distance of 425 kilometres on a ship in the North Sea near to an oil rig.

Irruptions

At various times barn owls may also disperse over a wide area, with the occasional bird flying across the North Sea to arrive in Britain. These events

The South-West Lancashire Ringing Group

Until the early 1990s the ringing of barn owls was a relatively low-key affair, with some counties providing remarkably few data, albeit for a variety of reasons rather than lack of effort. The South-West Lancashire Ringing Group (SWLRG) was perhaps the first to undertake the ringing of barn owls on a regular and organised basis. It was formed in 1968 with the object of encouraging barn owls to new and existing suitable areas.

A study area of 40 square kilometres was set up in a relatively quiet area of Lancashire to the south-west of Preston and adjacent to the River Ribble. It comprises intensively cultivated prime agricultural land, dominated by market gardening, cereals, potatoes and open pastures for horses. There are only a few hedgerows, but those that do exist, coupled with the well-vegetated banks of ditches, provide good habitats for large numbers of small mammals. Along with this, local conservation-minded 'keepers' have created small mammal-friendly headlands. All of these habitats together form a rich and varied wildlife habitat.

Within this area there are healthy populations of kestrels, sparrowhawks, little owls, tawny owls and a few pairs of long-eared owls, some of which use nest boxes. In the summer, this assemblage is joined by marsh harriers and, in the winter, by short-eared owls, hen harriers and merlins.

The decision as to where to locate an initial 100 nest boxes was based on the information provided by circulating a questionnaire to farmers and landowners in the area. But it was the history of where barn owls had previously been seen, or where they had previously nested, that was most influential in determining where the boxes were located, so that by the end of 2011 the group had ringed a total of 1,355, of which 28 were adults and the remaining 1,327 were pulli, or nestlings. One of the young lived to the ripe old age of 13 years, 4 months and 10 days.

There have been some interesting long-distance recoveries, including one in excess of 300 kilometres and another of more than 200 kilometres. Double broods have been recorded by members of the group on two occasions and a further seven have been reported to them by farmers.

Within this study, the group carried out a pellet analysis and, altogether, nine small mammal species were identified amongst a total of 475 prey species. Not untypically for an area that is located near the coast, field voles were the most abundant prey (number 219 = 46.10%), followed by common shrews (n104 = 21.9%) and then wood mice (n46 = 9.68%). Seven water voles were noted along with 18 house mice, but

Two owlets bred under the SWLRG's ringing scheme. Even with well-grown owlets the difference in age that comes with asynchronous hatching can be seen.

no water shrews. No harvest mice were recorded as this site is too far north. A further 22 pellet remains were unidentified.

The long-term information gathered by groups such as the SWLRG is invaluable to conservationists, so it is hoped that some of the many groups that have been formed within the past decade or so will also go on to provide such a historical record.

In autumn especially, barn owls may be found way out on the marshes, as is this one on the Essex coast. It seems likely that some dispersing birds use this 'east coast highway' in their search for a territory.

have been named on the Continent as *wanderjahren*, or years of wandering, and when they occur it is not impossible for hundreds to turn up in the most unlikely of places. For example, a *wanderjahr* occurred in 1929 when many were seen on ice floes in the former Zuiderzee, Netherlands, which is on a regular route for many migrating birds. The most recent of these occurred in 1990 when Denmark witnessed a mass arrival of young barn owls. In the following year, single birds that were ringed in Germany and the Netherlands were recovered in Britain, and these may have been part of that event.

Our knowledge of where barn owls travel to across Britain, and perhaps elsewhere, is important; so if you find a ringed barn owl, or any ringed wild bird for that matter, you should report it to the BTO. Even if you find a ringed barn owl at such a place as Camp Bastion in Afghanistan, as someone did on 4 April 2006, it should be reported. No doubt this bird was somehow transported with a military consignment by air and would have died on the way. Interestingly, it was ringed at Oxford on 5 June in the previous year, although its travel route is more likely to have been via RAF Brize Norton rather than by following the Ridgeway!

Part 3
Quis custodiet ipsos custodes?

'Who will guard the guardians?'
Juvenal, Roman poet and satirist
c55–127AD

10: A fragile relationship
What's your poison? • Rodenticides • Other poisons • A cleaner countryside? • Road traffic and general disturbance • Woods, water and bricks • What's your medicine?

11: Weather and climate
Deep and crisp and... • The ever-changing climate • Heatwave • Blowin' in the wind • A panel game • Rising damp? • Water under the bridge

12: Perspectives, thoughts and conclusions
The present status of the barn owl in Europe and elsewhere • The status of the barn owl in Britain • Looking back, going forwards • Some thoughts on practical barn owl conservation • A vision for the future • What might the future be for Britain's barn owls?

10: A fragile relationship

For many years now, man has shown great benevolence to barn owls. He has built windows into his barns to encourage them to nest there. More recently he has put up nest boxes for them to nest and roost in, and in a variety of ways he has provided areas for them to feed. All of these actions are positive and are movements in the right direction.

Yet despite these efforts there remain various issues that continue to threaten barn owls right across the world, and, while it might be thought that they are doing well in Europe and Britain, the reality is quite different.

What's your poison?

Amidst the massive agricultural changes that were introduced to our farmlands during the post-war decades, it was the pesticides and other agricultural poisons that were destined to wreak a great deal of havoc amongst wildlife, and barn owls did not go unscathed.

Poisons for killing 'pest species' have been around for many years, but it was not until some highly toxic ones were introduced on to our farmlands in a significant way during the late 1940s that serious problems emerged for many species of wildlife, and barn owls were not immune from those. The story of those poisons, the organo-chlorines, has been detailed (Newton, 1979; Ratcliffe, 1980) but, even so, an account using the salient points of that episode are worth including here.

The first of these poisons was dichlorodiphenyltrichloroethane, known colloquially as DDT, an insecticide that had found fame in the Second World War as an effective chemical in the fight against disease such as typhus. It was withdrawn at the end of that war, only to be re-introduced shortly afterwards as an agricultural pesticide and as a combatant against malaria. It had little direct effect upon humans, but its effect upon wildlife proved to be calamitous.

It was applied through crop spraying and from a farmers' point of view it was highly effective. On wildlife though, and here we are concerned primarily with birds, the effects were highly damaging, for after being absorbed in the body of an animal DDT rapidly changes to form DDE. It was this compound that was largely responsible for the thinning of egg shells (Ratcliffe, 1967), and this brought about a consequential decline in the productivity of birds, especially the raptorial species. This was the forerunner of a host of other pesticides that were introduced on to the farmlands of Britain, Europe and North America after 1955, as the usage of DDT started to decline.

These were dieldrin, aldrin, heptachlor and endrin, the so-called organo-chlorines, but – unlike DDT – these poisons were applied as thinly coated seed dressings, which were designed to protect crop plants against insect attack. Like all other seeds, these treated seeds were subsequently eaten by birds and other creatures, including small mammals and especially rodents. The effects of this contamination were to poison those creatures which fed upon the dressed grain, leading to poisonous residues building up in their tissues and their eventual death. This caused a drastic decline in many seed-eating bird species such as the finches, which in turn led to the dramatic decline of many birds of prey, such as peregrine falcons, sparrowhawks and kestrels which, being at the top of the food chain, accumulated the poisons in their bodies through eating contaminated prey.

After a lengthy investigation it was discovered that these pesticides were thinning the eggshells of those birds, causing them to break during incubation. As well as actually killing birds, the overall reproduction rate fell among those that managed to survive and breed. As a consequence, only a few young birds were entering the population to replace those that had died. Many observers blamed the severe crash in barn owl numbers which occurred during this period on pesticides, so this is worth looking at.

Kestrels were also amongst the birds of prey which suffered as a result of the organochlorine pesticides used in the immediate post-war farming decades.

While most barn owls would not have been affected by eating small birds, they would have been poisoned through eating contaminated small grain-eating mammals such as rats and mice. And we know through scientific research that it was the eastern counties of England which bore the brunt of these contaminants.

From the years 1963 to 1989 the former Institute of Terrestrial Ecology appealed to the public to send to them the carcasses of any dead barn owls that were found so that they could be analysed for chemical residues. Altogether 627 barn owl carcasses were received during that period and many of those were from the eastern counties of England; amongst these a number had suffered from the effects of HEOD; the metabolised product of aldrin/dieldrin.

Of those 627 carcasses some 143 were contaminated by these poisons. The most affected counties were Kent, with 40 per cent of its 15 carcasses suffering from the effects of poisoning, followed by Huntingdonshire (38 per cent: 21), Essex (33 per cent: 15), Lincolnshire (32 per cent: 37), Norfolk (22 per cent: 23) Cambridgeshire (16 per cent: 16) and Suffolk (6 per cent: 16). Elsewhere 137 were received from other parts of the country, but none was considered to have died as a result of HEOD poisoning (Newton *et al.*, 1997) because it is very unlikely that these poisons would have been applied in areas where livestock farming was the main practice.

Although there was ample evidence that small birds were affected by these poisons, there was little proof that small mammals were affected until recently, and the evidence for this has been obtained from an unusual source. Over a period of 30 months, it was found that 55 owls of 21 different species had died at the London Zoo, and of those it was considered that 22 had mysteriously died of dieldrin poisoning. It was then discovered that the mice the owls were being fed on had been living on a bedding of sawdust which had originated from dieldrin-treated timber and that the mice had become highly contaminated. Proof indeed that those poisons must have affected some small mammals, namely wood mice, on the eastern arable farmlands. There can be little doubt that it was the retention of relic grassland in those areas that probably prevented a greater catastrophe, although that is only part of the reason.

Following painstaking research, these pesticides were eventually withdrawn from use and, since then, there has been a significant increase in the number of peregrine falcons, while the recovery of the sparrowhawk has been nothing short of spectacular. Contrary to this, however, is that there has not been such a recovery in the number of barn owls, which suggests that there were other factors involved in their decline and not just poisons.

While attention was understandably focused at that time on the effects of HEOD, it unfortunately diverted scrutiny away from the damaging effects of habitat destruction that was going on in the background. Much of this occurred in the eastern counties as large areas of the countryside were turned over to intensive farming. In addition, it allowed harmful management techniques to go unchallenged, until it was too late, and the combined effects of those destructive farming methods are still with us. Even now, many commentators continue to assign the decline of the barn owl at that time solely to the effects of poisons. It is clear that those poisons did create havoc for a short while, but there has been a tendency to gloss over the effects of habitat loss that took place then, along with the effects of the severe winter of 1962–3, which we will look at later. The failure to grasp the reality of habitat destruction even today has proved to be a most serious mistake, but, as so often with this attractive creature, emotion has tended to obscure the facts.

Rodenticides

Where great attention has been applied by commentators to the effects of pesticides, there has not been the same attention given to the effects of rodenticides which, whilst not so spectacular in their effects as HEOD poisoning, may well be plying their trade in an equally effective but more unobtrusive manner.

It was shortly after 1945 that the rodenticide warfarin was discovered, and at that time it was considered to be the ideal poison for killing rodents. Warfarin is an anticoagulant which causes internal haemorrhaging and which, after sufficient dosage, eventually leads to death. The time-lapse for that is often one to three weeks, during which time an infected rodent will become progressively lethargic, so it becomes more vulnerable to predation. As a consequence of these effects, any creatures which feed on these infected rodents are also contaminated and probably will, in due course, also die.

It was in Malaysia that it was first discovered that the rats living in the oil palm plantations had become immune to the effects of warfarin. The barn owls that were also living there had been feeding on the rats with no ill effects. However, as a result of the rats' growing immunity to warfarin, more lethal poisons – popularly known as 'second generation rodenticides' – were introduced. These anticoagulants, namely difenacoum and brodifacoum, act in the same manner as warfarin in that they take between one and three weeks to kill a rodent. However, these contaminants are much more toxic than warfarin, and as a result of that the barn owls started to die. Eventually, warfarin was reinstated and the barn owl population started to recover.

In addition to these two poisons, in Britain there are two other products in commercial use, bromadiolone and flocoumafen, but the use of those is restricted due to their high toxicity. Even so, they are gradually making their way onto farmlands across Europe.

Following laboratory tests of brodifacoum and difenacoum, these poisons were found to be much more lethal to barn owls than warfarin, and tests proved that brodifacoum is more deadly than difenacoum (Newton *et al.*, 1990). From that examination it was reported that, although all barn owls in Britain are now widely exposed to 'second generation' rodenticides, not all are likely to receive a fatal dose.

More recently Professor Ian Newton has provided further details of the effects of rodenticide poisoning on barn owls. He described how 836 barn owl carcasses were examined by his team over the period 1983–98, with rodenticide residues being found in 28 per cent of them. Of most concern was the progression of the poisoning. From the period 1983–4, just 5 per cent of the examined carcasses were found to be contaminated, but by 1997–8 contaminated barn owls accounted for 40 per cent of those that were examined. It was pointed out that, although only 2 per cent of the overall sample of birds was considered to have died as a result of rodenticide poisoning, there was increased pressure to allow more toxic rodenticides to be released for wider use into the countryside. The conclusions of this study were that barn owls in the future might be at greater risk than they are at present.

There is growing concern amongst conservationists that, because these 'second generation' rodenticides are now less effective, the clamour to introduce more toxic poisons will become ever louder.

For example, in October 2012 a research team from Huddersfield University found that 75 per cent of all rats living in the Bristol, Wiltshire and Worcestershire area had acquired immunity against bromadiolone and difenacoum. However, they reasoned that this was a much wider problem which had been brought about by the incorrect application of these poisons. The conclusion reached was that the low dosages that had been applied had not killed the rats, but had left them immune to their effects. It was believed that the rats could have complete immunity to poisoning in ten years; therefore more liberal application of these poisons, and perhaps even stronger poisons, would need to be used to control the problem in the future.

In eastern France red kites are thought to be susceptible to bromadiolone poisoning through eating contaminated water voles which are killed because they damage the grasslands. As a consequence they are targeted with this poison at times of heavy population outbreaks which occur roughly every six years.

Although the highly damaging DDT and the organochlorine pesticides are no longer in use, agricultural poisons are still with us.

This method of control was also used in Spain during 2007 and 2008, where hundreds of tons of rodenticide-treated baits were put down over a very large area of about 350,000 hectares to control a huge plague of common voles.

Other poisons

On farmed land, slugs and snails are amongst our most misunderstood wildlife, although there is little doubt that they can cause serious damage to unprotected crops. With the possibility that Britain's weather is becoming increasingly wet, the threat to farmed produce from land molluscs is an ever increasing problem. In view of this, agricultural slug pellets are used in cereal and other fields to control slugs and snails, but these are also toxic to wood mice which eat the pellets.

The subject of poisons and their effect upon barn owls and other creatures is likely to dominate affairs in the future, and perhaps the greatest threat that conservationists will need to address is the danger of public complacency now that the pesticide scare of the '60s is over. Unless poisons are completely removed from the environment, or are selective through precision targeting, history teaches us that, in this sphere, one problem for barn owls is usually replaced by another. With a measured 30 per cent increase in the use of farmland pesticides in the UK between the years 1990 and 2006, it is not surprising to find that new products are regularly making their way on to our farmlands. One example is the neonicotinoids, which, until recently, were emerging on to the agricultural landscape of North America and Europe, including Britain. These are nicotine-based poisons which have been in use as rodenticides, in the form of alphachloralose, since at least the late 1990s.

In Canada the application of these poisons has been aimed at aquatic insects as well as a wide range of arthropods; thus they have been implicated in the poor breeding performance, and the subsequent decline, of barn swallows and other farmland bird species. The growing concern is that at present we know little about these poisons and their eventual impact upon wildlife. However, we do know that, although their toxicity is less damaging in the initial stages of contamination, their persistence in the environment and the potential for run-off – thus infiltrating the soil – makes these poisons highly controversial.

Within the neonicotinoids there is a range of products such as imidacloprid, a substance that has been studied in Spain and that has been implicated in the decline of the red-legged partridge. Its application is similar to that of the organophosphate insecticides which were largely responsible for the decline of the raptors in the 1960s. This poison is also applied as a seed dressing and, because of that, it presents a significant threat to seed-eating wildlife. In this study it was found that the partridges suffered weight loss, reduced egg fertility, eggshell thinning and increased chick mortality.

The researchers found that where red-legged partridges were offered an alternative feed to the dressed grain they would take it but, in the absence of an alternative, the partridges would eat the dressed seed. Their conclusions were that it was important to provide uncontaminated feeding areas for these partridges if they were to remain healthy, and they recommend the use of pesticides that are less toxic.

There is concern that neonicotinoids could pose a threat to wildlife reminiscent of the pesticide era of the 1950s and 60s. Birds may be affected by seed dressings and eggshell thinning, while small mammals, and especially mice, may also be seriously affected. In December 2013, the EU imposed a two-year ban on the use of three neonicotinoids: clothianidin, imidacloprid and thiamethoxam. At the time of writing, research continues into the effects of these pesticides.

A cleaner countryside?

The matter of poisons is an emotive subject and each year we hear about the illegal killing of raptors through poisoned baits. It could be argued, perhaps, that the legal but deliberate poisoning of rodents, which may in turn be caught and eaten by barn owls and other creatures, is tantamount to the same thing, even though barn owls are not the intended target. Rodent control on farmland is an important factor in preventing damage to crops, and it may become a bigger problem in the face of climate change, so is there a way round this without resorting to methods that are potentially harmful to barn owls?

In the Middle East there is a project involving barn owls and kestrels which interestingly combines the efforts of conservationists from Israel, Jordan and the Palestinian Authority. With a serious view to protecting crops from rodents, they have discarded the use of rodenticides in favour of using these natural predators. By providing nesting boxes, those two species have been encouraged to breed on the farmlands and are being used as biological pest controllers in a manner in which we have day and night shifts taking on rodent control, rather than resorting to poisons.

In northern Spain attempts have been made to control the numbers of voles not only by poisoning but also by burning the fields. However, perhaps learning from the Middle East experience, nest boxes for barn owls and kestrels have now been erected there with a view to controlling the numbers of common voles naturally through their biological predators. To date this appears to have had a positive effect (Paz *et al.*, 2012).

This approach to rodent control is being rolled out in a number of countries around the world, where barn owls are leading the clean war against mice, rats and other agricultural 'pests'.

Could this type of pest control be used in Britain? With the present trend for erecting nest boxes, it has the potential to be used as an effective rodent controller if approached in the right manner. This is particularly important in the south-east of England where arable prevails over livestock and where the effects of a warming climate may in time be felt more than in the west and north of

Britain. There, in south east England, irrigation may become an important issue in the future and this may well increase the populations of small mammals and especially voles, with their potentiality for plaguing.

Pest controllers may feel threatened by this, but perhaps their expertise could be used in ways to spearhead such a move away from poisons and into a more environment-friendly and positive manner rather than to chemicals which may harm barn owls and other creatures, including ourselves perhaps?

Road traffic and general disturbance

At the opening of the new millennium, Trevor Beebee (2001) drew attention to the fact that, although scientific study was important for biodiversity, beneath the surface lies the simmering and 'dominating influence' of the size of the human population. It was stated that this was an issue to which attention had been drawn in the past but which the various governmental and non-governmental wildlife conservation bodies had failed to publicly address, preferring to relate the problem to developing countries. Beebee pointed out that, according to satellite and photographic imagery, 10.6 per cent of England's land surface had been urbanised by the year 1991, and that each year from 1985 to 1992 some 15,000 hectares of rural land was taken over for building of some sort.

Following the 2011 census, the population of England and Wales was calculated as 56.1 million, an increase of 7.1 per cent on the previous census of 2001. Basing their prediction upon this current trend, the Office for National Statistics predicts that there will be a population increase of 4.5 million between 2011 and 2021. That equates to more than 1,000 additional people entering the population every day. The housing and infrastructure that will be needed to

As the human population increases, so the realms of the barn owls are increasingly pushed back.

meet the demands of this growing population will be substantial and, in relation to barn owls, is an issue that cannot be ignored.

Road traffic has been a constant problem for owls in Britain for many years, and as long ago as 1983 it was reported that 30.2 per cent of all barn owl deaths were road casualties, with this figure only being exceeded by the toll on tawny owls whose casualty rate was 31 per cent.

The figure for barn owls may be much higher now, although to date there has been no analysis of BTO ring returns to confirm that or otherwise. It may be that, in some instances, the conservation efforts that have been made to increase

The bright lights of the city are not attractive to barn owls.

the barn owl population are being nullified by road mortality. Apart from one detailed report from south-west England that was carried out by the Barn Owl Trust, on a national basis little has been remarked upon with regard to this problem, and perhaps the view is that nothing can be done about it.

The effects of road construction, road traffic and general disturbance upon barn owls is poorly understood across much of Britain, which is surprising when we consider the huge road-building programme that has gone on since the late 1950s and which, according to governmental announcements in the autumn of 2014, will continue into the future, albeit on a much smaller scale. General disturbance has often been quoted as a reason for the decline of barn owls in some areas of Britain, but very little research has been published on the effects of this.

According to the European Environment Agency, the noise from road traffic

Urban expansion

Barn owls are primarily birds of lightly wooded or open countryside. Consequently, any encroachment into, or destruction of, those habitats will have a negative effect upon barn owl numbers.

In the case of new roads, for example, there is a strong view that barn owls will stay faithful to the area surrounding the nest site, which is the focal point of the parents. In a number of instances they will need to fly further afield in search of prey, leaving them vulnerable to vehicle collision.

To the south of Ipswich, Suffolk, is the Copdock interchange, a place I used to drive through twice a day, five days a week. Before the mid-1980s the main A12 road passed to the left of the interchange. At that time there were three or four pairs of barn owls nesting in this general area, with good hunting grounds.

In the mid-1980s, as part of the Ipswich Southern Bypass, a new road was constructed that ran south from the interchange. Before then, the traffic went through the town.

Over the next few years barn owls would be seen hunting the roadside verges and their corpses were found dead on the roads. By the early 1990s all of the owls appeared to have gone, seemingly driven out either by noise and disturbance, or through road death. I left Ipswich in 2002, and the last barn owl I saw in this area was a flattened body, on 17 October, 1995.

Of course, this is just one area in Britain where development has caused the deaths of many barn owls either through road traffic or starvation as their hunting areas have been destroyed or degraded.

The Barn Owl Trust has done much to draw attention to this problem, and its publications on this subject are worth reading, though disturbing.

See www.barnowltrust.org.uk

The Barn Owl
10: A fragile relationship

Top: The new Copdock bypass shortly after it opened in the early 1980s. The scene above was taken just over 12 years later. In 1983 there were at least three, possibly four, pairs of barn owls nesting in this general area. Today there are not any. This is a scene that has been replicated throughout much of Britain over the past 50 years.

is having a detrimental effect on the lives of at least 100 million people across Europe, let alone all of the other disturbances that blight our lives. Are we really to believe that barn owls are not affected in a similar manner? For a creature that depends upon its hearing for hunting and that normally leads a quiet and inconspicuous life, a barn owl seen in close proximity to a busy road, or any other form of sustained disturbance, is not good news.

I have described one area of south Suffolk where new roads and disturbance in the mid-1980s were the likely reasons for the disappearance of at least three pairs from the area around southern Ipswich, but the Barn Owl Trust has done much more to highlight this problem.

Elsewhere there have been studies that have highlighted barn owl mortality on an alarming scale. In the state of Idaho, in the USA, a count taken over a two-year period on a 248 kilometre section of an interstate highway revealed that 812 dead barn owls were found, which was equivalent to 1.64 for each kilometre every year. However, the counts were only made every two weeks, and so, after adjustment was made for the bias of search and the removal of birds by scavengers etc., a reliable estimate suggested an average of 5.99 owls per year per kilometre of road. The authors (Boves and Belthoff, 2012) considered that without some form of significant immigration or management of the habitats, barn owls were likely to become extinct in this region primarily through road traffic mortality.

In the Champagne-Bourgogne area of western France, 674 dead barn owls were collected along a 517.8 kilometre length of motorway (two stretches of adjacent motorway each measuring 258.9 kilometres) over a four-year period. Of these it was found that roadside vole-rich habitats, alongside cereal fields that were either on the same level or below the level of the road, accounted for the greatest number of deaths (Baudvin, 1997). A more recent report over the years 1991 to 1994 found that road deaths amongst owls were continuing, with barn owls accounting for 86 per cent (142) of all owl deaths on motorways in the north-east of France. Road deaths also occur quite frequently in other parts of France on the newly created network of motorways (personal observation). This is a factor that has had a great impact upon barn owls in Britain and in time will affect other European countries where this may not be such a problem at present.

Globally, road traffic is an issue that affects many birds of the genus *Tyto*, and especially in developing countries, when the landscape is opened up to provide better communications. In the face of a rising human population, the number of barn owls that are killed by road traffic looks set to continue. Perhaps one of the most disturbing facts to emerge from these and other studies is that many of the road casualties were young birds in their first winter. This has meant that those birds were not allowed to disperse their genes, colonise new areas, or indeed replace older birds that will have died. Of most concern must be, however, why are those birds so often near busy roads in the first place?

Hunting for voles along grassy roadside verges can be lethal. Around the world, barn owls are in continual danger from road traffic.

Woods, water and bricks

We saw at the beginning of our story that after the Pleistocene much of Britain was covered by wildwood; within that scenario the barn owl population of Britain was considered to be a little over a thousand pairs. Although it is unlikely that we shall ever return to the days of wildwood, there is now a drive to greatly increase the amount of forest and woodland because it is felt increased woodland will eventually be good for the countryside and good for the general environment. While that is likely to be true, an increase in woodland will take away open countryside and will ultimately preclude some barn owls from hunting over it.

In 2010 the Forestry Commission declared that, following an inventory, the total woodland cover of Great Britain was estimated to be 2,982 hectares, which accounted for 13 per cent of the total land area; this was the highest amount of cover for nearly 300 years.

Following on from this, the Woodland Trust launched a campaign to double the amount of broad-leaved tree cover in the UK by planting 20 million native trees each year, rather than the 6 million that were currently being planted. Their stated aim is to double the present woodland cover in Britain over the next 50 years, bringing the nation into line with the European national average of tree cover, which is 44 per cent of the land area. Without commenting upon the practicality of such a venture, there is nothing wrong with this outlook, though in the long term it will mean a loss of habitat for barn owls.

In their early stages these woodlands may well have a hunting value. However, due to the reluctance of barn owls to enter enclosed environments where their plumage may be damaged, this value will decline as the trees get progressively bigger. The possibility of developing woodland pasture in some places is worthy of investigation, and developing wide rides in very large woodlands offers another.

With new woodlands emerging on a regular basis, some planted and some naturally regenerating, there exists the opportunity to manage some of them with barn owls in mind. Creating open woodlands for the long term will not only provide nest sites if large trees are promoted; they are excellent for storing carbon.

New woodlands are springing up across the country, occupying large areas of open countryside.

It is interesting to note that although Britain is less wooded than the European average it has a higher percentage of tree-nesting barn owls, so clearly Britain has a greater number of large farmland trees. Perhaps we shouldn't just be concentrating on promoting woodlands; should we also be promoting hedgerow trees? It is clear that on the European mainland they rely heavily upon buildings for nesting, and because of that their long-term future may be less bright in many places than it is in parts of Britain. In Poland, for example, they have a robust connection with human habitation, and the latest data suggests that there is a strong decline in their numbers, as they retreat from the majority of larger towns where once they were relatively common. This is not just a Polish problem, of course.

Elsewhere in Britain there is a great passion for restoring or creating wetlands, especially along the southern and eastern coasts of England where the lie of the land is more congenial to such projects. Large areas of farmland are gradually being ceded to the sea and, where this is happening, attractive areas for wetland wildlife are being created. But the coast is not the only place for such plans. To the south-east of Peterborough, in East Anglia, there is a long-term project to return over 9,000 acres of farmland to its former wetland status. The Great Fen Project is a scheme to progressively flood 14 square miles of land between the town of Huntingdon and the city of Peterborough. This project will restore the area to its former wetland status over a 100-year period.

Together, the woodlands and wetlands of the future will, to some degree, restore the landscape to its state prior to man's arrival thousands of years ago. But there were fewer people then and therein lies the difference. The clearing

A barn owl hunts this coastal strip. But for how much longer?

of the wildwood and the draining of the wetlands were done at a time when the human population was far lower than it is now, and consequently the demands upon the land were not so great. There can be no doubt that the needs of man are continuing to swallow up large areas of land at a fast rate – much faster than barn owls are succeeding in adjusting to it, if ever they can.

For example, at the time of writing, various plans have been put forward to open up large areas of the countryside for development. These include plans for high-speed rail links, housing projects, wind turbines, solar panel farms, airport expansion, road and other building projects.

All of these are potential problems for barn owls but, with care, thought, cooperation and some consideration given to planning, the damaging effects of these projects might be reduced. A suggestion in early 2014 that new housing should be built around existing villages appears to have received little support, yet for barn owls this might well be preferable to building large estates in the open countryside.

Apart from the problems of expansion, there may well come a time when the UK will need its farmlands to produce more food for its growing population. Should that happen, Britain would be in a poor position to feed its inhabitants. Thus food production would take precedence over everything, and many of the large grassy field margins that abound in the countryside would surely go under the plough.

To some degree these thoughts are speculative, but they are founded on historical and present fact and on our biological knowledge of this species. They are also driven by the knowledge that the countryside is not sustaining the wealth of wildlife that it was hoped it would do through environmentally based farming schemes. This is not speculation but evidence based on the latest report on the state of Britain's wildlife.

There are parallels to this situation elsewhere from which we might wish to learn. Following a study of the human impact upon elephants in West Africa, great concern has been expressed for their future (Barnes, 1999). Apart from the continuing problems of the ivory trade, alarm has been expressed at the general pressure that man is exerting upon their dwindling populations by taking more and more land for agriculture and other needs. This study considered that there was no future for elephants living outside protected areas, and that the future was not much brighter for those living in lightly protected parks and reserves. It was gloomily considered that there may only be a future for those living in a small network of well-protected parks.

Biologically there is a vast difference between elephants and barn owls, of course, but the principal of providing open countryside for them to live out their lives is the same. In Britain, open countryside is being lost to development day by day, and gently but steadily the realms of our barn owls are being slowly pushed back. In some places road traffic replaces the ivory hunters.

What's your medicine?

Once upon a time, before the people in Britain and Europe became enlightened, folklore and superstition were rife and, because of that, the barn owl was one of the most feared of all creatures. The sight of the white banshee flying silently across a moonlit village graveyard was enough to sober up the most intoxicated reveller as they made their way home from the local ale house, especially if the owl screeched in alarm as it too was surprised by the late night wanderer!

The word 'hag' is an interesting name that was sometimes used in Britain, until quite recently, to describe an old woman. The word may have its origins in Scandinavia, as the word in Norse appears to mean witch or evil spirit. The Scots once called the barn owl *Sgriachag*, which translated means 'screech hag' or 'screeching witch', while the Gaelic word 'hag' is derived from the name *Cailleach Bheur* – a Divine Hag. Elsewhere in Britain, the word 'hag' is Middle English and comes from the word *hægtesse*, which is an Old English name for 'witch'.

The link between barn owls and witchcraft is beyond doubt, but, if further proof were needed, we have no need to look any further than Mexico, where in August 2014 the distressing site of a caged barn owl being set on fire by women in Mexico was posted on YouTube. They were of the belief that the barn owl was in fact the incarnation of a witch, and as the owl screeches at its tormenters the excited crowd calls to the 'witch' to reveal herself.

This may seem cruel and dreadful behaviour, but it was not that long ago that, in Britain and elsewhere across Europe, people were sometimes burnt at the stake in the belief that they were witches. Whether Europeans treated barn owls in the same manner as they do in Mexico is open to conjecture.

However, Mexico is not alone in living in what might be described as the 'Dark Ages'. In many African and South American countries owls are still feared as portents of death and bad luck. In Madagascar, for example, the barn owl *Tyto sougmagnei* is looked upon as an evil omen; it is thought to be an endangered species, though its scarcity might be down to habitat loss rather than just persecution. The Madagascan name for the barn owl is *vorondula* or 'ghost bird', while at the Cape of Good Hope it is called *doodvogel*, or bird of death. There too, in South Africa, barn owls are persecuted.

Elsewhere in Africa, conservationists are concerned that Ugandan citizens are once again turning to witch doctors to cure them of disease, after the country was flooded with fake medicines from Asia that were meant to treat ailments such as malaria, but which failed. In 2014 the problem was further compounded by an outbreak of the Ebola virus, for which there is no readily available cure. In desperation, many people once again turned to witchcraft, with the ever-present threat of owl abuse.

We should not be surprised that even in the twenty-first century people who are not as well educated as modern-day Europeans should turn to medicines made from owls. It was not that long ago that people in Britain also used parts of owls for curing fevers and other illnesses. For example, in Yorkshire an owl broth was supposed to cure whooping cough, while in a number of places it was supposed that eating the eye of an owl would improve someone's sight. It is difficult to believe in today's modern world that until quite recently Britain had its fair share of 'witch doctors', and, in fact, some may still be around!

In India a number of owl species, including barn owls, are on the decline and concern has been expressed that, in order to emulate the world of Harry Potter, many are being taken from the wild and used as pets. That may be only part of the problem, however, for, like Britain in its immediate post-war years, Indian agriculture is going through a period of upheaval as many habitats are being destroyed and farming intensified in efforts to produce food for the burgeoning population.

Another part of the problem may be the Hindu 'Festival of Lights', known as *Diwali*, which usually falls in November each year. Although the owl is considered sacred in Indian culture and an animal of the Goddess Lakshmi, over the years various superstitions and false beliefs have created a demand for owls to be used in various medicines as well as black magic. Parts used include the skulls, feathers, ear tufts (those of the eagle owl are particularly prized, and consequently expensive), claws, heart, liver, kidney, blood, eyes, fat, beak, eggshells, meat and bones.

Although the hunting and trade in owl species in India is banned under that country's Wildlife Protection Act, it is believed that hundreds of owls are traded or trapped each year, and the barn owl is one of 15 species that have been recorded in the live-bird trade. Whether this persecution goes on in Britain is unknown.

All round the world barn owls are subject to persecution and abuse by a multitude of peoples and for all sorts of reasons. The late Sir Peter Scott, writing in Volume One of his travel diaries, recorded that, on 14 December 1956, his party landed on Banz, in New Guinea, where they were greeted by an excited group of natives, some of whom were wearing head-dresses made of barn owl feathers.

11: Weather and climate

If there is one subject that dominates Britain's day-to-day life, it is the subject of the weather. In summer, for example, it can change from being hot and dry one day to cold, wet and windy the next. Similar changes can affect the weather in winter, moving from mild, windy and sometimes wet weather, to extremely cold conditions with plenty of snow. These changes can affect the daily lives of barn owls and can cause great difficulties, especially during the breeding cycle.

Of even greater importance is the subject of climate change, and the potential effects that a warming climate might have upon the earth's wildlife. The concern expressed by many leading scientists regards the causes of climate change dominated by man-made actions which are driving up the amount of the gas CO_2 gas in the atmosphere, which in turn is leading to increasing global temperatures. If the trend for a warming climate continues, as many think it will, it seems likely that there could be serious repercussions for barn owls.

In the background, however, lurks the possibility that global cooling might be taking place. In September 2013, a new report to the UN Intergovernmental Panel on Climate Change (IPCC) explains that following a cold summer in 2013, there has been a 60 per cent increase in the amount of Arctic ice and that an area of ice half the size of Europe extends from the Canadian islands to the northern shores of Russia. This is before the onset of the winter ice which usually starts around the end of September. Some scientists are even suggesting that the world is entering a period of global cooling that will not end until the middle of the twenty-first century. Even so, there has been an underlying upward trend of the world's air temperatures over the past 150 years or so.

In looking at this subject we should remember that weather and climate are not the same thing. A very long hot summer is no more indicative of a warming climate than is a very cold and snowy winter indicative of climate cooling, although the protraction of these events over a long period of time might be more suggestive of climate change.

Deep and crisp and...

The effects of cold and snowy weather upon barn owls are poorly understood and less well documented than perhaps many other aspects of their lives, yet they have much to answer for. Deep snow has a detrimental effect upon the ability of barn owls to catch prey beneath it, and at such times many owls may starve to death. In addition to this, the effect of wind chill upon these owls, which have very little in the way of fat reserves, is also poorly understood.

Despite this, they do live in northern Scotland where it appears that a warming climate is enabling them to survive on some of the low-lying coastal areas and the lower parts of the river valleys. Indeed, those living in northern Scotland are the most northerly barn owls in the world. However, Scotland's barn owls could lose that claim at some stage, for barn owls have recently moved into some of Europe's most northern countries, such as Sweden and now Finland, and are showing signs of increasing their range as the climate becomes less harsh.

If our understandings of the effects of snow on barn owls are poorly documented, the effects of such winters are even less well understood. We saw earlier how cold weather affected them throughout much of the nineteenth century, and that Britain, like the rest of northern Europe, was in the grip of what has been termed 'the Little Ice Age' in which there were periods of severe cold and snowy weather alternating with very wet summer conditions. The weather events of that century, and indeed before then, have been painstakingly documented by climatologist John Kington (2010), and some items of interest require attention.

For example, 1879 has been referred to as a year without a summer, and its winter is considered to have been one of the coldest on record. Conditions were so cold in the Scottish Highlands that the onset of glaciation was noted. A heavy snowstorm in the north of England accounted for a snowfall of 30 cm, while 15 cm fell in Devon. At Thwaite in Suffolk, from where there is a run of historical weather records, the temperature fell to −10 °C, while there were further falls of snow of up to 15 cm across many parts of the country in April, at the time when female barn owls should be gaining weight to produce eggs.

In 1881 one of the worst snowstorms on record took place across southern and central England. It has become known as the Great Victorian Blizzard, and snow fell to a depth of 30–40 cm across the region. On a local basis, conditions were worse, with snow falling to a depth of 60 cm in Hampshire and 120 cm over Dartmoor, and snowdrifts stacking to a height of 3–5 metres. Many people died as a result of this, and 'countless birds perished'. It was an extraordinary year, with frosts recorded in June and very warm weather arriving in July, a period in which many heat-related human deaths occurred as temperatures soared as high as 38 °C. The hot weather continued into August, only to be followed by a battering of severe storms throughout the remainder of the year. It was during this period that the number of barn owls declined sharply, and the entire blame for that has been placed firmly at the feet of the gamekeepers.

These are but a few of the events that made the nineteenth century one of the most extraordinary centuries in recent documented history as far as weather is concerned. The latter decades were possibly the worst, but affairs began to improve by the turn of the century, as a period of warmer weather set in.

Over the course of the next century there followed a series of winters in which there were diverse bouts of severe weather, the first of which occurred in the winter of 1916–17 during the First World War and which affected Britain's bird life, although in a subsequent report no specific mention of owls was made.

This was not the case in Ireland where a decline of barn owls was noted and a report came in to *British Birds* which stated that 'This year some form of disease has attacked Barn Owls'. The report stated that altogether 160 were found dead, and that all of those were in a severely emaciated condition, with their bodies thin and stomachs empty. The author also reported that he had heard from several Irish correspondents who had found dead barn owls in their farm buildings.

At that time, the link between snowy weather and barn owl mortality had not been established, and so this episode serves as an example of how the 'mysterious deaths' of barn owls can be misinterpreted and the effects of bad weather overlooked. The next weather to affect Britain's birds was the winter of 1929, and it was this event that is likely to have sparked Blaker's survey of 1932.

The death of a barn owl is a sad affair, but it is important to gather the facts before attempting to reach a conclusion as to the cause. Food shortage brought on by bad weather can be a major cause of barn owl deaths.

A further bout of bad weather was observed in 1940 although owl mortality was not reported as a result of it, probably because the country's attention was focused on other matters. It was one of the worst winters of the century with severe cold, plus heavy snow falling in late January through to February. The most serious problem appears to have been extreme ice, the weight of which caused a great deal of damage to trees and overhead power lines. Although a decline of barn owls was noted by various observers during the war period, we do not know to what degree harsh weather played a part in this.

The next 'weather event' was the winter of 1947, when snow fell every day somewhere in Britain from 22 January through to 17 March. Even the Isles of Scilly, off the south-west of England, were not immune to its effects, for on 30 January the islands received a fall measuring a depth of 18 cm.

In times of harsh weather, even barn owls living on low-lying valley farms may suffer sudden and severe declines.

It remains the snowiest winter on record and this time owls were recorded amongst the great numbers of birds that were found dead. However, the neat round figure of 'two dozen each of tawny, little and barn owls' that were listed by Ticehurst and Hartley in their report must surely have been – quite literally – the tip of the iceberg.

While all of these winters were bad for barn owls, it was the winter of 1962–3 which was to prove the most devastating. It is still the coldest winter ever recorded in Britain, although not quite the snowiest. The bad weather began in the autumn of 1962, when snow started to fall in November. However, it was on Boxing Day that the weather really took hold, with heavy snow falling across much of the British Isles. The snowy weather ended in early March, although the severe cold and ice continued for much longer. The results from a survey afterwards found there had been a large drop in the number of barn owls, with several contributors to the survey reporting that barn owls had completely gone from their area. In many places populations were not to recover for several years while for a variety of reasons some never did.

The effects of this winter have been largely overlooked and nearly lost to the more spectacular pesticide episode of that period, and it is time that heed was paid to the effects of that winter. Further bouts of severe weather followed that winter, and even Colin Shawyer's survey of 1982–5 took place in the wake of the severe winter of 1979.

After this, there was another bad winter over the period 1986–7 when, amidst the very snowy weather that particularly affected Eastern England, a number of barn owls were found dead. In Suffolk there were 14 reported fatalities, but there will have been many others that would have died at their tree roost or nest sites and would have gone unreported. Several reports of these deaths appeared in the local and national press claiming that these owls had died of poisoning, but a subsequent investigation showed that starvation was the cause and not poisons (Martin, 1988). This demonstrates quite clearly the dangers of aligning the deaths of barn owls with extraordinary headline-grabbing notions without the evidence. The ravages of this winter were also likely to have affected the results for the species in the *New Atlas of Breeding Birds in Britain and Ireland: 1988–1991*. These showed that there had been a substantial decline in the distribution of barn owls since the previous atlas which covered the period 1968–72. Although there is little doubt that intensive farming methods were having an effect upon habitats, it seems distinctly possible that the aftermath of that winter had some bearing on the results for the barn owl during that survey. After that there have been no other incidents of a similar nature in the UK until the year 2009, when events once more took a turn for the worse. Somewhat unexpectedly, snowy weather set in across much of Britain during the second half of December and continued through to January and February: during this period an unknown number of barn owls perished. It was assumed that the weather led to many females being in poor condition and that, because of those weather conditions, 2010 proved to be the poorest breeding season for a decade.

This was the forerunner of what was to be a very strange year weather-wise, for in November, to considerable surprise, a large amount of snow fell across most parts of Britain followed by even greater amounts in December. By Christmas, over 100 dead ringed barn owls had been reported to the BTO, and by the end of January 2011 over 30 more had died. Once again this estimate is unlikely to be anywhere near to the real number that actually perished, because many would have died in isolated places, while unringed birds are unlikely to have been reported.

Obviously it cannot be known whether Britain is set for a run of cold and snowy winters, although there was a relatively brief period of very cold weather across Britain in February 2012 with a covering of 10–15 cm of snow. This episode lasted for around two weeks and was immediately followed by a very warm spell of bright and sunny weather succeeded by a lengthy period of heavy rain across most of Britain. This lasted from April until July and could be said to be another year without a summer. The British weather can indeed change very quickly.

It was probably as a result of these winter weather conditions that barn owls started to decline sharply in 2010, following their increase in population which started in the late 1990s (www. bto.org/birdtrends, accessed 2014-05-04).

Despite this run of cold and snowy winters, the official view is that the climate is warming and that there is only a very small likelihood of a severe winter happening on the scale of those experienced in 1947 and 1962–3. There are many problems that barn owls have to face during their lives, and the ever-changing weather pattern of the British Isles is just one of those. Yet despite the traumas of the weather they have experienced over the centuries, they are still here and will remain so, as long as there is food, shelter and space for them to live out their lives.

The ever-changing climate

The long-term effects of climate change were better understood at the end of the first decade of the twenty-first century than they were ten years earlier, and so it is possible to consider what the likely impact of a warming climate might be on barn owls in Britain. There will be other places within the wider Europe where barn owls may also be affected, but which are largely outside our terms of reference here, although Spain and some of the other countries bordering the Mediterranean provide a worrying scenario.

The barn owls of North Africa may come under threat as the Sahara Desert continues to expand and move northwards, while sea level will continue to rise if the polar ice caps melt as forecast, and that will eventually come to threaten many barn owls living in low-lying areas. It is expected that, in the northern hemisphere especially, the summers will be cooler and wetter or perhaps drier and hotter. Perhaps there will be a mixture of both types.

Although there is opposition to the view that climate change is taking place, there is now strong evidence from the Intergovernmental Panel on Climate Change that the climate is warming, and has been since 1850, although once again opinions are divided as to the cause and to the rate it is happening. There has been fierce opposition to the belief that this is taking place through man-made efforts, with some commentators holding the view that global weather patterns work in cycles of approximately a thousand years, albeit the present

European temperatures (1850–2013)
annual (upper), winter (middle) and summer (lower) periods in °C

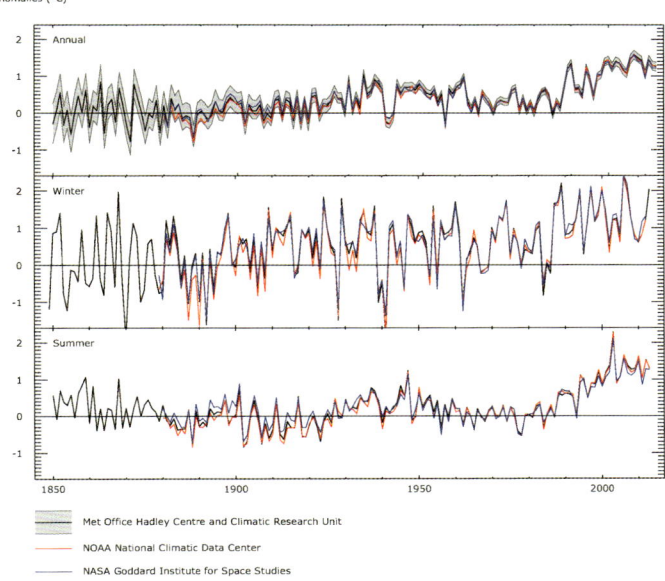

Global temperatures (1850–2012)
annual average and 10-year average

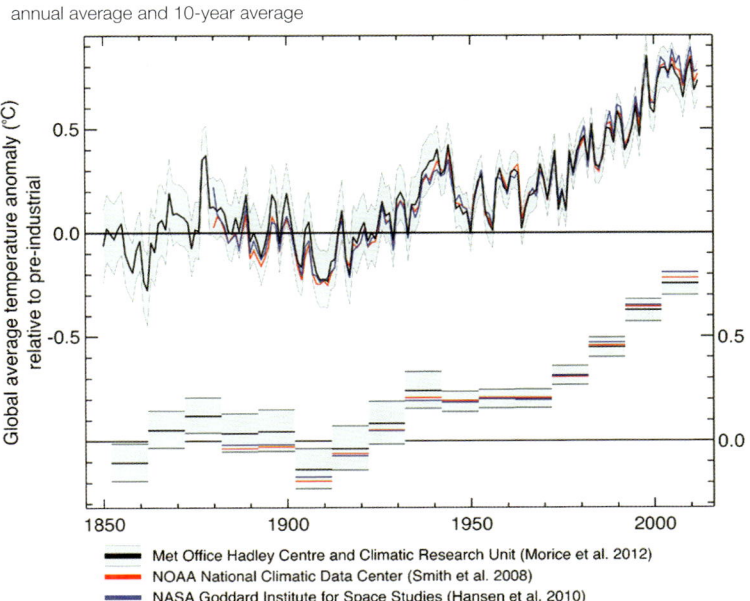

Global and European climatic trends.

change is taking place with man's help. The intention here is not to enter into this debate but to give a brief outline of how climate change may affect Britain's barn owls in the future. The graphs on the previous page show the European and World climatic trends since records began in 1850, with early indications suggesting this is likely to be the progressive trend through the first century of the new millennium.

Based upon a wide range of sources, such as palaeoclimatic data, historical documentary records and direct meteorological observations, John Kington presented the chronology of weather and climate during postglacial, historic and recent times. In his report he details the various climatic extremes that have occurred in the British Isles. These events range from severe drought to intense cold, and during their existence they brought great hardship to the human populations. In turn these events are likely to have had a great and negative effect upon Britain's barn owls. Here are just a few of the events that have brought problems to the countryside over the centuries and will no doubt have had an effect upon barn owls.

In 1305 Matthew of Westminster recorded, 'There was such burning heat and such a drought throughout the summer that the hay failed in most parts of the country and the beasts of the field died for want and a double heat oppressed mankind'. An event such as this would have had a disastrous effect upon the wildlife, including field voles, which would have had a terrible time without succulent vegetation. The effects upon the grain harvest and its likely consequences to mice would have also been serious. Insects, however, may have been more numerous and in that case would have benefitted shrews but also mice.

There were periods of intense cold such as the recurring 'Little Ice Age'. The first phase took place from 1540 to 1700 and marked the start of a period of severe cold in which there were glacial advances in Scandinavia, the Alps and Iceland. It is believed that during this period the climate of the British Isles may have been the coldest since the ending of the Ice Age. A 30-year period of intense cold followed the very cold winter of 1740, during which time there was mass starvation of the people in parts of the British Isles, especially in Ireland. The climax seems to have been around the year 1750 when the aforementioned glaciers reached their greatest extent. These were hard times for the European human population – barn owls too would surely have suffered.

In between these phases there were periods of more favourable weather, and Kington has pointed out that the 'rapid warming that occurred around 1700 well illustrates the remarkable shifts that can occur in the climate of the British Isles within a decade or so, from one mode of circulation to another'. The next phase in the 'Little Ice Age' appears to have been from 1740 to the early 1770s and was finally concluded in the years from 1800 through to the 1890s.

In the following century the climate improved, and from 1900 to 1939 Britain entered a period of warming. This was followed by a cool period from

1940 to 1979, at which point the climate started to warm once again, and by the early part of the new millennium unusual weather events were taking place.

For example, by early 2012 a severe drought, which had been building for nearly two years, affected most of southern and eastern Britain, resulting in water restrictions for the whole region. In keeping with the ironies of the British weather, though, this was immediately followed by a period of prolonged and heavy rain which fell almost continuously for several weeks across many parts and caused severe flooding. The critical months for very young barn owls are June and July, and these were the wettest months on record. There was a likelihood that many small mammal species would have suffered sharp declines, and in this period the population of barn owls fell away sharply.

During this time, reports from around southern England suggested that the ideal weather conditions in March and early April may have encouraged some barn owls to commence early breeding, with disastrous consequences. In a number of places the very poor weather led to food shortages as the small mammals struggled to survive. This resulted in a number of barn owls either deserting their clutches completely, or raising a very small number of young. In contrast, however, the RSPB reported that on their Hope Farm in Cambridgeshire their barn owls fared quite well with two nesting pairs, rather than just the one, while in Suffolk over 500 young were ringed from a total of 1,400 nest boxes: but these reports differed sharply from what was happening around the country.

In these times of climatic uncertainty it seems likely that the fortunes of Britain's barn owls will ebb and flow across the country as the weather continually changes, just as it has done in the past. The historical accounts suggest that the climate has, from time to time, been extremely unfavourable for them, but they also tell us that barn owls have persevered through adversity to the present day. It remains to be seen whether they will survive the rigours of future climatic change so well in the face of a man-made environment that is continuing to be the most challenging that they have ever had to face in Britain.

Whatever happens, we must be wary of assigning any decline in barn owl numbers to climate change rather than to our failures in managing the countryside in an environmentally friendly way. Every event which might suggest climatic causation should ideally be fully investigated before that conclusion is reached.

Heatwave

In the face of climate change, let us suppose that the climate becomes so warm, and the rainfall so low, that many crops and plants struggle to survive in the ensuing droughts that would surely occur. This is the scenario that some scientists and conservationists are predicting. In such an event, what would be the likely outlook for Britain's barn owls, let alone for us humans?

In the north-west of England such effects were observed in 1976 when Britain was subjected to a lengthy period of severe drought brought on by a very hot and almost rainless summer. At first the breeding season promised to be one of the best to have been experienced, but it soon became obvious, by the numbers of dead barn owls that were subsequently found, that it was going to be a disaster (Bunn *et al.*, 1982).

Initially it was unclear what the cause of this calamity was. Disease was a possibility, and of course suspicions of poisoning arose. The simple answer was that large numbers of field voles had died through lack of food as the succulent grasses upon which they feed had dried up. This led to large numbers of barn owls and their young dying because there was no alternative food for them to

Feeding habitats will undoubtedly be affected by a warming climate, but vegetation such as trees will also be affected. These Portuguese barn owls are nesting in a large cork oak. While this tree species is not present in Britain, there are other types of trees that we do have and which we should be encouraging as nesting trees, with the long-term view in mind.

turn to. Fortunately this was a one-off event so no long-lasting damage was done, and after a year or two the population recovered. But what happens if this type of event becomes a regular feature in the future?

In many southern European countries, such as Greece, Spain and Italy, where barn owls are fairly common, the climate is drier and hotter than it is in Britain, but in those countries the barn owls feed largely on mice and creatures other than voles. It may be that voles will continue to be the main prey of Britain's barn owls for many years to come, but we should be prepared for any eventuality. As we saw earlier, climate change is beginning to push back the boundaries of voles in the north.

Some of the owl species that inhabit the circumpolar boreal zones of the Northern Holarctic are showing declines that have been linked to climate change. The snowy owl is now considered to be less common than it used to be, and the encroachment of scrub and the loss of tundra are thought to be bringing about a decline in voles and lemmings. This once again highlights the danger of a species living on a restricted diet.

The northern hawk owl is another species which is largely dependent on voles. It, too, is in decline, a fact that has been tentatively attributed to climate change, possibly for the same reason, namely that encroaching scrub is bringing about a decline in the vole populations.

In view of this situation, the conclusions of 21 scientists from 17 universities, along with the American space organisation NASA, were presented at a conference in 2013. They were of the opinion that by the year 2100 the climate of Siberia, Alaska, northern Norway and Northern Canada will have reached that of a Middle European country, with a subsequent growth of vegetation. This scenario has been replicated across much of Europe in the last few decades as the amount of shrub land, as opposed to scrubland, has generally increased across Europe, and especially in the south.

Although grasslands in general are likely to respond well to climate change, the expectations are that intensively managed and therefore nutrient-rich grasslands will benefit while mature and less fertile grasslands (rough grazing) may not (Alcamo and Olsen, 2012); this is likely to have a negative effect upon field voles.

It is also suggested that, due to the climatic risks to fodder production, dairy and cattle farming may not be suitable in the long term; this would leave the redundant grasslands open to crop production, or even abandoned. It is thought that redundant grasslands could be turned over to shrub land or afforestation, and this is already happening across parts of Britain, as the redundant grasslands lose their appeal, or excess farmland is converted to woodland. According to the European Environment Agency this may be particularly relevant to the south-eastern corner of England.

Blowin' in the wind

In many countries, including the UK, there is a drive to cut the amount of CO_2 gasses that are being released into the atmosphere. This means that energy-producing initiatives that result in few or no emissions into the atmosphere are now highly promoted as the key to supplying 'clean' power. These include wave, solar, nuclear and hydroelectric power. In the early stages of the twenty-first century, attention is heavily focussed upon the exploitation of wind power through wind turbines, although solar panel farming is increasing in popularity.

The threat to barn owls from wind turbines has yet to be confirmed. It is true that the potential for them to be killed by the turning blades does exist, but an examination of their lifestyle suggests that the danger may come in different ways.

If wind turbines are erected on open ground which the owls use for hunting, the general disturbance and consequent deterioration of the surrounding habitats may well cause them to desert their territory. Another detrimental effect is likely to be the noise from the turbines. As we learnt earlier, barn owls rely mainly upon their hearing for hunting, and any intrusive background noise is likely to have a negative effect upon their ability to hear their prey. However, there is a need for research on this subject.

At present, perhaps the best indicator we have demonstrating how noisy wind turbines can be was highlighted in November 2011 when two Lincolnshire farmers won a settlement due to the noise that a newly installed wind farm was making. The turbines were half a mile away.

Wind turbines may be a threat to barn owls but not necessarily through collision with the turning blades.

Despite these concerns the RSPB is generally supportive of wind turbines. Their policy states that in general they support the implementation of wind farms in the 'fight against climate change', provided that there are no damaging consequences for 'important bird populations'. Even so, in 2007, when permission was given for a wind farm at Arecleoch in South Ayrshire, Scotland, they raised objections over the potential impacts that this wind farm might have on breeding barn owls, but despite their concerns, permission was granted.

A panel game

As a landscape feature, solar panel farms might not be looked upon as so offensive to the eye as wind turbines but, when viewed objectively, the effect that they are likely to have on preventing barn owls from hunting is obvious and potentially great.

There is nothing wrong in providing clean energy such as this, but solar farms are usually constructed on open countryside that is classed as non-productive farmland, yet this is the very type of habitat which is often attractive to small

Solar panel farms are now beginning to cover large areas of the countryside.

mammals. Of course, mice, shrews and voles may well be able to live beneath these panels but barn owls will be unlikely to reach them, unless the panels are sufficiently spaced apart – and even that might not be suitable, given their reluctance to enter enclosed habitats. For some barn owls these panels are likely to have much the same effect as a permanent blanket of thick snow.

Under current government thinking the plan is to develop a substantial number of these farms across the UK. It was reported in December 2012 that in Cornwall consideration was being given to allocating 5,120 acres of land for solar farms, and as a demonstration of that statement, approval for a farm of 15,720 panels covering just 36 acres of land was given in early 2013.

Elsewhere in the UK, there are a large number of solar panel farms either in existence or at the construction or planning stage, and together these will cover many hundreds of acres of open land, with a possibility that more solar farms will follow in the future. Together with the rising problem of agricultural poisons, solar panel farms might well have the capacity to bring about the biggest problem for barn owls since the post-war decades of the 1950s and 60s.

Rising damp?

For many years now, river valleys and low-lying coastal areas have been largely responsible for the general distribution of barn owls in Britain. This was first highlighted by Colin Shawyer when he published the results of his enquiry in 1987, and it is a situation that continues to prevail even now in many parts of Britain. The reason for this is that grassy riverside banks and neighbouring grazing meadows usually hold good numbers of voles and perhaps other small mammals, as we saw earlier.

By the beginning of the twenty-first century the flooding of lowland farmland appeared to be a more regular occurrence.

At the time of writing there are fears that, due to climate change, the incidence of river flooding is increasing and that we must expect this to happen more frequently in the future. The flooding of river valleys and coastal inundations are nothing new, of course, as this has happened many times before. However, the situation may now be more serious, with a knock-on effect for barn owls due to a greater reliance upon these river margins. This was demonstrated in north-west England when, during the course of one study, it was found that they disappeared from a particular area following the flooding of their grassland habitat. In December 2013 large parts of the Somerset Levels became inundated with deep floodwater which remained in place for many weeks. As a consequence of this, the fortunes for the barn owls of that area do not look particularly good for many years to come.

While inland flooding can affect the survival of many barn owls, coastal flooding is just as beset with problems. The most severe event in modern times occurred on the night of 31 January 1953, when a great storm surge powered down the North Sea, flooding large areas of the east coast of England as well as huge amounts of land in the Netherlands. Notwithstanding the large loss of human life, both in England and in Holland, this must have caused the loss of many small mammals, and there is some commentary which suggests this is true.

In Norfolk, the absence of barn owls in the Breydon area that year was attributed to the floods, while at Havergate Island in Suffolk, a lack of short-eared owls in the following summer was put down to the lack of rodents, which had been killed by the floods covering the island to a depth of several metres.

The flooding also occurred well inland, and altogether 640 square kilometres of farmland in the east of England were inundated. It seems reasonable to assume, therefore, that the flooding was ultimately responsible for the loss of some barn owls. Some might have flown inland to seek higher ground, but not all would have survived the turmoil. The present trend for managed retreat by intentionally breaching the sea defences and allowing the sea to encroach upon adjacent farmland has its attractions for many species of wildlife, but it also has its dangers for barn owls.

Storm surges on the east coast of southern England appear to have become more regular events since that time, and concern that the sea defences would be breached without warning and the coast would flood have been raised on several occasions in recent years.

Flooded farmland, River Colne, north Essex, 2010.

For example, on the night of Thursday, 5 December 2013 a powerful storm surge swept down the North Sea: parts of the east coast, from the Humber River down to Jaywick in Essex, were flooded. Of particular concern was part of the north Norfolk coast where many nature reserves were severely damaged; some barn owls would probably have been affected by this event. The weather system fortunately lacked the area of deep low pressure that was present in the northern parts of the North Sea in 1953. It was that deep low which suddenly rushed southwards to cause mayhem in East Anglia. Should such an event occur again, then the barn owls that live in that part of the Essex coast, or indeed elsewhere on the East Anglian coastline, would be in great danger.

Looking to the future, the likelihood of further flooding along the east coast of England is a real prospect, and John Kington has suggested that people residing in the coastal areas of Eastern England are 'living on borrowed time'. He pointed out that the Thames Flood Barrier is now being raised with such increasing frequency that thoughts are currently being given to building a much longer barrier of 16 kilometres between Sheerness in Kent and Southend in Essex. If that occurs, then in times of great surges the land immediately to the east of the barrier would be sacrificed to prevent the flooding of London, placing the barn owls there in danger.

In view of the concerns with sea-level rise that have been expressed by a number of scientists, should we be looking at barn owl conservation schemes other than those which are dependent upon the river valleys, fenland and coastal grazing areas? There was a view expressed in the 1980s that, due to winter severity, most of Britain's barn owls were living at or below the 150-metre threshold, but this may no longer hold fast in the long term. With a warming climate it may now be possible for parts of the higher ground to be recolonised in the future.

Water under the bridge

Not long ago I raised many of the potential threats to barn owls from climate and weather (Martin, 2008), but to date I see little changing in the barn owl's fortunes. Some years on, it seems that, unless there is a move away from concentrating many barn owl populations along the river valleys and in the coastal regions, in the long term many are facing an uncertain future.

In August 2013 it was reported that, following the floods of the previous winter, barn owls in the West Country had declined sharply, and that in Somerset their numbers were down by 60 per cent. One wonders what the situation will now be once an assessment is made of the damage following the horrendous floods of the 2013-14 winter. With little or no food to access, many will have died.

In the winter of 2014 the low-lying coastal areas of southern Britain took a terrible pounding from the weather. From Lincolnshire down to Somerset, large coastal areas were flooded by sea water as the defences were breached, while torrential and continuous rain caused many rivers to burst their banks and flood many square miles of farmland.

It seems likely that hard decisions will have to be made with regard to the future of the human population, as it slowly retreats inland from some vulnerable coastal areas. The threats from weather or climate change are just one of the major obstacles that barn owls will have to face in the future, as the human race defends itself from the elements.

As the politicians pointed out in the face of the floods on the Somerset Levels, human life comes first, then property, then wildlife.

12: Perspectives, thoughts and conclusions

'Truly this species is the farmland owl.'
Dobbs, A. (ed.), *The Birds of Nottinghamshire* (1975)

A look back to the beginning of our chronicle reminds us that a reliable calculation has estimated that at the peak of the wildwood there were only just over 1,000 pairs of barn owls in Britain. So with a population in the region of around 5,000 breeding pairs today, does this tell us that our expectations are too great, or does it tell us that, with all the effort that has been put into conservation efforts over the years, there should be a greater population than that which exists at present?

In closing the report on his study in south-west Scotland, Iain Taylor (1994) urged caution in promoting barn owl conservation at the expense of other farmland species, but this view seems to have been overlooked, which may have brought us, in Britain, to the point where we are today: a countryside where there has been a 60 per cent decline in the numbers of 3,148 different wildlife species that have been studied over the last 50 years (Burns *et al.*, 2013). It is now estimated that one in ten wildlife species is under threat of extinction in the UK which, to say the least, is a worrying state of affairs. Has the conservation of certain species been allowed to prevail over the interests of others? In our case, have farmers been encouraged to make provision for attractive barn owls while neglecting the needs of other, less spectacular, species? In my Preface the question was raised as to whether the barn owl was truly the 'Guardian of the Countryside', and upon reflection one cannot help but wonder at Iain Taylor's cautionary words.

The present status of the barn owl in Europe and elsewhere

With just a few exceptions, there is general agreement among barn owl students that most members of the worldwide family of *Tyto*, including the barn owls, are in overall decline, and that some of those are rare and perhaps in danger of extinction.

It is the island races that appear to be in the greatest danger – from tourism, logging, pesticides, road building and habitat destruction – but even some of the largest populations, such as *Tyto alba*, are under increasing threat from man's destructive forces. With an ever-growing worldwide human population these pressures will continue.

In the wider Europe the barn owl is now listed as a species of European Conservation Concern, Category 3, under the EU Birds Directive of 1979, and throughout the whole of this large area it is considered to be a declining species.

Although barn owls were once common across most parts of central and southern Europe, in many places they have probably been declining for many years. Their secretive behaviour may well obscure a local decline, especially if there were significant numbers to begin with. When a number of local declines take place in any large area, the decline may go unnoticed. It is only when they are completely gone that the loss manifests itself.

It is because of this that European populations are going to be difficult to estimate. According to the *European Atlas*, published in 1997, the overall population stood at between 120,000 and 172,000 (mean 141,000) breeding pairs. The report was of the view that Spain held the greatest number, with perhaps as many as 60,000 pairs. France came next with up to 30,000 pairs, followed by Italy and Germany, both with up to 10,000 pairs and Great Britain with up to 5,000 pairs.

It was believed that these countries held approximately 80 per cent of the European population, but with increasing amounts of road traffic, urbanisation, general disturbance, climate change and modern farming techniques, numbers now must surely be much lower. However, we shall not be sure of this until the next European bird atlas is published which, according to the European Bird Census Council, will be by the year 2020 latest (http://www.ebcc.info/new-atlas.html).

The status of the barn owl in Britain

The barn owl is now a green-listed species having previously been of moderate conservation concern (amber), yet despite the vast amounts of conservation effort that have been put into restoring its numbers it remains scarce or absent in many places. While it appears that there are more barn owls than there were 30 years ago, it remains to be seen whether this represents a stable breeding population or whether there is now a large floating non-breeding population.

The baseline for modern-day estimates was established in 1987 when it was believed there were around 4,500 pairs in England, Scotland and Wales (Shawyer, 1987). This figure was supported by a further survey in the years 1995–7, when it was thought there were between 3,000 and 5,000 pairs, with a reliable mean estimate of 4,000 pairs (Toms *et al.*, 2001). The latest estimate of the size of the population was published in *The State of the UK's Birds 2012* (Burns *et al.*, 2013) when the same figure of 4,000 breeding pairs was quoted, although the actual number of barn owls is likely to be higher. There can be no doubt that barn owls are now turning up in places where they have not been seen for many years, but whether many of those birds are breeding or are part of a floating population is another matter.

Looking at the various estimates that are available, it would seem that there may be as many as 5,000 to 6,000 breeding pairs present when conditions are favourable, with perhaps just as many non-breeding individuals in any one autumn period.

In his study of common buzzards, Robin Prytherch (2013) pointed out that, when he originally started his study in 1982, the number of breeding pairs was 13 and that by 2012 this had risen to 105. He explained that, when breeding performance began to be monitored in 1988, the number of young raised had steadily fallen from an average of 1.89 chicks fledged per pair to 0.56 chicks in 2007. He considered that by this time the number of breeding pairs had reached saturation point in the study area and that, although the overall average chick output per pair had declined, that was offset by a higher overall breeding population, although he acknowledged that it was not so good for individual pairs.

Whether we should adopt a similar outlook with barn owls may be a different matter, however, for they are more specialised in their diets than buzzards. The latter may take a much wider variety of prey ranging from earthworms to small and larger mammals, including rabbits, as well as birds of all sizes, including partridges, pheasants, wood pigeons, carrion crows and – on occasion – barn owls, to name but a few. Clearly, buzzards are not walking a narrow tightrope diet-wise, judging by the pace at which they are continuing to recolonise Britain.

The fact that Britain's barn owl population is constantly in a state of flux, and that there is no reliable way at present to monitor this situation, gives cause for some caution in assessing the present state of affairs. With so many nest record cards now being submitted and many young birds now being ringed, of which a worrying number are subsequently found dead, it is of some concern that an up-to-date estimate of the population cannot be given. The figure of 4,000 pairs was repeated in early 2013 with the presumption that there has been a 'substantial but unquantified population increase'. Quite understandably this provides only a vague indication as to how Britain's barn owls are truly faring, due to the difficulties of measuring their population.

Owls are probably the most difficult group of birds to assess in population terms, and it seems distinctly possible that any attempt to gauge the number of any species, and especially the barn owl, is fraught with difficulties and is always going to be a 'guesstimate', unless considerable time and resources are poured in to try and obtain a finer assessment.

According to the Bird Trends Report page on the BTO website, covering the years 1994 to 2013 (blx1.bto.org/birdtrends/species.jsp?s=barow&year=2014, accessed 2015-01-07), the Breeding Birds Survey, which is a diurnal survey, recorded an increase in sightings from 1994 to 2009, when records started to decline. Whether the decline is due to an actual decline in numbers or whether the owls have changed behaviour, thus making their detection more difficult, is unknown. The report also points out that the Nest Record Scheme has recorded a large reduction in nest failures and an increase in fledglings per breeding attempt.

At the same time as the upward trend for barn owls has been observed in this report, declines have been recorded for both kestrel and tawny owls, although our knowledge of Britain's tawny owls is poor. The relationships between these three species, and especially between tawny owl and barn owl, might be more complicated than is presently thought. It seems there is a new barn owl survey in prospect, but I would argue that a stand-alone survey is unrealistic. The intraguild relationships between these three species, at least, must surely be taken into consideration.

There will be occasions that will gladden the heart of all barn owl supporters, and one such year was 2014. This was considered to be the best year on record for the number of young barn owls that were raised. The previous year though, was contrary to this, and is considered to be the worst on record, so it is always best to ignore spectacular ups and the more dismal downs. It is the long-term trend that is important in determining our conservation outlook.

Looking back, going forwards

Our story started by highlighting the importance of young people in the future study of barn owls, and there can be little doubt that for students with an enquiring mind there is still much to discover about these fascinating birds both here in Britain and in the wider world. For those who might become interested in the barn owls, the world is their oyster.

For those who might become 'owlers', there are now plenty of opportunities to make this happen through the huge efforts by the volunteers who have put up so many nest boxes. They have laid the foundations for study opportunities and have created the enthusiasm for barn owls in which so many people are now involved. It is hoped that any future students will see the bigger picture outside the (nest) box.

In the British Isles there is much to be learnt with regard to the biological make-up of our barn owls. Passing reference was made earlier to the possibility that they could be slowly evolving into a distinct subspecies, and we need to assess that from time to time. The genetic traits of Britain's barn owls might make interesting reading at some stage in the future, and especially of those in Ireland, which have been cut off from other barn owls for longer than those of mainland Britain. It would seem that Ireland's barn owls are experiencing difficult times at present, and their dependence upon a very few prey species leaves them vulnerable in a variety of ways.

We saw earlier how the landscape was opened up for barn owls, following the clearance of the wildwood. Later we observed how the creation of the modern landscape, which was at the heart of the First Agricultural Revolution, stimulated their numbers but ultimately helped to bring about their long-term decline. Now, with the creation of so many wetlands, and the prospect of so much land being turned over to woodland, we are looking at a situation which once existed during the time of the wildwood, when perhaps no more than a thousand or so pairs existed in isolated pockets of open countryside. We may yet return to such a situation at some stage in the future, only by then things will be very different. When there were just a thousand or so pairs, the human population was considerably smaller than it is today. There were no motorways, airports, factories, houses, offices and all of the other paraphernalia and disturbance of the twenty-first century, so the opportunities for survival were likely to have been greater then than they are now, even though the number of predators would also have been greater.

Some thoughts on practical barn owl conservation

Throughout much of our story, great emphasis has been placed on protecting and enhancing the habitats, for it is their richness and wealth that is of greatest importance in barn owl conservation. Within those habitats there are many things that can be achieved and a few are listed here.

Nest boxes. While our owls must undoubtedly depend on young people for their future conservation, their present requirements seem to be catered for by volunteers from the older generations. Many of these 'old owlers' are either retired or approaching retirement. In the summer months, they dedicate many hours to inspecting nest boxes and sometimes helping with ringing, the birds. During the autumn and winter they repair nest boxes, or put new ones up, while some spend their time in the workshop making them.

These are the unsung heroes who are helping to plug the gap in nest site opportunities that presently exists in the countryside. All of these 'owlers' do it for the love of barn owls. I suspect, however, that there is more to it than just the love of barn owls, as many of these volunteers go on to do other things, such as taking

A 'mature owler' puts the finishing touches to a nest box.

part in other wildlife surveys. So perhaps in that way barn owls are moving in the direction of being the guardians of the countryside?

Choosing where to put up nest boxes might appear to be a simple task, but it is a waste of time, and perhaps money, if the chosen area is not rich in prey. It helps if some knowledge of small mammals is acquired; the presence of kestrels, too, usually means there are small mammals about.

A hunting kestrel suggests the presence of small mammals.

The shape of the box is not important but the larger the box the better. This will allow the owlets to grow strong, through exercise, within the nesting chamber. The size of the entrance hole is also likely to be important, although there does not appear to be any information on this from studies in the UK. The previously mentioned study in Finland found boxes with too large an entrance hole were rejected for breeding by many boreal owls due to the likelihood of predation by pine martens; this is something to bear in mind for the future. In

Creating the right-size entrance hole in boxes might help deter tawny owls from taking over, thus reducing the possibility of inter-species aggression.

addition, they also found that boxes with too large an entrance hole were often used by unmated, or bachelor, males or by inexperienced males and females. This is something worthy of study in relation to barn owls in Britain.

It seems that it was Iain Taylor (1994) who first employed the A-shaped box during his study in Scotland. He used these in trees but especially on the outside of buildings, where they fitted into the triangular apex of gable ended roofs. Externally, he also used upright square boxes. Both of those designs were without external perches or landing platforms, and through field observations you will find that these are not necessary. Barn owls have no more difficulty entering a box without a platform than have great tits, blue tits, pied flycatchers, tawny owls and many other hole-nesting bird species. The absence of an external landing ledge might also deter some non-target species, such as pine martens and grey squirrels, who could eat the young. It should also deter predators, such as the fast and powerful goshawk, from taking any unwary owls that might be perched there. Such an event was reported to have occurred quite recently in Hampshire.

Looking at things from the inside, nest cameras have revealed that adult and fledgling birds have no difficulty leaving the nest without assistance. They are perfectly capable of 'climbing' up the inside of a nesting box without any ledges

It is quite remarkable to find that barn owls will readily enter a nest with a very small entrance hole. I was once opening the door of a barn to collect pellets when I unwittingly disturbed a barn owl which did not usually roost there during the day. I was then stunned to see it unhesitatingly fly out through a slit window in the wall of this barn which was no further than one metre away from me. After it had gone I measured the gap and was astonished to find that it was only 9.5 cm wide! This may seem unbelievable, but it is perfectly true. I suspect that, as long as barn owls can fit their facial disc into an aperture, they will be capable of passing through it. It is a bit like cats and whiskers. The fact that this owl did not hesitate before flying through this opening suggests that it had used this 'window' to enter and leave the barn on previous occasions.

Suffolk barn with hole.

I once witnessed something equally remarkable when I was shown the opening to a nest site in an old elm tree. The owl literally had to squeeze its body through the hole to enter or leave the nesting chamber. This is something to remember if you wish to attract barn owls. A hole that is no bigger than 10 cm should be quite sufficient and may often deter the more robust tawny owl.

You might not always get what you expect in a nest box. Here a stock dove has taken advantage of a nest box with a conveniently sized entrance hole and an equally convenient landing platform at the entrance hole.

on the inside, just as blue tits have no difficulty in climbing the insides of nest boxes when they want to be fed or when they want to leave.

All nest boxes should have the entrance hole near the top. I previously suggested that, on internal boxes, the entrance hole could be low down, with a tray on the front for the youngsters to begin exploring, but, upon reflection, that design may be inappropriate for some situations. Where such a box is used in a barn with a large floor area, this design might still be safely used, but, where boxes are positioned high up, then it is possible that owlets might fall from the tray to the floor below where they will be ignored by the parents. A hole at the top will lessen the chances of that happening.

Nest recording. The BTO nest monitoring scheme exists to collect information on the breeding performance of all bird species, and recording the history of a nest is an extremely important part of owl conservation. For precise monitoring to take place it is essential that those nests which are studied should be in a settled and quiet environment. Iain Taylor pointed out that most of his nests were never visited by humans apart from himself, and that is likely to be good practice to follow.

Recording the nest contents is very important. In most schemes it is unlikely that time will permit this for all nests, so perhaps a concentrated sample of nests should be undertaken, rather than spreading resources too thinly. It is worth remembering that a brood of three youngsters might not reflect the number of young that originally hatched, or indeed the number that will eventually fledge. It may be that selecting a few nests to concentrate on might tell us more about the breeding biology of our barn owls than inspecting a whole host of boxes where only brief snippets of information can be obtained.

With the chosen nests, it will ideally be necessary to monitor the first egg-laying date, then the dates of the subsequent eggs until the clutch is complete, and then to follow the nests through until the actual fledging. The advent of small nest cameras means that in some instances it might be possible to capture that information from the comfort of an armchair. With nest boxes that are close to the site of monitoring this is relatively inexpensive, but for monitoring boxes that are, say, half a mile away from the monitoring area the technology becomes more expensive.

If you are interested in recording the nest contents of barn owls, you will need to be in possession of a permit, which can be issued through the BTO. For guidance on this matter, the best thing is to visit their website (see useful addresses at the back) and go from there. The BTO staff are always ready to provide help and guidance on this and other matters.

Studying behaviour. Simple observations of a wildlife species are not science in the accepted manner because they cannot be easily measured against comparable studies. However, they can detect a change in behaviour which may then lead to a scientific study, and this sometimes-overlooked subject is most important.

The latest update to the *Birds of the Western Palearctic* states that British barn owls behave in a different manner from those which breed on the Continent. It appears they breed more commonly in trees than their continental counterparts and they tend to hunt more frequently during the day. They also produce fewer second broods, and when they do the second broods are usually smaller than the first. It also seems that clutch size decreases as the season progresses, so clutches which are laid in late summer are likely to be smaller than those produced in late spring. There is also strong evidence to suggest that they tend to stay more faithful to their mate as well as to their nest site, but why should this be? It may be that field observations, coupled with more measured observations, might help to unravel all or part of these mysteries.

One question that a patient observer may be able to answer is whether barn owls leave a trail through the countryside which helps them find their way around. This requires an explanation.

Barn owls are well known for leaving copious amounts of white droppings (observed as chalky splashes) at various places, such as at the entrance to their nest sites or on top of their favourite perches, e.g. fence posts. There does not appear to be any information as to why they do this, but there must be a reason because it appears that no other owl does this on such a regular basis. Do they use these white splashes as route markers through their territories, helping them to find their way home, or are they randomly produced? Other owls produce white droppings, although not so copiously as barn owls, and not in such regular places. Earlier we discussed the likelihood that barn owls do not possess such good sight as other owl species, so do they randomly leave their droppings, or do they deliberately deposit them at specific places and use them as markers at night? Perhaps they use them to mark their territories?

Barn owls are renowned for leaving a trail of white droppings. Here we can see the inside of one barn and the exterior of another. Are these trails randomly made, or do they serve a purpose?

Community barn owl projects. Around 10 to 15 years ago it became fashionable for 'community barn owl projects' to be set up which were mainly focussed on putting up nesting boxes. On the whole they were successful in gathering public support and encouraging barn owls to breed where they had not done so for many years, but there they stopped. With so much backing, these might have been carried forward in establishing barn owl conservation projects that enveloped a wider brief.

A parish community, with suitable conservation support, might well contemplate purchasing areas of land that could be managed with barn owls and other wildlife in mind. These need not necessarily be large parcels of land, but areas which could be added to as opportunities allow. Such projects may well have added benefits in securing the tranquillity and peace of some village surroundings, thus providing an environmentally friendly atmosphere for barn owls. Perhaps parish councils have a role to play in setting up and managing such schemes, especially if they were based on establishing a trust; guidance for this is obtainable from the Charity Commission.

A vision for the future

Although no plan for the future of Britain's barn owls is offered here, a radical vision that might be looked upon as unworkable is presented in the light of the problems that have been raised earlier.

By their very nature barn owls are not easily confined to nature reserves, and so they are vulnerable to a whole raft of problems. However, at some stage we may wish to decide how best we can ensure their long-term future in a relatively safe environment. Should that day arrive, we may wish to draw upon the example of what is happening to the elephants in Africa and create specially protected areas, not just for barn owls but for a whole raft of species – particularly those with similar needs for large, open, and mainly undisturbed countryside.

It may be thought that, because barn owls are widely distributed throughout much of Britain, their future is largely secure, but an evaluation of the situation will reveal that there are only a relatively small number of areas where their numbers appear to be doing well. It may be, therefore, that these are the areas in which to focus our attention.

Some of the best places to see barn owls in Britain are North Norfolk, the East Anglian Fens, the Suffolk Coast and Somerset Levels (although the situation in Somerset has changed drastically following the floods of winter 2013–14). In addition, the map indicates other areas such as the Lincolnshire Fens, the counties of Wiltshire, Hampshire and Devon, Dumfries and Galloway, the Waveney Valley of north Suffolk and south Norfolk, the Northumberland coastal areas, and parts of the Wye Valley, through the Welsh Borders and up into Cheshire. This is where barn owls are present in reasonably good numbers and which could be a focus of attention in the future.

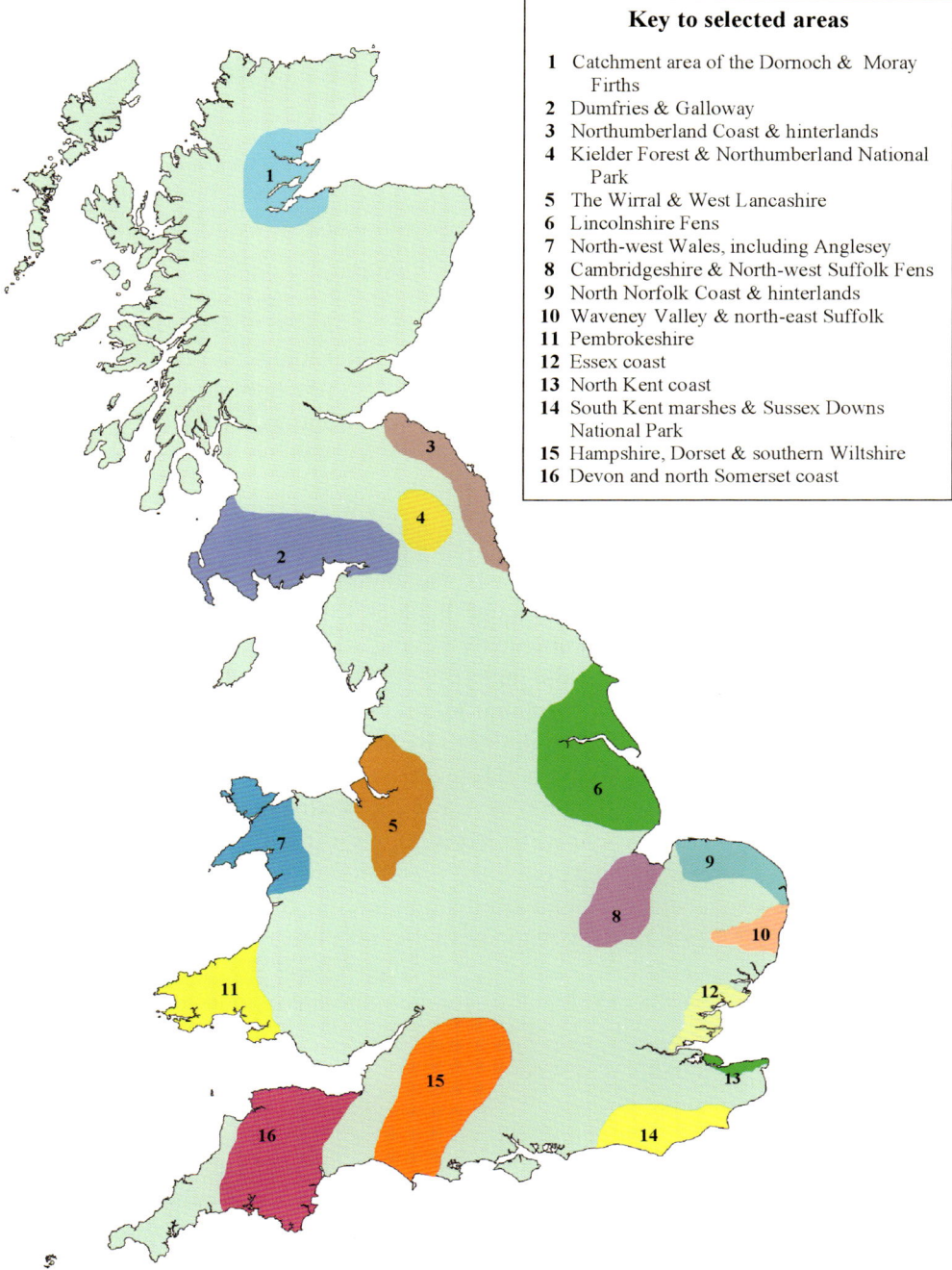

Lowland retreats.

I would label these places as 'lowland retreats' where ideally the aim should be to secure and enhance the barn owl populations that presently exist there, through a combination of man-made and natural resources and wildlife-friendly farming methods.

The word 'retreat' is appropriate as I suspect that, in the fullness of time, that is what many barn owls will have to do: retreat into specially protected areas that put farming and wildlife first. That does not mean we should abandon barn owls in the wider countryside, but it might mean that it will be necessary to leave those birds to the benevolence of farmers and the consideration of the planners.

If such a strategy as 'lowland retreats' should ever be put in place, then that is perhaps where many of our agri-environment schemes should be concentrated, rather than to try and disperse them thinly over the wider and more vulnerable countryside. If these areas were managed with wildlife in mind, they could well host a diverse range of habitats, which could then be managed with a multiplicity of species in mind. They could perhaps, be managed in a similar way to the National Parks.

Of course, the issue of road traffic would need to be addressed, and perhaps in-car technology has a role to play in this. The time has now arrived that fully developed vehicle controls can be enabled through satellite technology, which means that the speed of any road vehicle entering a sensitive area, such as the proposed 'lowland retreats', could be governed so that the minimum amount of harm was caused to wildlife by speeding traffic. Emergency vehicles would, of course, be allowed to over-ride this control, and vehicles travelling along major roads that bisect the 'retreats' might also be exempt from such speed restrictions. With tractors and other farm machinery now being controlled by satellite, this is something that perhaps we should be exploring for the future, and surely the motor trade has a role to play in this.

In an effort to prevent barn owl deaths on some of Norfolk's roads, light-reactive sensors are being fitted to some of the county's roads by the Hawk and Owl Trust. The idea is that car headlights will trigger a sound wave which will discourage wildlife from the vicinity of the roads. Such sensors have been used in Sweden, where it appears that not only have collisions with moose gone down but also the death rates of great grey owls. The Hawk and Owl Trust's imaginative scheme (SWORD) was launched in late 2010, and their website has information on this venture. How effective this device will be in areas where many barn owls are active in daylight, however, needs to be taken into consideration.

Such an innovation as SWORD relies upon barn owls crossing roads in specified areas. However, the proposal that suggests satellite-controlled sensors should be employed in sensitive areas would mean that all traffic within those areas would be controlled, and not just those in specified locations.

Perhaps both of these proposals are worthy of further investigation? These

A lowland retreat in the making? With the short-term provision of nest boxes, and attention to detail in respect of hedgerow management, does this have the potential to be a 'lowland retreat'?

ideas may seem unrealistic, but in the absence of any other initiatives further investigations along these lines must surely warrant future support. It would be simpler and cheaper to erect road warning signs, of course, but these would be ignored by most drivers.

The countryside has changed dramatically over the past fifty or so years, but in some respects the overall approach to wildlife conservation has not. We can no longer rely upon governmental departments to fight nature's corner and so, once again, it must be down to the people, as it largely was during the years of post-war habitat destruction, to put their weight behind nature conservation.

Some of the sites proposed here are presently protected sites within the Habitats and Bird Directive Sites as stipulated within the EU. They are also within the network of sites in Natura 2000, designed to protect biodiversity in the EU. Following the UK 2016 referendum vote to leave the EU we shall have to wait and see what fate awaits those sites. Leaving may provide the UK government the opportunity to wholly take these sites on, but within different legislation.

The proposal of lowland retreats might be looked upon as conflicting with the Wildlife Trusts' 'Living Landscape' project, but instead the way forward may be to amalgamate these schemes into 'Lowland Retreats' if the opportunity arose, and to extend these areas further inland where wildlife might not be presently abundant.

Earlier, the benefits of managing a wide range of species in hedgerows and

Mixed habitats within an arable landscape have a positive role to play in conserving barn owls.

Is it inconceivable to think that one day mixed farming might return to parts of eastern England? (North Essex, August 2012)

providing pollarded trees were noted, and ideally these should be encouraged. These are disciplines and tasks that will not be easy to bring about, but ideally they should all be incorporated into the areas mentioned. It takes time, patience, research, forward planning and some well-directed financial input to achieve that. It also takes manpower, and I see opportunities to expand this subject, if the imagination and the will are there. We should remember that not every ambitious young person who wishes to make their mark upon the world is academically inclined, irrespective of what the government of the day might like to think, and there are some signs that this is at last being recognised.

There is one problem with such a barn owl strategy, however, and that is the issue of gene flow. Unless there is an opportunity for genetic exchange between neighbouring populations, the long-term future may be bleak, and fragmentation of populations is an undesirable outcome. Those of the east coast of Britain may not quite be so affected but exchange between west and east populations might be more at risk.

Britain's barn owls, as we have seen, behave somewhat differently from those on the European mainland. It is likely therefore that they are already evolving in a different way from their continental relations who are able to disperse widely and exchange their genes with other populations. At present there does not appear to be any research going on with barn owl genetics in the British Isles. We have little or no idea as to how our major roads act as barriers to the interchange of genes across Great Britain. If they do, then perhaps the previously mentioned 'Ridgeway' has a role to play in this. Perhaps it already is performing that role, unbeknown to us?

History has shown us that with most wildlife species there is no 'quick fix' for their long-term survival. With the barn owl this is more relevant now than it was thirty or so years ago. However, the 'bridge technologies' are now in place, and so it would seem that the time might now be right to consolidate and move forward, so to restore diverse habitats in specially selected and secure environments for future generations. At the same time we also need to take heed within this framework of the plight of our other owls, kestrels and other rodent eating species, all of which appear to be declining.

What might the future be for Britain's barn owls?

Predictions are often wrong, but calculated comment, based on past history and the current state of affairs, provides an opportunity to lay out the facts and provide a tentative educated guess as to what the future might be for Britain's barn owls.

As this book draws to its conclusion a new report entitled *State of Nature* has been published by a group of 25 non-governmental organisations headed by the RSPB and including the Wildlife Trusts, The Mammal Society, Plantlife, BTO and Butterfly Conservation, to name but a few. It draws attention to the worrying state of affairs with our wildlife and states that those species which

A hedgerow sympathetically managed with wildlife in mind can be host to a myriad of species, each one playing its part within the food chain to help barn owls and to help increase farmland species biodiversity.

require specific habitats are the ones which are at the greatest risk rather than those whose requirements are broader, because the latter are able to switch from one habitat to another as necessary.

A further report by Butterfly Conservation in early May 2014 warned that a fall in numbers of moths was putting the biodiversity of Britain at risk. They provided evidence from 16 million moth records, dating back to 1769, that moth populations were in serious decline. They placed the blame for this on climate change, agricultural intensification and, most interestingly, the spread of urban sprawl.

Agriculture is perhaps the most important of all these issues. Following the UK's decision to leave the EU, there is considerable apprehension within wildlife circles as to what will happen to the environmental grants scheme. The opportunity now arises, surely, to undertake positive major reforms to benefit both the farming community and biological diversity.

Providing the nation with food is the most important function for Britain's farmers. However, with consideration and forward planning, might not some barn owls return to our arable farmlands? Nest boxes would be necessary in many places to encourage this, but, over time, as many farmland trees mature, natural cavities will develop. For conservation-minded farmers, this could well be a heritage to leave for those who follow, especially if good foraging areas for small mammals of all kinds are left undisturbed.

For some farming communities such environmental schemes may be worthless, and the resources of those farms may be better suited to producing food rather than trying to meet the demands of both consumer and wildlife. This is at a time when the UK is producing only around 55 per cent of its food requirements.

In June 2012 the total amount of land dedicated to agriculture stood at 17.2 million hectares, which accounted for 70 per cent of the land area. This was a decline from 17.5 million in the year 2000 (DEFRA farming statistics). Clearly, not all of the farming incentives and stewardship schemes that have been introduced through the Common Agricultural Policy (CAP) are working, as the late Derek Ratcliffe suggested.

In the present scenario, that at the time of writing embraces the European Common Agricultural Policy, most farmers rely upon the guidance and help of the wildlife conservation movement to accommodate wildlife on their farms. For barn owls the requirements are relatively simple for their long-term survival.

Surely there is no one who would disagree that we need more trees in our countryside, and that our existing trees need care and attention. At present, nest boxes are vital conservation tools, but we cannot rely on them in the long term.

The reliance of barn owls on field voles for food is in need of assessment. The reports emanating from the Kielder Forest, with regards to the effects upon the tawny owls there that are reliant upon voles for their survival, make disturbing reading. The danger of relying upon a restricted diet has already been drawn on earlier.

All round the world, creatures that require open countryside for their survival are under threat, and barn owls are no different. The clearance of woodland and forest for agriculture benefits the world's barn owls as long as they have nesting places, but this is of little benefit if the habitats upon which their prey depends are either destroyed or degraded. Poisons too can be extremely harmful to them through contaminated prey, but it may be that there is some light at the end of the tunnel with the likelihood that many agricultural poisons will be banned from Europe's farmlands in the next few years.

At the end of the day, however, despite all of conservation's efforts, the fate of the barn owl lies squarely in the hands of farmers. We can only guide and assist. We cannot enforce upon them the recommendations of this book and others from elsewhere.

Truly, this *is* the farmland owl, for ever since the time that farmers cleared the wildwood, the fate of Britain's, and indeed the world's, barn owls has rested on the way that they have managed their farms; and so it will remain. It is for them to decide the future of this iconic farmland bird.

The farmland sentinel – guarding Britain's farmland wildlife?

Appendix
The problems of sex identification in the barn owl *Tyto alba alba*

Neck ornamentation in the barn owl *Tyto alba alba* is considered by some authorities as being the defining method of separating the sexes in the field. This technique is determined by the amount of buff-coloured feathering on the neck of the females, which tends to be absent on males.

The subject of neck colouring as a method of identifying the sexes was raised by Bunn *et al.* (1982) who were of the view that 'often in females the buff extends down to the chest', while on males the white underparts 'tend to extend on to the breast'. Thus there is the suggestion that this is the general rule and not the decisive criteria for sexual identification. It should be noted here that many of the barn owls they studied were often active during the day. In view of this, the following illustrates some of the problems that may be encountered when sexing barn owls in the field.

The specimens shown in images A–C and G are taken from the collections held in the Colchester Museum.

Specimen A (Access number 7427) is a male. This has a very light neck, though on the left side of the facial disc and down on to the chest there is a very light suffusion of buff. Overall, this is a very light-coloured bird.

The colouring of the right profile of the specimen shown in B and C (Access number 7629) suggests that it could be a male. Although the left profile is a little darker, under the right conditions, this female could be mistaken for a male.

A Male

B Female, right profile

C Female, left profile

Specimen: Colchester and Ipswich Museum Service

This suggests that, although the absence or presence of neck ornamentation may be a guide to sexing barn owls, it may not be totally reliable unless confirmed by internal examination.

  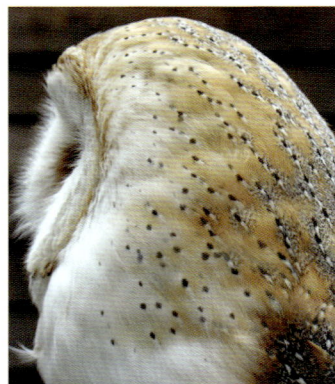

D Female *E Female, right profile* *F Female, left profile*

D–F show an interesting bird (photographed 21 August 2016) with light plumage on its right profile (E) and contrasting slightly dark plumage on its left (F). If this bird were seen in flight, an observer might think it was a male if seen from profile E and a female if seen from profile F.

From the 18 study skins in the Colchester Museum collection and the live bird (D–F), the overall impression is that, in general, there is an imbalance of neck ornamentation in barn owls with pigmentation tending to be heavier, in varying degrees, on its left side, but this is just a small sample from one part of Britain.

Because of the difficulties in sex identification that can be encountered, it may be that the spotting on the ventral plumage is a more reliable method of gender separation in barn owls. In his south-west Scotland study, Iain Taylor (1994) found that it was the amount of spotting on the underside of the birds that was the best way to separate the females from the males.

He found that the amount of flecking varied from bird to bird, but in more than 90 per cent of the males (number of birds examined (n) = 149) there was no flecking at all. In contrast to this, he found flecking on the vast majority (> 90%) of females he examined (n = 182).

This guide to sexing barn owls has been confirmed to me personally by Eden Falconry.

Specimen G (Access number 73105) is an example of what could be described as the perfect female. Apart from the deep buff suffusions on the chest, it has the spotting indicative of a female. It also has dark thighs, which are not so evident in the picture. It was found on the Essex coast, at Brightlingsea, in January 1972,

 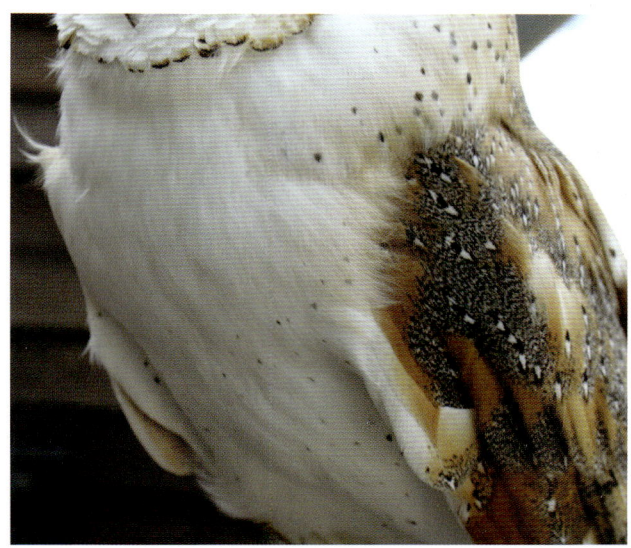

G Female

Specimen: Colchester and Ipswich Museum Service

H Young female. Note the spotting under the wings and down to the ventral parts.

and could possibly be an *alba/guttata* intermedia.

The conclusion is that British barn owls cannot be sexed in the field or in the hand by the methods of either neck ornamentation or underbody spotting. At present they can only serve as guides.

Although British barn owls are assigned to the race *alba alba*, in some respects they are notably different from their European counterparts. Perhaps the most remarkable thing about them, and which makes these illustrations necessary, is that some may be observed during daylight hours. This and other atypical behaviour, along with differences in plumage, might suggest that some of Britain's barn owls may be experiencing a process of subspecies formation.

My thanks to Sophie Stevens, Curator of Collections and Learning at Colchester and Ipswich Museums, for her kind assistance in this matter and to Eden Falconry for their kind and generous help (www.edenfalconry.com).

Scientific names

Scientific names of species mentioned in the text

Birds
(except Barn Owls)

Common name	Scientific name
Blackbird, Common	*Turdus merula*
" Red-winged	*Agelaius phoeniceus*
Buzzard, Common	*Buteo buteo*
Chaffinch, Common	*Fringilla coelebs*
Dunlin	*Calidris alpina*
Goshawk, Northern	*Accipiter gentilis*
Harrier, Hen	*Circus cyaneus*
" Montagu's	*Circus pygargus*
Jackdaw, Western	*Corvus monedula*
Kestrel, Common	*Falco tinnunculus*
" Lesser	*Falco naumanni*
Kingfisher, Common	*Alcedo atthis*
Moorhen, Common	*Gallinula chloropus*
Nuthatch, Eurasian	*Sitta europaea*
Osprey, Western	*Pandion haliaetus*
Owl, Boreal	*Aegolius funereus*
" Eurasian eagle	*Bubo bubo*
" Great grey	*Strix nebulosa*
" Little	*Athene noctua*
" Long-eared	*Asio otus*
" Northern-hawk	*Surnia ulula*
" Short-eared	*Asio flammeus*
" Snowy	*Nyctea scandiaca**
" Tawny	*Strix aluco*
" Ural	*Strix uralensis*
Peregrine falcon	*Falco peregrinus*
Pied flycatcher, European	*Ficedula hypoleuca*
Red kite	*Milvus milvus*
Redshank, Common	*Tringa totanus*
Redstart, Common	*Phoenicurus phoenicurus*
Red-legged partridge	*Alectoris rufa*
Sparrow, House	*Passer domesticus*
Sparrowhawk, Eurasian	*Accipiter nisus*
Starling, Common	*Sturnus vulgaris*
Stock dove	*Columba oenas*
Swallow, Barn	*Hirundo rustica*
Tern, White or Fairy	*Gygis alba*
Tit, European blue	*Cyanistes caeruleus*
" Great	*Parus major*
Water rail	*Rallus aquaticus*
Yellowhammer	*Emberiza citrinella*

Fish

Grunion	*Leuresthes sp.*
Perch	*Perca fluviatilis*
Roach, Common	*Rutilus rutilus*
Rudd, Common	*Scardinius erythrophthalmus*
Trout, Brown	*Salmo trutta*

Mammals

Bat, Daubenton's	*Myotis daubentonii*
" Greater horseshoe	*Rhinolophus ferrumequinum*
" Grey long-eared	*Plecotus austriacus*
" Natterer's	*Myotis nattereri*
" Noctule	*Nyctalus noctula*
Dormouse, Hazel	*Muscardinus avellanarius*
Fox, Red	*Vulpes vulpes*
Giant Panda	*Ailuropoda melanoleuca*
Marten, Pine	*Martes martes*
Mink, European	*Mustela lutreola*
Mouse, Harvest	*Micromys minutus*
" House	*Mus domesticus*
" Wood	*Apodemus sylvaticus*
" Yellow-necked	*Apodemus flavicollis*
Mole, Common	*Talpa europea*
Rabbit	*Oryctolagus cuniculus*
Rat, Brown or Common	*Rattus norvegicus*
Shrew, Common	*Sorex araneus*
" Pygmy	*Sorex minutus*
" Water	*Neomys fodiens*
Stoat	*Mustela erminea*
Vole, Bank	*Myodes glareolus*
" Common	*Microtus arvalis*
" Field	*Microtus agrestis*
" Root	*Microtus oeconomus*
" Water	*Arvicola terrestris*
Weasel	*Mustela nivalis*

Trees and plants

Alder	*Alnus glutinosa*
Apple (Crab)	*Malus sylvestris*
Beech	*Fagus sylvatica*
Birch (Silver)	*Betula pendula*
Bramble (sp.)	*Rubus fruticosis*
Dog Rose	*Rosa canina*
Elder	*Sambucus nigra*
Elm (sp.)	*Ulmus sp.*
Field Rose	*Rosa arvensis*
Hazel	*Corylus avellana*
Hawthorn	*Crataegus monogyna*
Honeysuckle	*Lonicera periclymenum*
Hornbeam	*Carpinus betulus*
Ivy	*Hedera helix*
Oak	*Quercus sp.*
Rowan, mountain ash	*Sorbus aucuparia*
Whitebeam	*Sorbus sp.*
Wild Cherry	*Prunus avium*
Wild Plum	*Prunus domestica*

* Snowy owl: Potapov and Sale (2012) have asserted that this species is monotypic and not of the genus *Bubo*. Therefore, I revert to the original scientific name *Nyctea scandiaca*.

References consulted

British Ornithologists' Union List (www.bou.org.uk/thebritishlist/British-Lists.pdf)

Gill, F. and Donsker, D. (eds.), *IOC World Bird List* v. 5.2 (2015) (www.worldbirdnames.org)

Natural History Museum, *Checklist of British Freshwater Fishes* (2005) (www.nhm.ac.uk)

Harris, S. and Yalden. D. W. (eds.), *Mammals of the British Isles* 4th edn (The Mammal Society, 2008)

Mitchell-Jones et al., *The Atlas of European Mammals* (Poyser, London, 1999)

The Wild Flower Society, *The List of British Plants*, (www.thewildlflowersociety.com)

Useful addresses

British Birds
4 Harlequin Gardens, St Leonards on Sea, East Sussex TN37 7PF
Telephone 01424 755155   britishbirds.co.uk

British Ornithologists' Union
P.O. Box 417, Peterborough PE7 3FX
Telephone 01733 844820   www.bou.org.uk

British Trust for Ornithology
The Nunnery, Thetford, Norfolk IP24 2PU
Telephone 01842 750050   www.bto.org

British Wildlife Magazine
1–6 The Stables, Ford Road, Totnes, Devon TQ9 5LE
Telephone 01803 467166   www.britishwildlife.com

Hawk and Owl Trust
Turf Moor Road, Sculthorpe, Fakenham, Norfolk NR21 9GN
Telephone 01328 850590   www.hawkandowl.org

Natural England
County Hall, Spetchley Road, Worcester WR5 2NP
Telephone 0300 060 3900   www.naturalengland.org.uk

Royal Society for the Protection of Birds
The Lodge, Potton Road, Sandy, Bedfordshire SG19 2DL
Telephone 01767 693690   www.rspb.org.uk

The Barn Owl Trust
Waterleat, Ashburton, Devon TQ13 7HU
Telephone 01364 653026   www.barnowltrust.org.uk

The Mammal Society
18 St John's Church Road, London E9 6EJ
Telephone 0238 0010981   www.mammal.org.uk

The Wildlife Trusts
The Kiln, Waterside, Mather Road, Newark NG24 1WT
Telephone 01636 677711   www.wildlifetrusts.org

The World Owl Trust
Millstones, Bootle, Cumbria LA19 5TJ
Telephone 01229 718080   www.owls.org

Websites

The Owl Pages	www.owlpages.com
The Barn Owl Conservation Network	www.bocn.org
Global Owl Project	www.globalowlproject.com
The International Owl Society	www.international-owl-society.com
Ancient Tree Forum (pollarding)	www.ancienttreeforum.co.uk
IOC World Bird List	www.worldbirdnames.org
Israel Birding Portal	www.birds.org.il/en
Strix Editions (wildlife art publishers and specialists)	www.strixeditions.co.uk
Iceni Post (online magazine for Norfolk and Suffolk)	www.icenipost.com
The Eric Hosking Charitable Trust	www.erichoskingtrust.com
European Ornithological Union	www.eounion.org
Met Office	www.metoffice.gov.uk

Barn owl projects

Somerset Wildlife Trust Community Barn Owl Project
   www.somersetwildlife.org/barn_owl_project_2014

Suffolk Wildlife Trust community barn owl project
   www.suffolkwildlifetrust.org/barnowls

The Wychwood Project
   www.wychwoodproject.org/cms/content/barn-owl-project

The contact details and website URLs are subject to change.

Credits

The author and publishers would like to thank the following individuals and organisations for their kind permission to use their photographs and other materials for the illustrations in this book.
Images are referenced by page number first with the position of the image on the page shown in brackets (t: top, b: bottom, l: left, r: right, b-r: bottom right, etc.).

All images not listed were supplied by the author.
Paintings reproduced on cover, frontispiece, and throughout: Terance James Bond
Chapter 1
Page 14 Deane Lewis/*The Owl Pages*; 15 Michael Daniels; 16 Colchester Zoo; 18 David Nixon; 23, 26, 38 Eric Hosking Charitable Trust; 25 artist: Dag Peterson; 28 Artur Vaz Oliveira; 34 Stanley Dumican
Chapter 2
42 Peter Hewitt; 45 David Nixon; 46 Ian Anderson; 49, 59(all) Eric Hosking Charitable Trust; 53, 58 Artur Vaz Oliveira; 54 Deane Lewis/*The Owl Pages*
Chapter 3
69 Artur Vaz Oliveira; 70 Ian Anderson
Chapter 4
83 Hazel Williams; 81 Kate Martin; 88(b-r), 91(b), 95(b), 96(both), 97(b), 99(l) Pat Morris; 89, 90(both), 91(t) John Dobson; 102 Peter Hewitt
Chapter 5
105 Jonathan Wright; 106–7, 109, 114, 115, 117, 119(l) Peter Hewitt; 112 Thomas Harris; 113(both) Artur Vaz Oliveira; 116 Eric Hosking Charitable Trust; 118 Ralph Hancock; 119(r) Pat Morris; 120 Colin Hawes; 121(t) Ian Anderson
Chapter 6
124, 130(bl) Ian Anderson; 127(all) Nigel Clarke; 131 Stanley Dumican; 138(b) Helen Read
Chapter 7
143, 147 Ian Anderson; 150 *icenipost*
Chapter 8
152, 154, 156 Ian Anderson
Chapter 9
167 Eric Hosking Charitable Trust; 169 Tony Duckels SWLRG
Chapter 10
174, 188–9 Peter Hewitt; 181 Artura Vaz Oliveira; 185 Ian Anderson; 187 Thomas Harris
Chapter 11
202 Artur Vaz Oliveira; 205 Wagging Dog Media Ltd
Chapter 12
213, 215, 217 Ian Anderson; 214, 229 Peter Hewitt

199 The European Temperatures graph is reproduced by permission of the Met Office; their terms of usage can be found at: www.nationalarchives.gov.uk/doc/open-government-licence,version/3/
The Global Temperatures graph is reproduced by permission of NASA; their terms of usage can be found at: www.nasa.gov/audience/formedia/features/MP_Photo_Guidelines.html

Every effort has been made to credit accurately all copyright holders. If we have been unsuccessful, we apologise and will, if notified, make any necessary corrections in future editions and reprints.

References and bibliography

Alcamo, J. and Olsen, J. E. 2012. *Life in Europe under Climate Change*. John Wiley and Sons. Ltd.. Chichester.
Attenborough, D. 2002. *The Life of Mammals*. BBC Books, London.
Balmer, D. E., Gillings, S., Caffrey, B. J., Swann, R. L., Downie, R. S. and Fuller, R. J. 2013. *Bird Atlas 2007–2011: The Breeding and Wintering Birds of Britain and Ireland*. BTO Books, Thetford.
Barnes, R. F. W. 1999. Is there a future for elephants in West Africa? *Mammal Review*, 29: 175–199.
Barn Owl Trust. 2012. *Barn Owl Conservation Handbook*. Pelagic Publishing, Exeter.
Batey, C. 2013. The distribution of Barn Owl nest-sites in relation to altitude in south-west England. *British Birds*, 106: 482–483.
Baudvin, H. 1997. Barn Owl (*Tyto alba*) and Long-Eared Owl (*Asio otus*) mortality along motorways in Bourgogne-Champagne: Report and Suggestions. 2nd Owl Symposium. Winnipeg, Canada.
Beebee, T. J. C. 2001. British wildlife and human numbers: the ultimate conservation issue? *British Wildlife*, 13: 1–8.
Birkhead, T., Wimpenny, J. and Montgomerie, R. 2014. *Ten Thousand Birds*. Princeton University Press.
Bontzorlus, V. A., Peris, S. J. and Vlachos, C. G. 2005. The diet of the barn owl in the agricultural landscapes of central Greece. *Folia Zool.*, 54: 99–110.
Boves, T. J. and Belthoff, J. R. 2012. Roadway mortality on barn owls in Idaho, USA. *Journ. Wildlife Management*, 76: 1381–1392.
Bunn, D. S. 1972. Regular daylight hunting by Barn Owls. *British Birds*, 65: 26–30.
Bunn, D. S. 1974. The voice of the Barn Owl. *British Birds*, 67: 493–501.
Bunn, D. S., Warburton, A. B. and Wilson, R. D. S. 1982. *The Barn Owl*. T. and A. D. Poyser Ltd, Calton.
Burns, F., Eaton., Gregory., *et al.* 2013. State of Nature. The State of Nature Partnership.
Carroll, S. P., Jørgensen, P. S., Kinnison, M. T., Bergstrom, C. T., Ford Denison, R., Gluckman, P., Smith, T. B., Strauss, S. Y. and Tabashnik, B. E. 2014. Applying evolutionary biology to address global challenges. *Science Express*, 1–16. www.sciencemag.org.
Čech, M. and Čech, P. 2015. Non-fish prey in the diet of an exclusive fish-eater: the Common Kingfisher *Alcedo atthis*. *Bird Study*, 62: 457–465.
Coleman, M. 1998. Elm – the forgotten tree. *British Wildlife*, 9: 137–143.
Dobinson, H. M. and Richards, A. J. 1964. The effects of the severe winter of 1962/63 on birds in Britain. *British Birds*, 57: 373–434.
Durant, J. M., Massemin, S. and Handrich, Y. 2004. More eggs the better. *Auk*, 121: 103–109.
Durant, J. M., Massemin, S., Thouzeau, C. and Handrich, Y. 2000. Body reserves and nutritional needs during laying preparation in barn owls. *Journ. Comp. Physiol.*, B., 170: 253–260.
Eaton, M. A., Balmer, D. E., Cuthbert, R., Grice, P. V., Hall, J., Hearn, R. D., Holt, C. A., Musgrove, A. J., Noble, D. G., Parsons, M., Risely, K., Stroud, D. A. and Wotton, S. 2011. *The State of the UK's Birds 2011*. RSPB, BTO, WWT, CCW, JNCC, NE, NIEA and SNH, Sandy, Bedfordshire.
Feduccia, A. 1999. *The Origin and Evolution of Birds*. 2nd edn. Yale University Press, Newhaven.
Fitzpatrick, F. 1934. Unilateral and bilateral ovaries in raptorial birds. *Wilson Bull.*, 46: 19–22.
Flegg, J. and Hosking, D. 1993. *Eric Hosking's Classic Birds: 60 Years of Bird Photography*. HarperCollins Publishers, London.
Flowerdew, J. 1993. *Mice and Voles*. Whittet Books Ltd., London.
Gill, F. and Donsker, D. (eds.). 2015. IOC World Bird List (v 5.2). www.worldbirdnames.org. (Accessed 2015.07.02).
Gill, V. 2011. British barn owls rely on humans. BBC News Report.
Gilling, S., Henderson, I. G., Morris, A. J. and Vickery, J. A. 2010. Assessing the implications of the loss of set-aside for farmland birds. *Ibis*, 152: 713–723.
Glue, D. E. 1974. Food of the Barn Owl in Britain and Ireland. *Bird Study*, 21: 200–210.
Glue, D. E. and Jordan, R. 1990. Baked Barn Owl pellet revelations. *BTO News*, 167–5.

Hagemeijer, W. J. M. and Blair, M. J. (eds.). 1997. *The EBCC Atlas of European Breeding Birds: Their Distribution and Abundance*. T. and A. D. Poyser Ltd, London.

Harris, S. and Yalden. D.W. (eds.), 2008. *Mammals of the British Isles Handbook*, 4th edn. The Mammal Society, Southampton.

Hunter, J. 1999. *The Essex Landscape*. Essex Record Office, Chelmsford.

Jánossy, D. 1979. Plio-Pleistocene bird remains from the Carpathian Basin. III. Strigiformes, Falconiformes, Caprimulgiformes, Apodiformes. *Aquila*, 84: 9–36.

Kessler, J. 2014. Fossil and subfossil bird remains and faunas from the Carpathian Basin. *Ornis Hungarica*, 22: 65–125.

Kington. J. A. 2010. *Climate and Weather*. Collins, London.

König, C., Weick, F. and Becking, J-H. 2008. *Owls of the World*, 2nd edn. Christopher Helm, London.

Korneliussen, I. 2005. Can wild animals have mental illnesses? sciencenordic.com/content/ida-korneliussen.

Korpimäki, E. and Hakkarainen, H. 2012. *The Boreal Owl*. Cambridge University Press.

Kurochkin, E. N. and Dyke, G. J. 2011. The first fossil owls (*Aves: Strigiformes*) from the Paleogene of Asia and a review of the fossil record of *Strigiformes*. *Paleontological Journ.*, 445–58.

Love, R. A., Webbon, C., Glue, D. E. and Harris, S. E. 2000. Changes in the food of British Barn Owls (*Tyto alba*) between 1974 and 1997. *Mammal Review*, 30: 107–129.

Martin, J. R. 1988. Barn owl mortality during the winter of 1986/87. *Suffolk Birds* 1988, 37: 12–15.

Martin, J. R. 2008. *Barn Owls in Britain*. Whittet Books Ltd., Yatesbury.

Martin. J. R. 2010. The East Anglian Heights – overland migration. *The Harrier*, 162: 7–16. Suffolk Ornithologists' Group.

Martin, J. R. and Martin, T. 1990. Perching on overhead wires by Barn Owls. *Trans. Suffolk Nats Soc.*, 26: 45.

Martin, J. R. and Mikkola, H. 2014. The changing face of Britain's Tawny Owls. *British Wildlife*, 25: 391–399.

Massemin, S., le Maho, Y. and Handrich, Y. 1998. Seasonal pattern in age, sex and body condition of Barn Owls *Tyto alba* killed on motorways. *Ibis*, 140: 70–75.

Mátics, R. 2003. Microevolution of the Barn Owl (*Tyto alba* Scop. 1769) in Europe. Ph.D. Thesis, University of Debrecen.

Meek, W. R., Burman, P. J., Sparks, T. H., Nowakowski, M. and Burman, N. J. 2012. The use of Barn Owl *Tyto alba* pellets to assess population change in small mammals. *Bird Study*, 59: 166–174.

Mikkola, H. 1983. *Owls of Europe*. T. and A. D. Poyser Ltd, Calton.

Mikkola, H. 2013. *Owls of the World: A Photographic Guide*, 2nd edn. Christopher Helm, London.

Millom, A., Petty, S. J., Little, B., Gimenez, O., Cornulier, Y. and Lambin, X. 2014. Dampening prey cycle overrides the impact of climate change on predator population dynamics: a long term demographic study on tawny owls. *Global Change Biology*. 1–12.

Mineau, P. 2013. Birds and insecticides – from organophosphates to neonicotinoids. Are we jumping from the frying pan into the fire? Symposium 4, 9th Conference of the European Ornithologists' Union. Norwich, England.

Mlíkovsky, J. 2002. *Cenazoic Birds of the World, Part 1: Europe*. Ninox Press, Prague.

Musgrove, A., Aebischer, N., Eaton, M., Hearn, R., Newson, S., Noble, D., Parsons, M., Risely, K. and Stroud, D. 2013. Population estimates of birds in Great Britain and the United Kingdom. *British Birds*, 106: 64–100.

Mushtaq-Ul-Hassan, M., Ghazi, R. R. and Nisa, N-un. Food preference of the Short-eared Owl (*Asio flammeus*) and Barn Owl (*Tyto alba*) at Usta Muhammad, Baluchistan, Pakistan, *Turk. J. Zool.* 31: 91–94.

Naish, D. 2014. The fossil record of bird behavior. *Journ. of Zoology*, 292: 268–280.

Newton, I. 1979. *Population Ecology of Raptors*. T. and A. D. Poyser Ltd, Berkhamsted.

Newton, I. 2013. Organochlorine pesticides and birds. *British Birds*, 106: 189–205.

Newton, I., Wyllie, I. and Asher, A. 1991. Mortality causes in British Barn Owls *Tyto alba* with a discussion of aldrin-dieldrin poisoning. *Ibis* 133: 162–169.

Newton, I., Wyllie, I. and Dale, L. 1997. Mortality causes in British Barn Owls (*Tyto alba*), based on 1,101 carcasses examined during 1963–1996. Proceedings of the Second International Owl Symposium Biology and Conservation of Owls of the Northern Hemisphere. Winnipeg, Manitoba, Canada.

Newton, I., Wyllie, I. and Freestone, P. 1990. Rodenticides in British Barn Owls. *Environmental Pollution*, 68: 101–117.

Nyagolov, K. and Ignatove, A. 2003. *Owls of Bulgaria*. Borina, Sofia.

Osborne, P. 1982. Some effects of Dutch Elm Disease on nesting farmland birds. *Bird Study*, 29: 2–16.

Palmer, P. 2013. Daylight hunting by Barn Owls – is England a special case? *Brit. Birds*, 106: 416.

Parker. A. 2000. *Watch the Birdie*. Cerebus Publications Ltd., Walsall.

Payne, R. 1971. Acoustic location of prey of Barn Owls (*Tyto alba*). *Journal of Experimental Biology*, 54: 535–573.

Paz, A., Jareño, D., Arroyo, L., Viñuela, J., Arroyo, B., Mougeot, F., Luque-Larena, J. J. and Fargello, J. A. 2012. Avian predators as a biological control system of common vole (*Microtus arvalis*) populations in north-western Spain: experimental set-up and preliminary results. *Pest Management Science*, 69: 444–450.

Pollard, E., Hooper, M. D. and Moore, N. W. 1974. *Hedges*. Collins, London.

Potapov, E. and Sale, R. 2012. *The Snowy Owl*. T. and A. D. Poyser Ltd, London.

Prytherch, R. 2013. The breeding biology of the Common Buzzard. *Brit. Birds*, 106: 264–279.

Rackham, O. *An Illustrated History of the Countryside*. Weidenfeld and Nicolson, London.

Ratcliffe, D. 1967. Decrease in egg shell weight in certain birds of prey. *Nature*, 208–210. Nature, London.

Ratcliffe, D. A. 1980. *The Peregrine Falcon* 1st edn. T. and A. D. Poyser Ltd, Calton.

Ratcliffe, D. A. 2007. *Galloway and the Borders*. Collins, London.

Read, H. J., Pollards and pollarding in Europe. *British Wildlife*, 19: 250–259.

Robb, M. and the Sound Approach. *Undiscovered Owls: A Sound Approach Guide*. The Sound Approach, Poole.

Roulin, A. 2004. Covariation between plumage colour polymorphism and diet in the Barn Owl *Tyto alba*. *Ibis*, 146: 509–517.

Roulin, A. and Dubey, S. 2012. The occurrence of reptiles in Barn Owl diet in Europe. *Bird Study*, 59: 504–508.

Roulin, A., Richner, H. and Ducrest, A. 1998. Genetic, environmental, and condition-dependent effects on female and male ornamentation in the Barn Owl *Tyto alba*. *Evolution* 52: 1451–1460.

Ruprecht, A. L. 1979: Bats (Chiroptera) as constituents of the food of barn owls *Tyto alba* in Poland. *Ibis*, 121: 489-494.

Salvati, L., Manganaro, A. and Ranazzi, L. 2002. Aspects of the ecology of the Barn Owl *Tyto alba* breeding in a Mediterranean area: Data are given on breeding density, nest-sites, reproduction and breeding diet of the Barn Owl along the urban gradient in Rome, central Italy. *Bird Study*, 49: 186–189.

Shawyer, C. R. 1987. *The Barn Owl in the British Isles*. The Hawk Trust, London.

Shawyer, C. R. 1998. *The Barn Owl*. Arlequin Press, Chelmsford.

Southern, H. N. 1954. Tawny Owls and their prey. *Ibis*, 96: 384-410.

Stamp, L. D. 1955. *Man and the Land*. Collins, London.

Taylor, I. 1994. *Barn Owls: predator prey relationship and conservation*. Cambridge University Press.

Toms, M. P., Crick, H. Q. P. and Shawyer, C. R. 2001. The status of breeding Barn Owls *Tyto alba* in the United Kingdom 1996–97. *Bird Study*, 48: 23–37.

Villar, N., Lambin, X., Evans, D., Pakeman, R. and Redpath, S. 2013. Experimental evidence that livestock grazing intensity affects the activity of a generalist predator. *Acta Oecologica*, 49: 12-16.

Watson, D. 1997. *The Hen Harrier*. T. and A. D. Poyser Ltd, Berkhamsted.

Yalden, D. 1999. *The History of British Mammals*. T. and A. D. Poyser Ltd., London.

Yalden, D. W. and Albarella, U. 2009. *The History of British Birds*. Oxford University Press.

Zuberogoitia, I., Martinez, J. A., Zbala, J. and Martinez, J. E. 2005. Interspecific aggression and nest-site competition in a European owl community. *Journal of Raptor Research*, 39: 156–159.

Online references

British Ornithologists' Union (BOU). 2013. The British List: a checklist of birds of Britain, 8th edn. *Ibis*, 155: 635–676.

British Trust for Ornithology, www.bto.org/about-birds/birdtrends/2013.
www.bto.org/volunteer-surveys/ringing/publications/online-ringing-reports

(BWP) Cramp, S. 1985 and update. *Birds of the Western Palearctic*, Vol. IV. Oxford University Press.

Index

Africa 20
Agricultural Act, 1947 72, 79
agricultural depression 67
agricultural land, amount of 228
agricultural revolution
    first 61, 64, 66
    second 72
agri-environment schemes 222
Americas 22
    North America 11
amniotic vertebrae 19
amphibians, as prey 78
anatomy 12–18
    feet 15, 16, 18
    skull 13
Asia 22
Attenborough, David 81, 101
Australasian 20, 22
Australian barn owl 22, 23

Balkans 30
Barn-door owl 39
Barn Owl Monitoring Project 82
Barn Owl Trust 126, 162, 181
bats, as prey 78
bay owl 20
beak *see* bill
beech 31
    as pollards 138
behaviour 218–19
bill 13, 45
Billberg, Gustav 13, 16, 36
biodiversity 82, 136
biological diversity 141
biological pest control 179
Biological Records Centres 71
birch, silver 30
blackbirds, common, as prey 78
    red-winged, as prey 77
Bodmin Moor 35
breeding and releasing 135
breeding, condition of female 145
Bristol University 52
British Isles 21, 29, 31
    separation from Europe 21, 29, 31, 32
    status 210
British Ornithologists' Union 37
broods
    difference in behaviour 151
    production of 150
    manipulation of sexes 148
brown rat 66, 91
BTO (British Trust for Ornithology)
    Nest Record Scheme 212, 217–18

buildings, as nest-sites 36, 126
    as nests in inhabited buildings 128
    loss of buildings in Britain 126
    loss of buildings in Europe 128
Bunn, Derek 48, 51, 81, 108, 109
butterflies *see* invertebrates
butterfly conservation 227
buzzard, common 211

Cambridge University 51
camouflage *see* cryptic colouring
cannabalism 158
    in hen harriers 158
    in short-eared owls 158
    stress factor 159
captive breeding 149
Caribbean 20
Carpathian Basin 17, 29
carrying of prey 115
chick survival *see* owlets
church owl *see* names
church towers, as nesting places 129
climate 19, 79
    change 30, 104, 193, 198–201
    Intergovernmental panel on 198–9
clutches *see* eggs
coastal marshes 63
conservation 212–18
    community barn owl projects 220
    involvement of young people 212
    nest box schemes 213–15, 217
courtship 143–5
    activity prior to breeding 144
    breeding condition 144
    over-wintering condition 145
    timing of 143
cryptic colouring 46–8

dark-breasted barn owl 26, 29, 41, 42, 45, 164
Dartmoor 35
daylight activity *see* diurnal activity
description 41
    wing lengths 41
development 190
Devon 58
dispersal *see* ringing
distribution
    in Britain 33–6
    of the barn owl *Tyto alba* 21–9
disturbance 21, 58, 59, 180–4
    of nests 159
    road traffic 180–5
    effects of noise 181–2
diurnal activity 47, 56, 105–12

DNA 13, 20, 26
Doggerland 32
dormouse, common 90, 91
drought 201–3
   effects on cattle 200
   efffects on voles 202
   effects on owls 203
dry stone walls 86
Dudley Stamp, L., *Land Utilisation Survey* 72
Dumfries and Galloway 220

eagle owl 118, 119
East Anglian Heights 165
   as a dispersal route 165–6
east coast flooding 206–8
echo-location 52
eggs 146
   clutch, timing of 145, 147
   incubation of 148
   measurements of 146, 150
   monitoring of clutch 160
   production of 147–8
   reduction of clutch 159
   second clutch 46, 157
   size of clutch 145
   weights of 150
elm 124–6
   as nesting habitats 31, 125
   disease 33, 123, 125
Enclosure Acts 65
England 33, 35
   eastern 123
   north-west 36, 107
   West Country 36, 208
Environmentally Sensitive Areas (ESAs) 74
Environmental Stewardship 86
Epping Forest 139
Essex 36, 128
Eurasia 28
Europe 20, 24, 26, 30, 123, 125, 209–10
   distribution 21–9
   population of barn owls 129, 210
   woodland 141
European Union 223, 227
evolution 11–12
eye, description of 53, 54
   development in young 55, 56, 155

facial disc 45, 56, 57
Falkland Islands 25
farmers 228
farmland 63, 65, 72, 82
   flooding of 205–7
   loss of 67
   under-utilised, 85
feathers, collecting at roosts 122
feet *see* anatomy
Fens 33
fish, as prey 16–19
fishing owl 17
fish owls 18
fledging 157
flight 49–51
flooding 205–8
   coastal flooding 207–8
food
   requirements 153–4
   small mammals 20–1
food passing 116
forests 21; *see also* woodlands
France 26

Galápagos 20, 22
   barn owl 22
gamekeepers 65, 66
gene flow 161, 225
Germany 11, 26, 27
Glue, David 68, 96
goshawk, northern 117, 118, 215
grassland 16, 17, 74, 77, 98–103, 111
   effects of climate change on, 203
   protection of 74
great grey owl 45

habitats 21, 67, 136, 225
   feeding 123
   loss of 79
   open countryside 21, 24
hatching of eggs 151
Hawk and Owl Trust 222–3
hawk owl, northern 44, 203
head 54–5
headlands 95
hearing 57–9
   effects of noise on, 181–4
   use in hunting 57
hedgerows 61, 84–95
   creation of during Enclosures 65
   destruction of 67, 73
   diversity of 91–5
   management of 65, 86, 93, 94
   small mammals 88–91
hornbeam 31
   as pollards 138
Hosking, Eric 48
human population 80, 180
   urban expansion, effects of 182–3
hunting 112–16

efficiency 109
in rain 113
methods, quartering, post-hopping 113–14
opportunistic 77

Iberian Peninsula 30
Ice Age *see* Pleistocene
identification 43
incubation 148
Industrial Revolution 66
Inter-specific Aggression Index 119
intra-guild aggression 116–20, 212
invertebrates 78, 136, 138, 227
butterflies 78, 227
moths 78, 79, 227
Ireland, separation from Britain 31, 32
irruptions 166–70
Israel *see* Middle East
ivy 141–2

January isotherm 27

kestrel
common 31, 43, 117, 212
lesser 133
Kielder Forest 104, 228
kingfisher 19
Kington, John 208

land bridges 22, 31
Land Utilisation Survey *see* Dudley Stamp
legs *see* feet
Little Ice Age 66, 200
little owl 117
lizard *see* amniotic vertebrae 19
long-eared Owl 26, 28, 119
longevity 162
lowland retreats 221–3

Mammal Society *see* pellets
measurements 41, 44
Mediterranean 21
melanistic keratin 50
Mesolithic 33
Middle East 28, 35, 179
biological pest control scheme 179
migration *see* ring recoveries
mink 96
mole, common 103
Montagu's harrier 36
mortality 161
collision with overhead wires 55
road collisions 161
seasonal 162

starvation 161
weather 194–8
moths *see* insects
moult 46
mouse
harvest 91, 98
house 91
wood 30, 31, 74, 90
yellow-necked 84, 90

names 36–9
barn-door owl 39
church owl 36–7
white-breasted barn owl 38
white owl 36, 37
nest boxes 51, 63, 124–5, 132–6
conservation programmes 133
ecological impact 140
maintenance of 133
monitoring of 132–3, 135, 140
quality of 133
nest recording *see* BTO
nests 146
away from roads 162
entrance hole, size of 216
in buildings 21, 37, 66
height above sea level 35
loss of 123
scrape 146
straw stacks 130
New Zealand 20, 52
nictitating membrane 54
noise *see* disturbance
Norfolk 206–7

oak, as nesting sites 31, 136
sudden oak death disease 137
origins 16–19
ovaries, number of 147
owlets 151–7
description of 151–2
development of 152–5
feeding of 150–3
fledging 157
manipulation of sex ratios 148
level of young for long-term survival 160
survival of 152–3, 157–62
weights of 154

Palestinian Authority *see* Middle East
Pannonian Sea 16, 19
Parker, Alan 38, 48
pellet analysis 67–79
collecting at roosts 70, 122

Mammal Society studies 75–7, 159–60
    of short-eared owls 158
    skulls of waders 78
perching 114
    on overhead wires 55
Peregrine falcon 175
persecution 66
pest control *see* poisons
pesticides *see* poisons
Phillips, Frank Gibson 48
Phodilinae 12–13
Phodilus, the genus 13, 20
phylogenetics 13
pied flycatcher 215
pine marten 215
Pleistocene 21, 27, 30–2
    Great Ice Age 22, 29, 30
plumage 42
    cryptic 46–8
    of owlets 154–7
    primary feathers 48
poisons 21, 173–80, 228
    neonicotinoids 178–9
    organo-chlorines 173–5
    rodenticides 176–8
    slug pellets 178
    see also red kite
pollarding 136
    benefits of 136–8
polygamy 148
population 209–12
    European estimates 210
    British estimates 210–11
    sustainability, level of 160
prey
    diversification of 159
    selection of 77

Ratcliffe, Derek 82, 228
Ray, John 36, 37
relationships with owls and other birds 116–20
red kite 177
reptiles, as prey 78
ringing 166–9
    BTO ringing scheme 163
    dispersal 164–6; *see also* East Anglian Heights
    European recoveries 164, 170
    selected UK recoveries 165–6
rivers 95–8
road traffic 21
    death from 137, 162, 182, 184
    noise from 58
roosts 120–2
    farm buildings 121

tree holes 120
    usefulness in bad weather 121
Roulin, Alexandre 29
RSPB (Royal Society for Protection of Birds) 52, 66
    1929 Survey 67
    wind farms 204

Scotland 33, 36, 42
Scott, Sir Peter 192
sea level 22, 30–2
Second World War 63, 72
set-aside 74, 76, 77
sex identification (Appendix) 231
sexual dimorphism 41
Shawyer, Colin
    1987 survey 205–6
short-eared owl 15, 17, 30, 119
shrews
    common 31
    pygmy 31
    water 96, 97
sight 52–56, 109
    binocular vision 54
    research on 52
sightings, seasonal occurrence 144–5
signalling to conspecifics 112
silver birch 30
skeleton 14–15
skull(s) 13
Smithsonian Institution 37
snow, effects of 193–8
snowy owl 30, 44, 203
solar panels, and possible effect on barn owls 204–5
Somerset levels 65, 206, 208
South West Lancashire Ringing Group 132, 168–9
sparrowhawk, Eurasian 43, 56, 175
Stamp, L. Dudley 72
State of the Nation's Birds 2013 82, 119
status of barn owl in Britain 210–12
stoat 30
straw stacks, for nesting 147, 130
Strigidae 13
Strigiformes 13
Suffolk 36–9, 63, 84, 207
superstitions 191–2
    Africa 191
    India 192
    Mexico 191
    Scotland 191
Sweden 25, 31

talons *see* feet
tawny owl 31, 33, 44, 52, 104, 118, 119, 148, 215
Taylor, Iain 63, 82, 84, 112, 132

technology 222
Tengmalm's, or Boreal, owl 119, 132, 148
territory 105–6
   advertising presence 114
Thames Flood Barrier 208
tits, blue and great 215
trees 139
   as nest sites 21, 31, 138
   biodiversity value 138
   destruction 33
   loss of 21
   photosynthesising 141
trends 212
Tyto, the genus 11–13, 16, 20, 21, 57
   T. a. alba 12, 41
   T. a. guttata 26, 29
   T. alba 20, 24–36, 50
   T. bargei 19
   T. contempta 19
   T. crassirostris 23
   T. delicatula 22
   T. deroepstorffi 23
   T. detorti 26
   T. furcata 18, 19, 21, 50
   T. gigantea 21
   T. insularis 20
   T. neddi 21
   T. prigoginei 20
   T. punctatissima 22
   T. soumagnei 23
   T. thomensis 20
   evolution 24
   in decline 209
Tytonidae 12, 16, 20
Tytoninae 13

ultraviolet light 52
Ural owl 119

voice 51–52
   contact calls 51
   dialects 52
   inheritance 51

phonograms 20
   vocabulary 20, 52
voles 77
   bank 30, 31, 88, 89
   common 27, 33
   dependance on 101–4
   field 30, 31, 82, 104
   plagues 100, 101
   poisoning of 177–8
   root 33
   virus 104
   water 96, 97

Wales 30, 33
watching barn owls at roosts 121
weasel 31
weather 108
   contrasting 197
   effects of hot 198, 200–3
   severe winters in 20th century 67, 196–7
   severe winters in 21st century 197
weights 44
Western Palearctic 29
wetlands 187
Wheat Act (1932) 67
White Owl 38
Wildlife and Countryside Act 136, 149
wildwood 33, 185, 228
   numbers of barn owls in 209
Willughby, Francis 36, 37, 132
wind, effects on hunting 113
wing 43–4
   aeronautical research 50–51
   shape of 44
   wing-loading 50
witchcraft 191–2
   good luck charms 192
   superstition 191
   use of owls as medicine 191
woodland 63, 137, 228; *see also* forests
   increase of 185–6

yellowhammer 52